AMERICA'S IMAGINED REVOLUTION

Southern Literary Studies

SCOTT ROMINE, SERIES EDITOR

AMERICA'S IMAGINED REVOLUTION

The Historical Novel of Reconstruction

Tomos Wallbank-Hughes

LOUISIANA STATE UNIVERSITY PRESS   BATON ROUGE

Published by Louisiana State University Press
lsupress.org

DESIGNER: Barbara Neely Bourgoyne
TYPEFACES: Minion Pro, text; Helvetica Neue LT Pro, display

An earlier version of chapter 4 appeared as "'Can We Imagine This Spectacular
Revolution?': Counterfactual Narrative and the 'New World Peasantry' in W. E. B.
Du Bois's *Scorn* and *Black Reconstruction*." *ELH* 87, no. 1 (2020): 179–210.

LIBRARY OF CONGRESS CATALOGING-IN-PUBLICATION DATA
Names: Wallbank-Hughes, Tomos, author.
Title: America's imagined revolution : the historical novel of Reconstruction /
    Tomos Wallbank-Hughes.
Description: Baton Rouge : Louisiana State University Press, 2024. | Series:
    Southern literary studies | Includes bibliographical references and index.
Identifiers: LCCN 2023045211 (print) | LCCN 2023045212 (ebook) | ISBN
    978-0-8071-8154-6 (cloth) | ISBN 978-0-8071-8235-2 (pdf) | ISBN
    978-0-8071-8234-5 (epub)
Subjects: LCSH: Reconstruction (U.S. history, 1865–1877) in literature. | American
    fiction—19th century—History and criticism. | Literature and society—Southern
    States—History—19th century. | American fiction—20th century—History and
    criticism. | Literature and society—Southern States—History—20th century. |
    Historical fiction, American—History and criticism. | LCGFT: Literary criticism.
Classification: LCC PS374.R38 W35 2024 (print) | LCC PS374.R38 (ebook) |
    DDC 813/.409358—dc23/eng/20240202
LC record available at https://lccn.loc.gov/2023045211
LC ebook record available at https://lccn.loc.gov/2023045212

for Ruth

CONTENTS

ACKNOWLEDGMENTS

Thinking back on writing a book about anachronism was always likely to make me feel anachronistic, especially when two (but what feels like more) years of writing coincided with time going haywire. I have relied on many people to keep me on my personal rails while time went off its own. I began an earlier version of this project at the University of Nottingham under the direction of Sharon Monteith and Tony Hutchison. Without Sharon's wealth of knowledge on the cultural and literary history of activism and the U.S. South, there wouldn't have been much of a project. Her encouragement for my ideas, along with a readiness to challenge the more aberrant ones, have improved my work to no end—she also taught me to write more clearly, for which I am thankful (hopefully my readers will be too). Tony asked the kinds of challenging questions that helped me to see the broader implications of my ideas, get to grips with what I wanted to say, and say it more directly.

In the Department of American and Canadian Studies at Nottingham, Matthew Pethers has been a generous reader and interlocutor; Robin Vandome, Graham Thompson, Richard King, and Catherine Rottenberg all provided advice; and Steve Gallo, Scott Weightman, Hannah Jeffery, Hannah Lauren-Murray, Jimmy Brookes, Mark Eastwood, Patrick Henderson, and Olivia Wright made Nottingham an enriching and enjoyable place to be. At the University of Warwick, starting a postdoc alongside Harry Warwick made it much easier to adapt to a new institution at a strange time. Mark Storey and Stephen Shapiro provided advice and support. I enjoyed being in reading groups with Harry, Stephen, Tom Waller, Harry Pitt-Scott, Sean O'Brien, Christine Okoth, Christine Emmett, and Mike Niblett.

At different stages of writing, Tim Armstrong and Ed Sugden provided helpful and generous feedback, and comments from Louisiana State University Press's reviewer and Scott Romine improved the manuscript. Through the British Association of Nineteenth-Century Americanists, I have met a group of scholars who have been universally welcoming. Along with several already named, I am thankful to Katie McGettigan and Tom Wright. Further afield, I am grateful to Brook Thomas, for sending me unpublished work and providing material on Reconstruction; to Jack Matthews, for reading and commenting; and to Blake Spitz, for advice on W. E. B. Du Bois's archive. Scott Romine, the editor for LSU Press's Southern Literary Studies series, and acquiring editor James W. Long have been patient and enthusiastic in helping me navigate the daunting process of publishing a first book. Midlands3Cities and the Leverhulme Trust provided funding for me to research and write.

My friends have been a welcome distraction for the years I've been working on this project and much longer: Phil Jones, Isa Cipirska, Rich Jones, Zillah Holford, Richard Chevin-Dooley, Amy Chevin-Dooley, Alex Shenton, Ciara Shenton, Peter Bray, Emily Andrews, Matthew Birchall, Dan Nixon, Ade Harrison, Chris Wilson, Calum Murphy, Alice Thatcher, Harri Murphy, Rich Wilkinson-Dallimore, Libby Wilkinson-Dallimore, thank you! Jenny Swann and Schölin Tipping generously gifted me books, and Jenny cut a hole in her hedge for me to park in. My parents, Rhian Hughes and Richard Godden, and sister, Mabli Godden, have always been generous and understanding (and have listened to me moan at length). Pete, Krystina, and Phil Wallbank are also good family to have. My biggest thanks are to Ruth Wallbank-Hughes, to whom this book is dedicated and without whom I could not have written it or done much else besides: for sixteen years and counting, you have been my best friend, believed in me absolutely (often to my astonishment), and been silly with me through it all.

AMERICA'S IMAGINED REVOLUTION

Introduction
Revolution and the Historical Novel of Reconstruction

An unfinished revolution, a missed opportunity, a tragic defeat: Reconstruction holds a near mythic place in the American historical imagination. As a moment of egalitarian possibility, supplanted by a retrenched white supremacist order, its legacy is defined by the allure of the incomplete, the unfulfilled, the unwritten. This sense of foreclosure has everything to do with Reconstruction's qualified and yet unavoidable relationship to that seemingly most un-American thing, social revolution. Once, the ambiguous connection had pejorative implications. Before W. E. B. Du Bois memorably declared Reconstruction "a tragedy that beggared the Greek," because capital defeated the revolutionary aspirations of enslaved people, reactionaries had more commonly bemoaned that emancipation had placed the bottom rail on top in the South.[1] This commonplace metaphor implied a temporary, carnivalesque reversal requiring violent correction. Turning such bromides into popular history, Claude Bowers's 1929 bestseller, *The Tragic Era,* depicted Radical Reconstruction as a melodramatic revolutionary aberration, a departure from progressive national principles that lasted just long enough to foreclose the promise of the Lincoln Republic.[2]

Thankfully, Reconstruction's revolutionary implications have shifted with the period's fortunes in the popular imagination. Following Eric Foner, Reconstruction is now commonly understood as America's "unfinished revolution." Building on two decades of revisionist history, Foner invoked a tragically curtailed experiment in using the newly developed powers of the nation-state to protect interracial democracy and "free" labor: an unfulfilled horizon that presaged the "second Reconstruction" of the civil rights movement or awaits fulfillment by a third Reconstruction today.[3] For understandable reasons, revolutionary incompletion is the mode in which Reconstruction has been reclaimed for broadly progressive purposes. This narrative follows the recursive plot suggested a half-century before Foner by Du Bois: "The slave went free; stood a brief moment in the sun; then moved back again toward slavery."[4]

But does incompletion tell the full story? I want to begin by noting a risk involved when the era's revolutionary dynamics, and Du Bois's complex account of them, are condensed to his pithy summary of their narrative arc. At the heart of this book lies a fairly simple claim about what we miss when we frame Reconstruction in terms of its incompletion: we still struggle to understand American slave emancipation as a record of actually existing revolution, as Du Bois insisted it was. This is in part a narrative problem. We lack a framework for narrating the uneven paths revolution takes in a society defined by plantation slavery. In this book, I turn to literary form to read Reconstruction less as a revolution unfinished than one complexly lived through, imagined, and narrated, making the case for the historical novel as a form that helps us to trace those uneven paths.

The classic European historical novel of the nineteenth century gave shape and direction to the revolution that constituted its particular historical moment: the transition from feudal to bourgeois society. It did so in the form of the epic.[5] But for the writers explored in this book—principally George Washington Cable, Albion Tourgée, Frances Harper, Charles Chesnutt, and Du Bois—the destruction of slavery did not provide such a narrative arc. In the period following Reconstruction, these authors stretched the temporal and generic resources of the historical novel; lacking an epic framework, and yet finding in historical fiction a means for describing the epochal dimensions of the recent past, they advanced a more precarious, experimental historicism that shaped a different temporality for understanding revolution. By making revolution Reconstruction's *problematic,* their novels challenge the way we relate the unfinished and revolutionary as concepts, enabling us to question how the era continues to trouble our temporal, representational, and historical models of revolutionary change.

Identifying revolution as Reconstruction's (and the Reconstruction historical novel's) problematic does not mean advocating that the period's political gains outweigh its losses in the scales of historical justice. My concern is instead with the narrative frameworks we adopt for revolution and the understandings of historical change, stasis, and repetition that follow when we apply these narratives to the aftermath of slavery. Though not primarily empirical, these narrative questions illuminate an empirical baseline: I am asking what it means to treat slave emancipation as a revolutionary zero condition. Leaving aside for a moment the important qualifications about the juridical process that gave legal form to the social fact of slavery's abolition, if we cannot imagine a violent, uncompensated, and (relatively speaking) immediate emancipation on a scale unseen anywhere else in world history, other than Haiti, as revolution, it is hard to imagine what the concept is for.[6] This is so even if the experience of freedom—or just as pertinently for the postbellum South, the transformed characteristics of unfreedom that emerged from the struggles of the late nineteenth century—do not easily translate into the formal terms of achieved civil rights or constitute a narrative of progress.

As the prevalent sense of Reconstruction's foreclosure suggests, we struggle to think about revolution without a progressive narrative arc. The "constitutional revolution" following abolition was an important attempt to integrate formerly enslaved and functionally rightless free Black people into a republican nation-state as citizens.[7] But the truncated development of legal rights is only one narrative frame and one that measures revolution in terms of the incomplete legacies of republican constitutionalism.[8] Equally important, emancipation created a vernacular politics across the South that made exercising the rights and protections debated in legislative proceedings into an often semi-paramilitary struggle over the character of work, everyday life, and kinship that reshaped the social terrain in ways unrecognizable from chattel slavery.[9] The outcome did not resemble a just social order; the specific problems of narration I trace in this book lie in that contradiction. Another way of putting this is that the sheer depth and duration of the racial terror required to reconstruct the institutions of white supremacy in the face of changes that shattered mastery's legal and social edifice across the South attends to the epoch-making force of emancipation.

Commenting on the "momentous discontinuity" emancipation introduced into American history, Barbara Fields notes that "there is something profoundly unsettling in the contemplation of a change immense in scope and purchased at great cost, yet so ambiguous that it is impossible to say with full conviction whether it is a change for the better or for the worse."[10] How to narrate such a process? This introduction begins to outline how literary form dramatizes competing accounts of historical time that have shaped our understandings of Reconstruction and revolution, thereby helping us to read the revolutionary dynamics of a moment that remains at the limits of our models for narrating historical change.

Reconstructing Revolution

An example helps to introduce the idiosyncratic historicism I have mentioned. Sutton Griggs's novel *Imperium in Imperio: A Study of the Negro Race Problem* (1899) tells the story of the formation of a revolutionary Black nation-state in the post-emancipation South. Or rather, it doesn't quite tell that story. Instead, a partially narrated revolution hangs over the novel's retrospective plot, constituting what one of Griggs's chapter titles calls "unwritten history."[11] The novel's structure creates a revolutionary horizon that retroactively reshapes what would otherwise be, as the nod toward the nonfictional in the subtitle suggests, a more familiar history. Opening soon after emancipation, the novel encompasses the struggle for Black education, the formation of Black political leadership, disfranchisement, segregation, lynching, and the internationalization of American racial terror in the Spanish-American War: it narrates the full arc from postbellum revolutionary promise to reactionary defeat.

But Griggs relays this history in unusual form, framing himself as the editor of a nonfictional manuscript, written by one Berl Trout. As we are informed in the preface, Trout is secretary of state in, and traitor to, the revolutionary Black state, whose history remains largely untold, even as it implicitly shapes the lives of the characters on whom the novel focuses its action, Belton Piedmont and Bernard Belgrave (the state's eventual leaders). A formal structure that Tess Chakkalakal and Kenneth Warren suggest hangs "curious[ly] . . . between utopian and historical fiction" forces the reader to reinterpret historical landmarks in this fictionalized account of the transition from Reconstruction to redemption in the U.S. South.[12] Griggs's strained temporal structure acts like a thought experiment. Given the revolutionary state's retroactive presence, a narrative of a foreclosed freedom struggle and resurgent white supremacy demands to be read as a concrete genealogy of revolution.

This temporality is first apparent when Belton (who will ultimately renounce the state he has led) organizes a petition by Black students to protest the segregation of teachers at newly founded Stowe University. A peaceful invocation of the political consciousness of future race leaders melodramatically transforms into an act with immediately radical, even revolutionary, implications. The white teachers retreat in the wake of a mass of Black students who "flaunted a black flag" and "marched out of doors two by two singing 'John

Brown's Body lies mouldering in the grave and we go marching on'" (*II* 29). This incongruous intrusion of insurrectionary violence is clarified by an aside on the event's historical significance: "The errors in the South, anxious for eternal life, rightfully feared these schools more than they would have feared factories making powder, molding balls and fashioning cannons. But the New South, the South that, in the providence of god, is yet to be, could not have been formed in the womb of time had it not been for these schools. And so the receding murmurs of the scowling South that was, are lost in the gladsome shouts of the South which, please god, is yet to be" (25).

Griggs adopts a strange temporality to invoke the imaginative pull of the novel's terminal event: he narrates the protest simultaneously from the perspective of two different "New South[s]" that are "yet to be" in very different senses. On the one hand, Griggs's narrator speaks with the knowledge of a revolutionary horizon whose details, only briefly glimpsed in the preface, are unknown to the reader. He frames a familiar political history (of Black education and uplift) as antecedent to this fictional revolutionary moment. Importantly, the reader later learns that Belton joins the Imperium while at the college (though we don't yet know it, revolution is in the making). On the other hand, the aside looks forward from the 1870s to the time of writing, suggesting the emergence in Griggs's near future of a new struggle for Black rights within the postbellum U.S. civil compact, characterized by a long, gradual process of enlightenment and reform. The grammar is poised, like the action of the novel, between tenses. More importantly, it shifts between a retrospective impulse to narrate revolution historically, as a radical departure that makes alien the reader's understanding of recent history, and a prospective impulse to locate a usable politics in an unbroken past.

Griggs's historical-formal thought experiment underpins the generic strangeness immediately obvious to the novel's modern readers. Its tensions give meaning to the way the narrative swings between realistic documentation of political and historical events and melodramatic, sometimes grotesque, treatments of the same. This is a novel in which acts of moderate, even conservative, Black organization routinely portend apocalyptic conflagration: in which, for example, a conventional anti-segregation set-piece shades quickly from Belton's ejection from a Louisiana train carriage into him miraculously surviving a lynching and killing a white scientist who captures his seemingly dead body for a racist medical experiment. The exaggerated shifts of Griggs's plot reflect a treatment of narrative time that asks readers to rethink everyday political struggle in the postbellum South as the product and symptom of revolution rather than the sign of revolution's curtailment. This is so even when what we might read as the novel's political "message" is ultimately concerned with more moderate reforms to the political situation at the time of writing. By destabilizing the historical narrative of post-Reconstruction politics, Griggs's open-ended novel calls into question the reader's willingness to imagine the South's recent history as one of revolution, even when the outcome of this process cannot be expressed in the familiar terms of an achieved state structure founded on a set of civil rights.

Even though *Imperium in Imperio* does not explicitly treat the events most commonly associated with Reconstruction, its narrative temporality exemplifies the historicism explored in this book. Reconstruction conditioned a particular kind of historical novel whose formal distinctiveness rests on the attempt to unite the seemingly incompatible temporal registers of Griggs's narrative. This literary form locates two competing senses of time in the period: one associated with historical narrative and the other with political narrative. The authors I discuss write about Reconstruction with an activist intention. They share a sense that the novel form could be used broadly in the tradition of abolitionist fiction to promote political intervention in the South and advocate for the rights of freed people. Yet in representing Reconstruction as an unfinished political process, they confront a changed historical terrain: their own positive and prospective political programs (whether reformist or radical) distort as mimetic windows for interpreting the recent past. The attempt to resolve these imperatives makes visible a history that, though it might seem static, has been shaped by revolutionary change. Though not so explicitly structured as thought experiments, these novels do something similar to *Imperium in Imperio:* they estrange assumptions about politics that nineteenth-century authors brought to their work as well as associated accounts of historical time that have shaped understandings of the nineteenth century.

Not the least, this estrangement applies to the awkward relationship between Reconstruction and revolution as political temporalities that define the era. In its narrowest, most procedural sense, *Reconstruction* has a recursive meaning. In the aftermath of the Civil War, it was often presented as a political process that would enable sectional reconciliation. Set against the Confederate rebellion, the term implied restoration of the southern states to a national constitutional order. However, since this restoration involved the destruction of an entire social system—chattel slavery—the recursive political implications of Reconstruction clashed with an inflection more suggestive of social revolution.[13]

This tension animated conflicting visions of the emergent American political order after the Civil War, but it also foregrounds what Reinhart Kosselleck notes was a broader historical irony of revolution's emergence as "a linguistic product of our modernity."[14] In its early modern sense, the term *revolution* framed historical time in analogy with the cyclical, naturalistic motion of the stars. But following the American and French Revolutions, this cyclical register took on the implications of political reversal, implied by the words *rebellion* and *revolt,* to designate a human *over*turning of the existing order that creates a fundamentally new regime. In the wake of the rebellions and reactions that shaped the Age of Revolutions, this modulation signified a new "temporalization of . . . history" defined by a constitutive tension between progress and revolt.[15] On the one hand, *revolution* described a novel, rational human project premised on radical upheaval, both of a political regime and the naturalistic determinism of historical time. On the other hand, this politicization of the future gave history a progressive sense of direction that was anathema to the unruly contingency of actually existing revolutionary struggle.[16]

These tensions shaped the emergent self-consciousness of a European bourgeoisie that sought to locate its origins as a new ruling class in the same social struggles that brought the proletarian masses (in the French empire, the enslaved people of Saint Domingue) violently onto the stage of history as political subjects. By the mid-nineteenth century, in retreat from these proletarian struggles, intellectuals began to reinterpret the bourgeoisie's role as the class subject of revolution. They did so by framing private property and the nation-state as the process's guiding principles. Revolution's definitive rending of historical time came to be interpreted as a discretely political (rather than broadly social) process.[17] Of the nation-states emerging from the Age of Revolutions, the United States was the one whose foundational revolution was most often (and earliest) understood in these terms: as the creation of a more perfect constitutional, rather than a fundamentally altered social, order. In no small part, this was due to the institution of slavery. As Saidiya Hartman points out—reworking Hannah Arendt's observation that the social question in the United States was "hidden in darkness" by slavery—a narrow framing of politics functioned ideologically to equate the social with a seemingly unbridgeable race problem.[18] Maintaining slavery meant limiting revolution to its political referent.

These domestic and international histories fed a distinctively American discourse for sundering revolution from its social horizons: the jeremiad. Much reunionist discourse framed the Civil War in jeremiadic terms, as a radical transformation that nonetheless returned the institutions of the nation-state to their righteous founding ideals (from which slavery had apparently diverged).[19] This narrative resolved change, recursion, and progress by viewing Reconstruction through the lens of a Romantic theory of revolution most influentially expressed before the Civil War by the nationalist historian George Bancroft. For Bancroft, "the outbreak of a revolution is the pulsation of the time, healthful or spasmodic, according to its harmony with the civilization from which it springs."[20] The American Revolution embodied a providential transhistorical ideal toward which the convulsions and recursions of political life moved history, as into "harmony." The United States, then, was "bound to allure the world to freedom by the beauty of its example" because it fulfilled a project of the transatlantic bourgeoisie: it turned revolution from a temporal and institutional break into a process by which the nineteenth century became synchronous with its (bourgeois) origins.[21]

Contemporaries and early historians of Reconstruction reached for this vision of revolution as an internally coherent national zeitgeist. However, the sheer social upheaval created by emancipation strained at the narrative of how revolution was supposed to proceed in an American context. This was the case even for writers committed to the most conservative invocation of revolutionary change. At the beginning of the twentieth century, Columbia University historian William Dunning established what for a half-century became the standard account of the period. He did so by modeling the affect of an emergent academic historical discipline on the disavowal and displacement of revolution. For Dunning, dispassionate history meant disowning a narrative of revolutionary melodrama analogous in its misplaced passions to the project of Radical Reconstruction. The "reckless and revolutionary policy" of the radicals, he argued, had plunged the entire nation into a juvenile (if necessary) obsession with "the picturesque details of Ku-Klux operations and carpetbag legislation" that distracted from the real plot of the revolutionary story. The latter was "to be found in the record not of the vanquished but the victorious section."[22] Once the South was liberated from the childlike misrule of its Black population, Dunning claimed, the revolutionary dimensions of Reconstruction passed from a regional tragedy to a national *Bildung*. Viewed from this perspective, the Civil War instigated a "revolution . . . in the whole national character and feeling" that integrated a mature (avowedly Anglo-Saxon) nation-state from the broken pieces of sectional strife.[23] Dunning frames revolution as a Burkean constitutional process anathema to the tumult of the postbellum South. But his providential Anglo-Saxonism holds two revolutions in unstable, constitutive opposition. His narrative found such popularity because, however ambivalently, it located the ordered, providential sweep of national progress within the anarchic clash of revolution and counterrevolution. This conflict, rather than constitutional process, was the motor of history.

As much is demonstrated by the fact that popularizations of Dunning's narrative fixed attention squarely on the "picturesque details" (and geographical region) that the professional historian disavowed. Exemplifying this popularizing mode, Bowers began *The Tragic Era* by positing: "That the Southern people literally were put to the torture is vaguely understood, but even historians have shrunk from the unhappy task of showing us the torture chambers."[24] In these chambers, Dunning's revolutionary *Bildung* reverts to a tragedy in which emancipation triggers a social revolution that betrays Lincoln's jeremiadic errand. For Bowers, after Lincoln's death, congressional Republicans and emancipated slaves played the part of the French Revolutionary Terror, co-opting the Union's righteous victory over the Confederate rebellion and forcing southern Democrats to resort to their own necessarily revolutionary methods to protect the Constitution and white supremacy. Although he celebrated the latter in rabidly racist terms, Bowers (a populist western Democrat) framed the Redeemers' victory over Radical Reconstruction as pyrrhic from the perspective of the nation-state. Even after white rule was returned to the South, a decade of anarchy meant that "power passed during the revolution, from the agriculturalist to the industrialist and the financier," so that "the Jeffersonian Republic that came in with the revolution of 1800 gave way to the Hamiltonian Republic brought in by the counter-revolution of 1865–78. The tables had been turned. The age-old fight would continue, the spirits of Jefferson and Hamilton leading as before, but the advantage, under the new order, had passed to the latter."[25]

Despite their political differences, Dunning and Bowers describe Reconstruction as a competition between transhistorical epoch-making forces (coded as national) and foreclosed insurrectionary upheavals (specific to the South). Oddly, both processes have the same name, *revolution* (which for Bowers is apparently interchangeable with *counterrevolution*). This temporal and definitional tension indicates how Reconstruction strained a discourse that was designed to resolve revolutionary foreclosure and transition and to make clear distinctions between legitimate and illegitimate historical change. This strain was not limited to Reconstruction's historical detractors; it also characterized contemporary antislavery efforts to promote Reconstruction as the fulfillment of the U.S. revolutionary tradition.

In *The Negro in the American Rebellion* (1867), formerly enslaved abolitionist William Wells Brown uses "the part which the Negro took in suppressing the Slaveholders' Rebellion" to demand protection for Black people as citizens of the nation-state.[26] Rather than a straightforward historical narrative of Black participation in the Union war effort, the book takes the form of a genealogy that accumulates instances of Black resistance to the Slave Power. Denmark Vesey's and Nat Turner's insurrections accompany participation in the Revolutionary and Civil Wars as evidence of Black fidelity to "the revolutionary struggle of our fathers for their freedom."[27] While Brown's unorthodox jeremiad frames this loyalty as a transhistorical continuity, much of the resistance he recounts is at best ambivalently national. His juxtapositional form—favoring extensive quotation of previously published accounts and fragments of testimony over narrative—compounds the interpretive ambivalence. As a result, the referent of his "American rebellion" is ambiguous: the slaveholders' rebellion, Black rebellion against the slaveholders, and a broader (even metaphysical) antislavery rebellion against a national Slave Power that outlasts the Civil War all overlap, making emancipation into the contingent product of competing violent insurrections as much as a national errand. Despite Brown's political appeal to a Bancroftian revolutionary zeitgeist, it is not clear that emancipation constitutes one of history's "legitimate revolutions," which proceeds "by the gradual expansion of its institutions to suit the onward march of society."[28]

Despite fracturing the temporality of revolutionary legitimacy, Reconstruction seemed to portend revolution all the same. The abolitionist and expatriate German "'48er," Carl Schurtz—who experienced revolution in Europe before fighting for the Union—recognized this contradiction as early as 1865, highlighting its repercussions for narratives of revolutionary incompletion. Reporting on "conditions in the South" for the U.S. Senate, he claims that "the general government of the republic has, by proclaiming the emancipation of the slaves, commenced a great social revolution in the south, but has, as yet, not completed it. Only the negative part of it is accomplished."[29] Schurtz warns that planter rebellion and "negro insurrection" will follow if Andrew Johnson returns power to the states before "means are found to effect a final settlement of the labor question according to the logic of the great revolution."[30] He cautions: "Nothing renders society more restless than a social revolution but half accomplished, it naturally tends to develop its logical consequences, but is hindered by adverse agencies that work in another direction; nor can it return to the point from which it started. There are then continual vibrations and fluctuations between two opposites which keep society in the nervous uneasiness and excitement growing from the lingering strife between the antagonistic tendencies."[31] Schurtz's providential logic captures the sense of foreclosure implicit in a myth of revolution as the project of the American state, whether this foreclosure is plotted as errand, *Bildung*, or tragedy. Anything short of state-managed transition to a free labor society, it seems, constitutes pure negation: movement without direction.[32] But as he acknowledges, history moving aberrantly is still history moving, and moving irreversibly. Wielding an understanding of revolutionary legitimacy imported from Europe and recast in the mold of the American jeremiad, Schurtz raises the representational problem of how to imagine and narrate a historical change that proceeds aslant revolution's preconceived logic but still sets historical time on new rails.

This representational problem continues to define the relationship between the unfinished and the revolutionary. One counterintuitive implication of Foner's now commonsense phrase *unfinished revolution* is that it raises the question: where should we look for history's finished revolutions? The phrase announces a deferred connection between emancipation and revolution, privileging a revolutionary terminus that by definition renders the South a partial case. For Foner, this foreclosed moment looks like a complete transition to an activist, civil rights–protecting liberal state.[33] Dunning, Bowers, Brown, and Schurtz offer very different perspectives on Reconstruction from each other (and from Foner), but they all approach it as a national zeitgeist. Through this lens, they do not identify a singular positive revolutionary content in Reconstruction, but with varying degrees of consciousness, they depict it as a moment that sets revolutionary time out of joint.

It is this disjointed temporality that historical novels of Reconstruction dramatize. They do so through a narrative equivalent of the photographic negative, allowing us to see how slave emancipation refracts the concepts through which revolutionary time has been understood, past and present. Schurtz's representational dilemma, then, *is* the formal dilemma of the historical novel of Reconstruction. I am interested in thinking with novelists as they work through the ambiguity that comes from thinking of Reconstruction as revolution. Employing versions of the temporal distension I have identified in *Imperium in Imperio,* the novels discussed in the following chapters give imaginative form to emancipation as an "event" in the sense intended by Alain Badiou: an epochal occurrence that, even as it eludes positive categorization, demands fidelity to transformed conditions that fundamentally alter existing means for understanding the passage of history.[34] The pressure of maintaining fidelity to emancipation's event led writers to pursue a literary form adequate to dramatizing a series of important questions about the nature of revolution as conditioned by slavery: how do you narrate an epochal change that also feels like a retrenchment? In what direction does history travel if it does not progress? What narratives of race, class, and region can encompass both the fact of continued domination and the experience of ruptured power? These questions frame revolution as Reconstruction's unavoidable problematic, rather than as a historical substance to be measured and tallied until we hit the requisite quantity to apply the name.

Reconstructing Literary History

By the term *historical novel of Reconstruction,* then, I mean something more specific than novels that are about the period but written after it. I mean a recognizable and coherent—if short-lived—aesthetic form that gives shape to Reconstruction as revolution by submitting the generic constructs of historical narrative to the questions posed in the previous section. Because, if Reconstruction strained the temporal models of revolution, the attempt to represent its emergent historicity at the end of the nineteenth and beginning of the twentieth centuries (the period covered here) also stretched the literary genre most associated with revolutionary transition.

Discussing the contemporary historical novel, Fredric Jameson asks a question that helps conceptualize my account of a form shaped by a problematic. He asks:

> Is it still possible that the word revolution is historically and even dialectically ambiguous? . . . To use the same word, revolution, for historically different transitions from one mode of production to another is to suggest an identity between them which is misleading . . . This ambiguity suggests some doubt as to whether the historical novel—historically a narrative

form generated by the passage from the old order to a bourgeois society, as well as the representation of the historical passage—can function as a useful generic category for novels which issue from and represent wholly different kinds of historical convulsions.[35]

Rather than abandon the category, Jameson reads it in relation to a phenomenon (revolution) that is not the same in all time and all places, invoking the "multiplicity and differentiation of standpoints" on revolution that might emerge when the "generic term is [treated as] metaphorical or analogical."[36] By subjecting the resources of a genre "generated by the passage from the old order to a bourgeois society" to the social conditions of slavery, Reconstruction historical novels imagine a convulsion that did not lead to the civil, institutional, and political categories associated with the bourgeois-democratic nation-state, the locus point for a model of transition that has been central to accounts of the historical novel as well as accounts of revolution. These novels produce their sense of an epoch in tension with an expected and foreclosed narrative of transition.

We can approach this formal stretching as a way of producing knowledge about the past, as an act of theoretical production in the sense conceived by Louis Althusser: rather than a positive model of revolution, these novels present Reconstruction's revolutionary history "in the rigor of a problem."[37] They allow us to read revolution contrapuntally, through the contradictions, tensions, aporias, and tautologies that writers navigate as they plot their own and a culture's models of historical transition onto the resistant terrain of the Reconstruction South. This, then, is a precarious genre that produces its sense of revolutionary change in tension with a broader political purpose. But precisely this openness to formal and historical precarity in political fiction provides a window onto the literary culture of the South's long nineteenth century, one in which "the nation's region" is not a storehouse of tradition but a terrain for theorizing revolution.[38]

Because these are, in a sense, historical novels in spite of their political content and purpose, it is necessary to discuss their political function—not least because it is as political writing that scholars have begun to recover Reconstruction literature as a field. Sharon Kennedy-Nolle articulates an emerging consensus when she argues that "it is primarily for its role in reconstructing the American South and its citizenry in a postwar nation that Reconstruction literature is important."[39] It makes sense to think about Reconstruction literature in relation to its political purposes. Indeed, the authors explored in this book all conceived of writing as an activist pursuit that intervened in the history it narrated to continue something of Reconstruction's work in the present.

In addition to publishing fiction, George Washington Cable wrote essays advocating for civil rights and the abolition of the convict lease system. He was forced out of the South when using his literary reputation as a native voice on the region for these political ends involved direct social contact with Black political allies.[40] Albion Tourgée was a Radical Republican "carpetbagger" who moved to North Carolina after fighting in the Civil War. He was influential in drafting the state's Reconstruction constitution, which ensured Black representation on juries, universal manhood suffrage, and homestead laws protecting tenants from large landowners. As a judge, he investigated the Ku Klux Klan at great personal risk and later argued Homer Plessy's landmark anti-segregation defense at the Supreme Court.[41] Conceiving imaginative writing as an instrument for political change, Tourgée modeled his literary endeavors on abolitionist fiction: he republished his breakthrough novel *A Fool's Errand* (1879) with a lengthy second part, modeled on *A Key to Uncle Tom's Cabin* (1853), that detailed the historical actions of the Ku Klux Klan fictionalized in the novel; he also adapted the book into a Tom Show–like stage production. As a critic, he attacked literary realism for dispensing with the didacticism of the abolitionist generation and making an aesthetic virtue of moral ambivalence.[42]

Chesnutt turned from a career teaching freed people in Reconstruction-era North Carolina to writing in an attempt to use fiction as a form of political education. Seeing Tourgée's success writing Reconstruction with a "necessarily limited intercourse with colored people," Chesnutt wondered in his journal: "why could not a colored man, who has lived among colored people all his life . . . write a far better book about the South than judge Tourgée or Mrs. Stowe has written?"[43] "Fifteen years of life in the South, in one of the most eventful eras of its history," left Chesnutt determined to "write for a purpose" that he understood as war of position. Writing "not so much [for] the elevation of the colored people as the elevation of the whites," he envisioned a literary "organized crusade" against a political order that could not be "stormed and taken by assault" but "must be mined, and we will find ourselves in their midst before they think it."[44]

Harper began writing novels late in an activist life. Her magazine fictions, *Minnie's Sacrifice* (1869) and *Sowing and Reaping* (1870), were serialized in the Black newspaper the *Christian Recorder* as Reconstruction unfolded. These stories continued Harper's long engagement with activist print culture, instrumentalizing the Black press's "weaving of the poetic and the political" for the cause of Reconstruction.[45] Later she used *Iola Leroy* (1892)—the first novel she published in book form, explored here in chapter 3 alongside Chesnutt's *The House behind the Cedars* (1900)—to look back on Reconstruction, renew the era's activist imperative, and give historical shape to a career spent writing and speaking in the service of abolition, the women's movement, temperance reform, and civil rights. Finally, Du Bois's career-long fusion of scholarship and activism had as a central plank his ambition to upend popular narratives of Reconstruction as a period of Black misrule. This desire stretched from his early reassessment of the Freedmen's Bureau, in a 1901 edition of the *Atlantic Monthly* and his 1909 paper on Reconstruction at the American Historical Association, to his magisterial radical history *Black Reconstruction* (1935). Less well known, and examined in chapter 4, is the fact that Du Bois's revisionist project involved his first, still unpublished, attempt at a (historical) novel, *Scorn: A Romance,* in 1905.

Even this brief summary highlights the political function of the period's writing that has concerned scholars shaping the field of Reconstruction literature. Increased attention to the period's print culture has complicated the story of sectional "reunion and its discontents."[46] Moving beyond the paradigms of "the romance of reunion," literary studies have revealed how fiction shaped the imagined geographies and ideological parameters of a messy political process, reminding modern readers that "the Civil War made possible many worlds."[47] Part of what constitutes Reconstruction literature as a renewed critical object is the way it deployed changing ideas of civic legitimacy to shape the unfolding national compact.[48] Within this process of ideological legitimation and contestation, literary conceptions of the South as an internal colony, and of Reconstruction as a colonial encounter, helped to racially segregate the broadened ideas of citizenship and nationalism deployed by Reconstruction writers.[49]

The explicitly political character (even instrumentality) of this writing partly explains its neglect on the syllabi and by the literary institutions that have shaped the canon. If these texts are not traditionally literary (let alone obviously "good" literature), they seemed important only as documentary evidence for the more developed historical study of Reconstruction. In response, scholars have begun to recover Reconstruction's *literary* history and to distinguish a literary approach to Reconstruction by focusing on how the textual construction of the fantasy life of the postbellum nation-state informs still unfinished battles over the parameters and exclusions of American citizenship.[50] By contrast, I want to put some pressure on the ideas of citizenship, nation-state, and racial formation in play when Reconstruction literature is framed, either in celebratory or critical mode, as the imaginative corollary to an ongoing national (or nationalist) project. The forms writers employed to imagine Reconstruction *historically* as well as politically provide a record of experiences not easily incorporated into, or analogized with, the unfinished business of the activist civil rights state. This is not to downplay the radical importance of the struggle for legal citizenship in a former slave society; rather, it is to emphasize that the emergent historicity plotted in these novels challenges the sense of continuity gleaned from viewing Reconstruction literature through the lens of unfinished civic contestation.

At issue is the conception of historical time and the kind of knowledge about the past (and present) we get from reading literature. One motivation for recovering Reconstruction literature, informed by literary studies' "temporal turn," has been to develop what Cody Marrs and Christopher Hager call "an internal periodization of the century"; such a periodization is designed to trouble the temporal trajectory that relegated Reconstruction from literary history in favor of a modernizing narrative in which the Civil War clears the way for the development of realism, naturalism, and later modernism.[51] To this end, critics have foregrounded continuity, extension, and recursion as Reconstruction's literary temporalities.[52] Marrs proposes that Reconstruction print culture provides an aesthetic record of a "long Civil War" that "enables us to reconceive the shape of Reconstruction as a literary-historical period, which resembles a parabola, moving in waves as the fight over emancipation morphs and modulates."[53] In an otherwise very different account, Brook Thomas argues that the literary resonances of Reconstruction complicate the symbolic end date of 1877—and narratives of sudden, tragic reversal that date implies—thereby extending a "period of Reconstruction" into an "era of Reconstruction."[54]

While this book focuses on novels written during Thomas's era of Reconstruction, I do not believe that timelines of extension and continuity do more justice to the lived experience of the period's upheavals and the narrative cultures they produced than revolutionary convulsion, fracture, and crisis. Revolution might seem like a disconcertingly homogeneous mode of periodizing compared to the deconstructive impulses of a temporal turn attuned to the "dissonances in historical metanarratives that have often underpinned the nineteenth-century Americanist field."[55] However, narrating emancipation as revolution need not "reproduce the nationalist narratives that frame the Civil War as a triumphal endpoint and moral cleansing of the republic."[56] Nor is the alternative to this view a continuity that renders Reconstruction into the ongoing "central theme" of American history (literary or otherwise).[57] Building on the work of critics and theorists who have opened up the temporal dimensions of nineteenth-century literary studies, I make the case for revolution as a contentious, uneven, and dynamic narrative timeline, or "problem-space," which writers debated and reconstructed to give meaning and form to the epochal significance of Reconstruction.[58]

Literature periodizes but not under circumstances that it has chosen. Each of the novels I discuss has a clear political stake in reviving the era's radicalism following the wave of political violence, electoral fraud, and state neglect that saw revanchist Democrat regimes return to power across the South (whether we date the completion of this counterrevolution to 1873, 1877, or the 1890s). As political novels, they make a claim on Reconstruction as a continuous present in which they aim to intervene, but in constructing this present, the political frameworks that they wield begin to become historical, revealing a recent past in which things have changed irrevocably. Foregrounding how writers plot this tension, I frame the period's literary historical significance more in terms of its ephemerality than continuity over time. These novels demonstrate many of the shared features that might have constituted a more permanent, transmissible genre, but without the settled narrative of transition from which the historical novel draws its "readily adaptable model" and through which revolution is so often understood, they constitute a foreclosed genre.[59] To adapt Toni Morrison's account of slavery's legacies, this is not a genre to pass on.[60] But as an imaginative means of theorizing the past, it does something that seems increasingly difficult today: it makes visible the thoroughgoing historical change that underpins a history all too easily imaginable either as static or heroic.

Presented in this binary form, emancipation can seem, as Hartman argues, like a "nonevent," one characterized by persistently racialized distinctions between political life and social relations that conditioned the peculiarly "occluded emergence of the social question" during Reconstruction.[61] This aspect of Hartman's account of slavery's afterlives—which runs together change and progress in an otherwise generative critique of liberalism's racialized dimensions—has influenced an understanding of emancipation's temporality that makes it anathema to revolution.[62] The same might be said for emancipation and the historical novel.[63] But if we limit our understanding of historical change (and literary historicism) to these terms, we miss what Steven Hahn suggests is "a much larger universe of politics" animating emancipation's revolutionary scope.[64] We also overlook one of slavery's key cultural afterlives: the compulsion writers felt to grapple with revolution as a means for understanding their recent past. The reproduction of forms of Black unfreedom after slavery is part of this narrative, not its antithesis. These novels do not plot revolution as a romantic overcoming of the past but, instead, through an idiosyncratic version of what the historical novel's most influential theorist, Georg Lukács, refers to as "necessary anachronism."[65] This uneven temporal perspective allows us to reconnect the afterlives of slavery and emancipation to a revolutionary history from which they are too often separated.

Reconstructing the Historical Novel

The texts discussed in the following chapters are political novels; they are also novels of the recent past: the earliest, Cable's *The Grandissimes* and Tourgée's *A Fool's Errand,* were originally published in 1879.[66] While Cable's is the most obviously "historical," because it depicts an old Creole world in decline following the Louisiana Purchase, its nearness to its allegorical subject complicates chronological distance as a measure of historicity, as do all the novels. At the other end of the spectrum, Chesnutt's *The House behind the Cedars* and Harper's *Iola Leroy* are passing fictions that, though set during Reconstruction, engage self-consciously with the occlusion of the era in racial genre fiction at the end of the century. So, why think of these texts as, or in relation to, historical novels at all?

These questions of recency and politics are inherent to the form. What Lukács called the genre's "historical sense" has little to do with chronology. Instead, it describes a move from a purely period sense of the past—defined by distant manners, customs, and fashions (inflected by the present's ideologies)—to a necessarily dialectical perspective that seeks to capture the relationship between the structuring forces of historical change and the situated collective experience of that change.[67] So conceived, the historical novel uses the past (however recent) to represent *history as a process* and to raise theoretical questions about what history is, how it moves, and how consciousness of that movement differs between (and constitutes) periods.[68] It is this aspect of the form—rather than a family relation to literary realism implicit in the act of attempting to capture the past authentically—that concerns me.[69] Of the writers I discuss at greatest length, only Cable and Chesnutt tend to be included in the pantheon of American realists, and then only tentatively, because their interest in documenting regional lifeways intersects with the generic slipperiness and explicitly political purpose that characterizes my texts. These novels mix genres: as political fictions, they make use of melodramatic and didactic elements of sentimental fiction; their plotlines hue to the conventions of romance. Nevertheless, they all adapt a historicizing impulse for a moment and a social terrain in which the "relentlessly serial nature of life in history" does not correspond to an epic sense of direction.[70]

Representing such a terrain requires a particularly self-conscious deployment and concentration of anachronism. As Lukács describes it, anachronism is the counterpoint to historical fiction's epic dimension. For all his focus on the historical emergence of the bourgeois nation-state as modern epic, implicit in Lukács's argument is an account of anachronism as the quality that creates an immanent engagement with revolutionary process.[71] Anachronism results from the attempt to represent history's emergence in the everyday, to root structures that "led up to the present . . . but whose later significance contemporaries naturally could not see" in the political contingencies of the moment from which they unfolded, rather than with a detached perspective.[72] This situated historicism—in which the writer imaginatively inhabits the space of an everyday life from which they are separated by the same revolutionary social transformation whose lived experience they seek to represent—requires, as James Chandler stresses in his account of Romanticist historical consciousness, not only a diachronic act of periodization ("the historian's code") but also a synchronic one of translation (a "textualization of culture").[73] By occupying and translating a system of manners and customs that it selects as the representative ground of an everyday life transformed by revolution, the historical novel opens up a necessarily anachronistic perspective on the past.[74] This divided perspective involves a reading as much as a writing of history: it raises questions about what connects and what sepa-rates past and present, and roots these questions in the relationship between revolutionary crisis and epochal change.[75]

Because it can seem at once the archetypal site of continuity between past and present and a space of revolutionary convulsion, the everyday life of the Reconstruction South is fertile ground for this kind of representation. In a symptomatic sense, anachronism characterizes even the most triumphal accounts of Reconstruction as a nationalist epic. In his contribution to a se-ries of articles on Reconstruction in the *Atlantic Monthly* in 1901, Woodrow Wilson called time on Reconstruction. "We have come out of the atmosphere of the sixties," he proclaimed, "the time seems remote, historic, not of our day. We have dropped its thinking, lost its passion, forgot its anxieties, and should be ready to speak of it, not as partisans, but as historians."[76] For Wilson, "the sixties" could serve as synecdoche for a generational epoch because, in a Hegelian process, the struggle to quash first slavery and then social revo-lution in the South produced a national "revolution of consciousness" that revealed force to be the true basis of U.S. nationhood. In the crucible of a radically anachronistic section, a progressivist nation discovered its imperial future.[77] However, his claim that Reconstruction "is still revolutionary matter," fit only for a historian who is "dangerously cool"—a "partisan" as much as the detached social scientist celebrated by Wilson's contemporary William Dunning—suggests that Wilson's epochal narrative of national integration is difficult to close satisfactorily as epic.[78]

A year later, Wilson's friend Thomas Dixon put this to the test. The first novel of Dixon's Reconstruction trilogy, *The Leopard's Spots: A Romance of the White Man's Burden* (1902), depicts Reconstruction's defeat as a progressivist, white supremacist epic for the era of the Spanish-American War. His hero, Charlie Gaston, represents "the young South," a generation who dream not of "local supremacy," like their slaveholding fathers, but of "conquest of the globe."[79] By overcoming "the farce of '67," this generation promises to bestow the nation with "the rising consciousness of Nationality and World-Mission" required to prosecute imperial rule in "the foulest slave-pen of the Orient" (*LS* 435). Gaston arrives at this conclusion after his Reconstruction experience confirms the oft-repeated words of his mentor, Dr. Durham, which form the novel's mantra: "you can not build in a democracy a nation inside a nation of two antagonistic races. The future American must be an Anglo-Saxon or a Mulatto" (383). But despite the novel's triumphalism, "the impossible position of the negro in America" is not something it resolves (382). Although Dixon stridently endorses segregation and disfranchisement, neither quite answers the problem of how to locate the future American in "the racial absolutism of the Anglo-Saxon in the South" (333). The quasi-postcolonial experience that allows the Reconstruction South to serve as a modernizing parable of "the white man's burden" leaves it "literally chained to the festering body of a Black Death!" (Dixon's preferred metaphor for Reconstruction as both racial catastrophe and historical retrogression) (436).[80] Since Dixon makes clear that a return to slavery and the sectionalism he equates with it are decadent impossibilities, his South remains, like "the position of the negro," "impossibl[y]" divided between imperial futurity and regional anachronism.

As in much white supremacist writing on Reconstruction, the ideal of southern whiteness behind Dixon's epochal progress narrative is only one step from a regressive nightmare. This ambivalence pervades his account of a lynch mob that transforms before Gaston's eyes into "a great crawling swaying creature, half reptile half beast, half dragon half man" (*LS* 380). In a novel that endorses a racially pure body politic—and makes southern racial violence a national rite of passage to achieve it—Dixon's framing of the white mass as an impossibly hybrid "creature" locates in the South a political body not so easily purified: one that remains "a nation within a nation." Tellingly, when Gaston imagines the anti-Reconstruction spirit as the basis for a new national consciousness, he turns to Haiti for images of Black insurrection as the contemporary "world-crisis" located in the South (437). The novel is poised between narrating a revolution overturned in the production of a new national (or world) spirit and a different kind of revolution whose anachronistic legacies haunt an epic origin myth.

This may seem a far cry from the novels I focus on. After all, the pairing of Wilson's *History of the American People* (1902) with the second novel of Dixon's trilogy, *The Clansman* (1905), provided D. W. Griffith with an urtext for his cinematic spectacle of Reconstruction history, *The Birth of a Nation* (1915). With Griffith's film, "American movies were born . . . in a racist epic" that soon became the popular cultural archetype of what Du Bois dubbed "the propaganda of history."[81] If a twinned sense of Black revolutionary disaster and redeeming white (counter)revolutionary spirit is antithetical to the politics of the writers I address, the hesitations in Wilson's and Dixon's periodization suggest how even the most symptomatic, instrumentalized attempt to resolve Reconstruction's revolutionary anachronism exceeds the bounds of epic closure.

This problem explains both the paranoia of Dixon's apparently triumphal racism and the sheer repetitiveness of his narrative, recapitulated over three lengthy volumes. More than just a function of Dixon's pathology, this indicates a formal pattern, shared by the novels I discuss, in which writers seem to resolve the anachronisms created by plotting Reconstruction as revolution, only to generate narrative energy (and length) by grappling with the temporal unevenness such a plotting creates. This *formal* treatment of revolutionary ambiguity pervades novels with radically different political aims, variously taking shape as the racist national epic of a revolution overturned in Dixon's *The Leopard's Spots* (1902) and *The Clansman* (1905); the pro-abolitionist tragedy of a revolution betrayed in Albion Tourgée's *A Fool's Errand* and *Bricks without Straw* (1880); nostalgia for an old world lost in Thomas Nelson Page's *Red Rock* (1898) and Joel Chandler Harris's *Gabriel Tolliver* (1902); a revolution allegorized and deferred in George Washington Cable's *The Grandissimes*; a subterranean revolution, undiscovered in Sutton Griggs's *Imperium in Imperio*; a revolution passed through and misrecognized in Charles Chesnutt's *The House behind the Cedars* and Frances Harper's *Iola Leroy*; or a revolution repeatedly retold in W. E. B. Du Bois's *Scorn*.

Whether in the guise of Dixon, Wilson, and Griffith's progressivism or Page's nostalgia, the (troubled) epic became the dominant mode for narrating Reconstruction for much of the twentieth century because it helped to map a segregationist nation-state's imagined geography. By framing the consequences of emancipation as strictly "the Southerner's problem," it exported them to a region coded at once as backward and in the vanguard of national life: "you are the real provincial," the opening of Page's *Red Rock* screams at a national readership whom it teaches how to control a colonial subject population.[82] However, as Raymond Williams observes, the epic is only one key for revolution and one that harmonizes most readily with a "post-revolutionary generation," for whom the contradictions of revolutionary process have been resolved by a new hegemonic formation.[83] The years of dominance without hegemony that followed Reconstruction in the South produced different narrative possibilities. What marks out the writers I explore, who sought to oppose rather than support that unstable system of dominance, is that they tarry with the anachronisms of revolutionary change; they plot revolutionary development not as the epic birth of a nation but as it was conditioned by the combined and uneven development of the Unites States and its internal colony.

In doing so, they show that an epic model of transition exhausts neither the concept of revolution nor the narrative form of the historical novel. It is worth remembering that even the account of bourgeois revolution on which Lukács drew is not one of linear transition. Instead, in *The Eighteenth Brumaire of Louis Bonaparte* (1852), Karl Marx roots his narrative of what he considered to be the defining revolutionary experience of the first half of the nineteenth century in anachronism. He imagines the series of failed alliances between the revolutionary Parisian proletariat and factions of the bourgeoisie competing for state power after the February Revolution as a grotesque (anachronous) body: "Each party kicks from behind at that driving forward and in front leans over towards the party which presses backwards. No wonder that in this ridiculous posture it loses its balance and, having made the inevitable grimaces, collapses with curious capers. The revolution thus moves in a descending line. It finds itself in this state of retrogressive motion before the last February barricade has been cleared away and the first revolutionary authority constituted."[84] Marx's critique of the bourgeois-democratic state form is a narrative of revolutionary failure, but it is also an account of the contradictions of actual revolutionary experience, driven by the bourgeoisie's attempt to contain the proletariat and peasantry. In critiquing a liberal fantasy of the bourgeoisie as revolutionary subject, Marx built a central principle of his historical materialism—that "men [*sic*] make their own history, but they do not make it just as they please; they do not make it under circumstances chosen by themselves"—on a narrative of revolutionary anachronism.[85]

Anachronism, then, is a historical materialist (rather than historicist) temporal resource for comprehending the relationship between the *experience of historical crisis* and a *narrative of historical direction*. Its temporal nuances are especially important for imagining social change in a slave society.[86] As Hartman argues, slavery seemed to make everyday life the terrain of racializing processes beyond the pale of politics, thereby rendering history static. As much is evident in the ubiquitous attacks on "social equality" (as code words for racial integration and interracial marriage) that met any and all political agitation against the status quo. Crucially, for the writers studied here, this seemingly ossified terrain—potentially the sign of the social question's occlusion—is the backdrop against which revolutionary change (although not transition) becomes most apparent and narratable. By placing the historical novel's epic dimensions in relationship to the stubborn anachronisms of postemancipation social life, Reconstruction historical novelists turn a temporal quality that Lukács discussed in relation to the bourgeois nation-state and industrial capitalism into a representational medium for considering what Ernst Bloch (Lukács's intellectual confidant and subject of his occasional critical ire) referred to as the "objectively nonsynchronous" experience of historical time and revolution at the periphery of those systems.[87]

Emancipation transformed the social relations governing everyday life in the South, even as it produced newly repressive forms of racialized domination. For that reason, the various practices, ideologies, relationships, and customs that signify the stuff of the everyday—of the social—are of central concern throughout this book. Each chapter explores a literary lens that a writer, or writers, uses to access the nonsynchronous temporalities of social life in the South: Cable uses the allegorical terrain of Creole New Orleans to represent the so-called caste system as a space of social transformation and political retrenchment; by balancing a politicized (and didactic) narrative irony against sincere attachments to regional custom in the South, Tourgée explores revolutionary dilemmas about the state and everyday life; Harper and Chesnutt use the sentimental poetics of passing fiction to question the historical continuity implied by the color line as an emergent discourse of racial custom; finally, Du Bois experiments with counterfactual narrative to track the untimely social formation of a post-emancipation peasantry. By focusing on how novelists plot the tension between treating these representational fields synchronically (as means of representing continuities between past and present) and diachronically (as spheres of social life transformed by the abolition of slavery), each chapter demonstrates a particular political paradigm for revolutionary change being stretched by Reconstruction.

Chapter 1 reads instabilities in Cable's allegorical treatment of Creole New Orleans in *The Grandissimes* (1880) and his shorter fiction as representative of the pressure that race and region place on the liberal narrative of transition he advanced in his anti-segregationist political writing. Cable's political writing criticizes what he frames as an exoticized, historically fixed, southern caste system for its failure to produce liberal separations between public and private life. This distinction between liberal modernity and an exotic, backward caste system plots a (blocked) progress narrative and informs Cable's subtly racialized desire for a distinctly southern road to liberalism. However, in his fictional representations of New Orleans, Cable represents the caste system as a much more contingent site of struggle on which social life is radically transformed, even as it does not progress toward a liberal public sphere. This chapter argues that the allegorical structure of *The Grandissimes*—in which New Orleans's early-nineteenth-century Creole elite acts as an ambiguous parabolic substitute for the epochal decline of the contemporary Plantocracy—expresses a condition of revolutionary interregnum defined by nonprogressive historical transformation.

Cable's antebellum allegorical framework depicts a historical moment caught in a temporal loop. This bears similarities to his friend Mark Twain's allusions to the period in *Adventures of Huckleberry Finn* (1885), originally serialized in the *Century Magazine* alongside Cable's anti-segregationist essays. Huck's and Tom's cruel charade of "set[ting] a nigger free that was already free before" indicts the tragic deferral of Reconstruction's promises, but Cable's fiction collapses allegorical distance to create a more complex temporality than Twain's more famous "time of the evasion."[88] Of these two archetypal white southern liberals, I focus on Cable because his allegorical interregnum frames a radically changed social life that pressures the historicism underpinning his politics. Where commentators since the civil rights movement have used Cable to celebrate and critique southern liberalism, I highlight how his quarrel with transition as revolution's narrative form challenges the assumption (common to his celebrants and critics) that progress is the historicist mode for conceiving emancipation.

Chapter 2 reads Albion Tourgée's Reconstruction novels, *A Fool's Errand* and *Bricks without Straw* (1880), alongside his case for the defense in *Plessy v. Ferguson* (1896) to explore republican questions surrounding the role of the state as a revolutionary agent. Tourgée plots Reconstruction's failure as the result of a historical impasse between two monolithic sections (North and South), equally sincere in their devotion to divergent social systems. His literary irony enables him to advance a politics premised on the transformative potential of a powerful nation-state to uproot deep-seated social customs and sincerely held beliefs at the same time as he depicts the social as an organic space beyond and prior to state power. This ambivalence, rehearsed and reframed in the *Plessy* defense's ironic discussion of segregation as *the* southern "custom," results from Tourgée's attempt to historicize an era in which it was difficult to discern whether revolution was something done to the state or something the state did. I argue that Tourgée's strained irony (and strained republicanism) plot new revolutionary dynamics conditioned by slavery. His work provides a point of departure for a critique of cultural theory that depicts racial continuities in republican civic ideology and possessive individualism as proof of emancipation's nonrevolutionary status.

Chapter 3 elaborates on segregation as an image of social custom by turning to fin de siècle passing novels to theorize Reconstruction's revolutionary event: taken here to be the uncompensated abolition of slavery as a system of human property. I argue that Chesnutt and Harper use the passing novel's allusive poetics, along with the political strategies of sentimental fiction, to question an emergent consensus in the period about the continuity between slavery and segregation. Their novels pick up on a symptomatic feature of turn-of-the-century passing novels: slavery's status as a metaphor through which to express (and protest) this continuity. Their treatment of Reconstruction as an elusive but persistent historical setting figures a moment of fracture that the abolitionist-derived representational strategies of passing fiction cannot represent. By depicting slavery's shift from a system of property to a metaphor for emergent Jim Crow racial segregation—and treating this shift as a fraught and anachronistic period discourse of the 1890s—Harper and Chesnutt question how to protest new forms of racial domination without passing over Reconstruction.

Chapter 4 moves from the problem of the revolutionary event to that of the revolutionary subject. It explores how W. E. B. Du Bois developed and revised a peculiarly recursive and elliptical form of counterfactual narrative between his first, and still unpublished, novel, *Scorn: A Romance,* and his Marxist history, *Black Reconstruction.* Written in 1905, *Scorn* is an experimental speculative history of revolution on the plantation that spans and retraces the period between the 1840s and the turn of the twentieth century, focusing on Reconstruction. I argue that Du Bois's unfinished novelistic experimentations with time and narrative—experiments that bemused his publisher and led them to decline *Scorn*—inform his later theorization of Reconstruction by questioning the positivist category of the revolutionary subject from the perspective of the plantation South. Between the two texts, Du Bois revises a counterfactual form that imagines the revolutionary potential of a Black peasantry only to undo itself in the process. Through this long process of speculation and undoing, Du Bois marshals the anachronisms of the historical novel to frame the peasantry as a precarious and untimely class. He also unites two temporally conflicting perspectives on revolution: the embedded experience of the political subject and the changing structural conditions of the plantation. As a culmination of productive tensions explored throughout the book, I root Du Bois's iteration of revolutionary anachronism in the plantation economy's structural reproduction of a precarious surplus population in the years following Reconstruction.

That my book closes with Du Bois's historical novel of Reconstruction reflects the influence of his thought throughout. Du Bois was the most explicit and persistent of these writers to theorize Reconstruction as revolution. However, the genealogy offered here demonstrates that he was not the only one. Treating Du Bois's experiments with a novel he was never able to publish as central to his thought about Reconstruction underlines an important feature of the fictions these writers created. Writing from within a historical moment that did not provide the conditions familiar from revolutionary epics, these writers adapted historical fiction to create temporal resources for narrating revolution otherwise: what is unfinished is not so much revolution as its narration. That their formal experiments did not extend into a tradition with the stability and recognizability of a major genre is testament both to their political insight and the revolutionary contradictions that shaped life in the postbellum South.

In *Black Reconstruction,* Du Bois writes that "the unending tragedy of Reconstruction is the utter inability of the American mind to grasp its real significance."[89] As well as attacking the racist propaganda of a generation of historians and cultural producers, Du Bois's words indicate the tremendous narrative shift required to plot slave emancipation as revolution. Although his own long engagement with the period suggests that communicating Reconstruction's "real significance" remained a difficult task, narrative culture in the era's aftermath indicates that a group of novelists located this significance in a similar place to Du Bois. Their work helps us to conceive Reconstruction as America's imagined revolution.

1

Liberalism and George Washington Cable's Impossible Allegories

In his commencement address at the University of Mississippi in 1882, George Washington Cable sought to detach the possibilities literary regionalism offered to southern writers from the dangers of sectional culture. A renowned author of historical short fiction about Louisiana, Cable's breakthrough novel, *The Grandissimes* (1880), had cemented his fame as one of the nation's foremost regionalists. It also sharpened the political critique of the postbellum South implicit in the short stories that made his name, collected in 1879 as *Old Creole Days.* In a booming national marketplace for local color fiction that was fast discovering the Reconstruction South as a locale suited to the genre's combined orientalist, nostalgic, and expropriative imperatives, Cable occupied the peculiar role of being at once the representative voice and immanent critic of his region's cultural mores.[1]

Mediating this position, his speech takes issue with the very cultural-geographic identifier he was coming to represent. "When the whole intellectual energy of the southern states flew to the defense of that one institution which made us the South," he argued, "we broke with human progress, we broke with the world's thought."[2] In Cable's view, the idea of the South was the product of a collective flight from history to what he elsewhere calls "the plantation idea."[3] Having compounded this anachronism after emancipation by way of "a semi-barbarism . . . the substitution of a Negro tenantry for Negro slaves," the former slave states were (re)making a sense of place premised on nothing more than a premodern labor regime and a caste system.[4] For Cable, in the wake of national reunion, the task of the true regionalist was to reconnect locality with a modernizing historical development in which, these anachronisms being abolished, "there will be no South. We shall be Virginians, Texians, Louisianians, Mississippians . . . and over and above all be Americans."[5]

The speech encapsulates Cable's literary-political project: to plot a native southern liberalism along a temporal axis in which immersion in the historical lifeways of a particular region (for Cable, New Orleans) dissolves sectional backwardness into the progressive horizons of the nation-state.[6] But his developmental schema produces an altogether more spatially and temporally uneven rhetorical telos. Framing his cosmopolitan vision against the conservatism of the New South movement, Cable declares: "There is a newly coined term . . . which I would gladly see met with some disrelish: the New South. It is a term only fit to indicate a transitory condition. What we want—what we ought to have in view—is the No South! Does the word sound like annihilation? It is enlargement. It is growth. It is a higher life."[7] Giving expression to a historical worldview in which "there will be no South," Cable reverts to a strikingly negative definite article, "*the No* South." Distinguished from an Old South that slips into history and the merely transitory New South, the No South is a negative model for the telos of historical transition that conflates epochal change with the spatial apotheosis—"enlargement," "growth," "higher life"—of an apparently residual provincialism.

This tension is symptomatic of Cable's political self-fashioning. Coming to national prominence as federal enforcement of the Reconstruction Amendments waned and opposing New South demands that "Home Rule" required the legal entrenchment of white racial dominance, Cable framed himself as advocate (and discoverer) of a peculiarly southern road to the kind of liberal public sphere that would enable "a voluntary Reconstruction" in the South.[8] To this end, he often imbued the same regional social customs and experiences that he otherwise attacked for blocking the development of liberal juridical-political values—customs and experiences he attributed to an atavistic caste system—with ambivalent political potential. Beyond this symptomatic feature of Cable's politics, though, his rhetorical flourish models the quite different allegorical structure of his fiction. Cable's historical fiction is populated with No Souths, imaginative time-spaces that convey an anachronism irreducible to a historicist model of stalled progress. I argue that these fictional time-spaces help us to think with and beyond the symptomatic features of Cable's politics. In line with his authorial persona as both detached observer of and immersed speaker for his region, Cable's No Souths are not just allegories for (stalled) historical change; they are also hermeneutic allegories about the way that immersion in a time and place shapes how it can be read and written. *The Grandissimes,* in particular, explores the difficulty of interpreting and representing the materials of a social life that has been fundamentally changed but whose conditions are anathema to the future Cable sought to use regional lifeways to engineer.

This slippage between symptom and self-consciousness has drawn scholars to Cable's writing, insofar as it characterizes two broad accounts of the relationship between liberalism and the idea of the South. From the 1960s, scholars began to recover Cable as the archetypal beleaguered white southern liberal whose affective connections to his region, paired with opposition to segregation, provided tantalizing evidence of a neglected usable past: in the wake of the civil rights movement, maybe the symptomatic archetype of the white southerner could be turned, via Cable, toward less reactionary ends.[9] By contrast, critics including Barbara Ladd, Bryan Wagner, Saidiya Hartman, and Stephen Best argue that Cable's writing manifests the disavowals of color-blind liberalism at a national level. In this view, Cable's self-conscious provincializing of liberalism represents a national symptom: the disavowal of the forms of state power that continued to structure racial domination after emancipation.[10] The tension between these accounts presents an opportunity to read Cable differently. Instead of positioning him as representative of either liberalism's deep racialized continuities or its unfinished reformist possibilities, I understand his regional historicism as a precarious conduit for reading revolutionary anachronism.

This complicates the view that Cable's writings frame Reconstruction as "a fable of arrested development."[11] By constructing allegories that not only represent a region's historical change but also pose ways of reading historical change regionally, Cable explores a different kind of arrest: that of liberal historicism when faced with the social life of the Reconstruction South. In reading *The Grandissimes*—a book that is as much an allegory about reading as about history—we have to read with the text; we have to read the interpretive disparity Cable opens up between the moment in which he writes and the moment he represents, a crossover that creates a historical sense in tension with Cable's political desires. In turn, these disparities estrange our own horizon on Reconstruction, enabling a theorization of the era as revolution that was obscured over the course of the second half of the twentieth century, as perspectives on Reconstruction's unfinished business (and Cable's place in it) became ineluctably shaped by the gains and limits of the civil rights movement. The reading I offer, then, is not Cable's per se but a reading that his anachronous historical form makes available by stretching perspectives on Reconstruction, past and present. In this sense, Cable's allegorical hermeneutics characterize the kind of theoretical work that the historical novel of Reconstruction does.

The Plantation Idea

Cable's politics were underpinned by a historical schema that explained the South's divergent development from the nation-state roughly according to the contours of free labor ideology. He argued that over time, states with plantation regions had tragically departed from a shared national origin that he called "the village and town idea—the notion of farm and factory, skilled labor, an intelligent many, and ultimate wealth through an assured public tranquillity." In regions where, by contrast, "the corner stone of the social structure was made the plantation idea—wide lands, an accomplished few, and their rapid aggrandizement by the fostering oversight and employment of an unskilled many," social development had in effect been frozen by the legally enshrined "supremacy of an untitled but hereditary privileged class, a civil caste."[12]

Cable encapsulates what he frames as the South's peculiar, and peculiarly entrenched, social and legal hierarchy by drawing on a strand of nineteenth-century abolitionist thought, influenced by British missionary literature, that analogized American slavery and racism to the Indian caste system. This analogy appealed to American abolitionists because its orientalist overtones "highlighted the atavistic and anti-republican aspects of racial hierarchies," making them seem external and anathema to the "true" character of American democracy.[13] As Oliver Cromwell Cox pointed out in *Caste, Class, and Race* (1948), this normative aspect of the comparison underpinned an emergent Cold War liberal account of segregation that shaped popular and social scientific understandings of race in the midcentury United States. By developing an anti-Marxist analysis of segregation that painted the South's Jim Crow order as a historically static (and stable) hierarchical system, fundamentally opposed to the apparently meritocratic and fluid patterns of American life, a "modern caste school of race relations" bracketed racism from questions of class exploitation and colonial domination that shaped capitalism in the United States and beyond.[14] Caste came to describe racism as the product of an anachronous psychological attachment to hierarchy, a tragic flaw that ironically reinforced the egalitarian promise of American democracy.[15]

As Cox also argued, the caste analogy appealed to twentieth-century race relations theorists because in its nineteenth-century guise, it was an essentially descriptive, rather than analytical, way of imagining hierarchy: it was rhetorically flexible.[16] In the Reconstruction context, caste depicted the persistence of racism after emancipation as an exotic colonial anachronism. As Charles Sumner recognized, speaking a year after the passage of the Fourteenth Amendment, if "an essentially barbarous" institution that "appears in barbarous ages" had survived the abolition of slavery and the creation of a new national citizenship, then it could only be "unconnected and out of place . . . a perpetual discord, a prolonged jar,—contrary to the first principle of the universe."[17] This made the controversial extension of nationally protected civil rights into new areas of everyday life that Sumner advocated seem like an inevitable "operation of that law which governs Universal Man": progress.[18] Cable employs a similar schema as Sumner, developing a popular regionalist tendency to depict the post-Reconstruction South as a colony and Reconstruction as a process of imperial management.[19] But bridging Sumner's liberal universalism with the regionalist's immersion in the local mores that civil rights legislation sought to reconstruct, Cable draws out the rhetorical (and temporal) ambiguity of caste.

Cable argues that the South's ruling group is "not, as it is commonly miscalled, an aristocracy, for within one race it takes in all ranks of society; not an aristocracy, for an aristocracy exists, presumably, at least, with the wide consent of all classes, and men in any rank of life may have some hope to attain to it by extraordinary merit and service; but a caste; not the embodiment of a modern European idea, but the resuscitation of an ancient Asiatic one."[20] His idea of caste does two things at once. He refuses a common temporally distant feudal metaphor for the South's social system (which would code it simply as backward) in favor of a contemporaneous colonial one. Even if the contemporaneity of this "resuscitated" "ancient" system still implies a modernizing process—in the Victorian colonial imagination, the "Asiatic" presumably becomes European—the modernity against which Cable positions caste is not in any simple sense American democracy or republican free labor. Instead, he sketches the ideal principles of a liberal public sphere (his "village and town idea")—consent, meritocracy, fluidity—in the image of what he elsewhere appeals to as "our whole South's better self": the image of the southerner as aristocrat.[21] Even as he disclaims that the southern elite, as it is, constitutes an aristocracy, by framing the plantation idea as a "resuscitated" caste system rather than a residual feudal one, he imagines a modernizing process that seems to move forward and backward in time at once. Anachronous barbarism dissolves into anachronous modernity.

Reading Cable's political writing, one is often confronted with the sense that he argues two things at once. This duality enables him to imagine the peculiarities of southern social life as at once stalled in time (prehistory to a national modernity) and the crucible of the future. This ambiguity is present in the essays that made Cable's name as not only the South's leading regionalist but also its most prominent white reformist. Cable published "The Freedman's Case in Equity" and "The Silent South" across the two 1885 numbers of the *Century Magazine*. Exemplifying the magazine's attempt to draw a new "serious" literary regionalism from the politics of national reconciliation, Cable's essays appeared alongside installments of Twain's *Huckleberry Finn*, Henry James's *The Bostonians*, and a new series (for which Cable also wrote), "Battles and Leaders of the Civil War": a collection of personal reminiscences from both sides of the conflict that sought to capture a moment "when the passions and prejudices of the Civil War have nearly faded out of politics, and its heroic events are passing into our common history."[22]

Rather against this grain, Cable's controversial essays dwell on an ongoing conflict over Reconstruction in the South while attempting to negotiate the *Century*'s reunionist historicism. In the essays, he attacks a spurious legal notion of privacy employed by the Supreme Court to blunt Reconstruction in the recent *Civil Rights Cases* (1883). In that ruling, the Court deemed that the 1875 Civil Rights Act's provision of federally protected equal access to public accommodations infringed "private rights between man and man in society" that only the states could govern.[23] While Cable argued that this logic was a sop to the caste system—which confused public and private, so that any attempt to establish "public equity" raised "the huge bugbear of Social Equality"—he nevertheless provincializes the valences of "privacy" at play in Reconstruction legal debates, so as to locate political possibility in the new situation created by the Court.[24] A political situation in which Reconstruction had become "each state's private affair," "to be settled by each of the States separately in the light of simple equity and morals," presented the South with an opportunity to find the basis for bourgeois distinctions between public and private, necessary for public equity, in its own distinctive, "separate," and (according to the Supreme Court) "private" experiences of everyday life ("FCE" 409).

Cable reimagines modernization as a process implicit in the plantation South's social conditions, rather than something external. To borrow a vocabulary from Sharon Monteith and Suzanne W. Jones, the "plantation idea" provides a speculative "novum" through which to reimagine the transformation of the regional "datum" he wished to abolish.[25] This produces a worldview in many ways symptomatic of the racialized contours of the social life Cable sought to reform, but it also complicates the whiggish historicism that generally underpinned the attempt to unite liberal nationalism with regional difference (implicit in the *Century*'s literary project). The heretical regionalism of Cable's politics, therefore, needs to be read through and against the anachronistic historicism of his fiction.[26] This requires an understanding of the particular social experience that shaped the fate of liberal reform in the plantation South in the wake of emancipation, an experience in which Cable was personally immersed.

For reformists, Reconstruction represented "a crisis of the free labor ideology inherited from the pre-war years."[27] Across the country, intensified industrial labor discipline and the spread of organized labor undermined belief in a harmony of interests between labor and capital. In the Reconstruction South, the idea central to the work of the Freedman's Bureau that the plantation offered a field for free labor was fractured by emancipated households resisting cash crop monoculture (especially cotton) and refusing to see production for the market as a "natural" transition toward freedom. Locating freedom in the sanctity of capitalist labor, reformists effectively allied with planters in "a community of interest" in the "revitalization of the plantation economy."[28] As Cable's protestations about the "*semi*-barbarism" of Black tenantry suggests, what resulted in cotton-producing regions was "a hybrid economic 'form,'" rather than a single new mode of production. In this terrain, legal defenses of contract freedom, ideologies of free labor, and speculative bursts of faith in a new commercial future (of the kind that motivated both reformist optimism and New South boosterism) sat unevenly alongside new, diversified, and geographically spreading mechanisms of bondage and tied tenancy.[29] As the commercial outpost of the Mississippi Valley's cotton economy, Cable's New Orleans was a flashpoint for these contradictory promises: the symbol of a "new" South whose extractive mode of development embodied economic modernity as much as social backwardness.[30]

This historical tension was the biographical condition for Cable's writing. While he took aim at New South boosterism, he sustained himself as a historian and fictionalizer of New Orleans by working as an accountant for a cotton factorage. There he became an early investor in the New Orleans Cotton Exchange (one who, as his biographer Arlin Turner specifies, "felt something of a founder's concern" for the organization).[31] This institution represented the coexistence of two capitalist horizons in the plantation South: the Exchange attempted (and ultimately failed) to rationalize the emergent, decentralized credit system of the postbellum Cotton economy—embodied in the repressive regime of the "country store"—by bringing it into an awkward relationship with a nationally integrated financial system. After Cable's political campaigns made him a pariah with New Orleans's elite, selling stock in the Exchange helped him to fund his move to Massachusetts to take up the life of a professional literary reformer.[32] Even as he sought to give representative shape (and a name, "caste") to a social system that presaged liberal modernity, then, Cable was immersed in a tangle of regional specificities that represented the nation-state's distorted capitalist future as much as its precapitalist past.

From this social position, Cable's work plots a transition in the very fabric of society that cannot but be fractured. While we can read his fiction for the way it resolves or disavows elements of this fracture, we should acknowledge that the "juxtapositions of the modern and the archaic [that] constantly jarred the New South" are not just his fiction's backdrop; they are its self-conscious hermeneutic problem, its creative principle.[33] Cable's early short stories, collected in *Old Creole Days,* plot this fracture through a representation of historical time in which colonial and early national New Orleans functions awkwardly as both a synchronic allegory for the era of emancipation and as a historical moment surpassed diachronically by that era. The stories depict early-nineteenth-century New Orleans poised on the verge of an epochal transition, even though they critique the failure of this transition to effect progressive social change. The collapsing Old World of European colonization is such a rich setting for Cable because it hangs between allegory and history, expressing a sense of transition caught in a loop.

Take the over-mortgaged ancestral plantation house in "Belle Demoiselle Plantation" that collapses, House of Usher like, into the "merciless, unfathomable flood of the Mississippi."[34] The crumbling edifice captures the sense of inexorable epochal shift animating the collection. But caught precariously between a metonymic allegorical frame (the Creole plantation signifying the collapse of the contemporary plantocracy) and a superseded historical origin (the contemporary plantocracy replacing an older Creole elite), it is an over-determined signifier. The collection's very investment in regional distinctive-ness hangs on this impossible allegorizing of change and stasis in the same objects, most significantly the plantation. Recognizing as much, the story's narrator preempts Cable's invocation of the No South by slyly commenting that "there was no place like Belle Demoiselle" (*OCD* 135). This representa-tional "no place" symbolically renders a contemporary historical shift from slavery to a new capitalism into a gothic repetition of its own allegorical frame: it is at once apocalyptic and recursive. The repercussions of this tem-porality are captured succinctly in another story, "Jean-Ah Poquelin," when the ghostly leper and brother of a former slave trader removes himself from his dead brother's plantation to make way for an American "'Building and Improvement Company' which had not yet its charter 'but was going to' and which had not, indeed, any tangible capital yet, but 'was going to have some'" (192). An old order is passing, but even the sentence's circuitous syntax in-scribes the uncanny fact that something about the new world is best expressed by the persistence and return of the old.

This allegorical temporality typifies Cable's attempt to think through Re-construction as revolution because it employs New Orleans as a setting in which past and present seem inseparable, yet the whole point is to separate them, to make the distinction. As much is ensured by Cable's characteristically insistent narrators, regional and historical guides too arch to quite be called didactic but who nonetheless intervene in Cable's digressive sentences to point and prod interpretation in an epochal direction. The opening of his 1882 novella, *Madame Delphine,* walks readers off "the central avenue" of modern New Orleans: "into the quiet, narrow way which a lover of Creole antiquity, in fondness for a romantic past, is still prone to call the Rue Royal. You will pass a few Restaurants, a few auction-rooms, a few furniture warehouses, and will hardly realize that you have left the activity and clatter of a city of merchants before you find yourself in a region of architectural decrepitude, where an ancient and foreign-seeming domestic life, in second stories, overhangs the ruins of a former commercial prosperity, and upon every thing has settled down a long Sabbath of decay" (*OCD* 1–2). The story then literally shifts back in time to the 1830s. But Cable's hedged second-person staging ("prone," "hardly realize," "foreign-seeming") refuses to let a parallel between past and present, based on a shared sense of stasis and a literal shared location, be seamless. A landscape marked by signs of "decay" and "former commercial prosperity" encourages readers to draw a diachronic line between before and after. Even the alignment of the temporally *ancient* with the spatially *foreign-seeming*—typical of Cable's account of caste—is overwrought: the narrator stresses that the romantic image of a "land where it seemed 'always afternoon'" is an ideological construction created by "writers of the day more original than correct as social philosophers" (6).

The story's knowing treatment of the authorial (and ideological) construction of regionalist nostalgia encourages readers to ask whose "day" they are occupying. This is not quite the familiar Faulknerian temporality of the postbellum South as a "country [where] everything, weather, all, hangs on too long" (or in Cable's allusive words, it is "always afternoon").[35] In Cable's stories—ironically much closer to the emancipatory event that Faulkner's gothicism displaces and elongates—the past might not be dead, but it is certainly past. The impossible narrative spaces and insistent narrative voices of *Old Creole Days* raise the question of how to interpret a scene that is not just ambiguous but that also demands to be read both ways, as history and as allegory, and what's more, a scene that demands to be read as allegorizing both arrest and epochal shift. More than a puzzle to be resolved, Cable bakes this interpretive quandary into his form, his syntax, his narrative voice; he makes it central to the act of reading, enjoying, and interpreting a regional distinctiveness premised on a temporality suggestive of Antonio Gramsci's description of the revolutionary interregnum, in which "the old is dying and the new cannot be born."[36]

In relation to the collapse of Apartheid South Africa, Nasser Mufti argues that interregnum, rather than transition, becomes the narrative basis of the historical novel when the historical shift that the form maps is not toward the unification of civil society around the nation-state but a political struggle that lacks "the standpoint of an accomplished history."[37] He notes how in such novels (as for Gramsci) interregnum is not just a symptomatic condition but "a field of intelligibility": "interregnal time" offers a way of reading historically that is not determined retroactively by the development of liberal civil society.[38] If Cable's politics demanded that the plantation South become modern and liberal, his attachment to regional particularity is premised on the admission that such a transition had not happened. But read for their representation of historical *time* as much as regional identity, the allegorical locales in *Old Creole Days* suggest an epoch in the absence of transition.

In Cable's shorter fiction, these locales constitute allusive scenes or archetypes, divorced from explicit politics. *The Grandissimes* is a more explicitly political text, one that connects regional critique of caste to a historical vision. It is as a language for reading the past—a "field of intelligibility"—that Cable develops the Creole caste system as an allegorical object in *The Grandissimes*. Attempting to articulate the historical shift the novel plots, its protagonist, Honoré Grandissime, muses that "there are but two steps to civilization, the first easy, the second difficult; to construct—to reconstruct—ah! There it is! The tearing down! The tear'—."[39] Articulating a historical transformation allegorized to Reconstruction, Honoré returns to the "tear" that separates past and present. Where words fail this fictional scion of an elite Creole family, the novel is Cable's attempt to give form to what he calls "life in Creole type" (*G* 15–16): to find, in his characteristic allegorical structure, a regional historicist language (a "type" in both senses of the word) that responds to Honoré's problem.

For Gramsci, the future is only visible from the interregnum as "morbid symptoms."[40] Cable's political investments in the idea of "the South" are symptomatic in many ways. Accordingly, before turning to *The Grandissimes*, it is worth limning in more detail the debate in which he most prominently attempted to provincialize his liberalism in relation to Reconstruction politics. I will then be able to show how Cable's allegorical form in *The Grandissimes* allows us to read beyond the symptoms of his politics.

Reconstructing the Private

The essays that announced Cable nationally as the white South's most prominent social critic—"The Freedman's Case in Equity" and its follow-up, "The Silent South"—respond to the political situation created by the Supreme Court's invalidation of the 1875 Civil Rights Act in the *Civil Rights Cases*. While not the most politically efficacious plank of Reconstruction legislation, the Civil Rights Act—forced through Congress in tribute to the recently deceased Sumner—was an important political battleground. In the eyes of Reconstruction's critics, it represented a significant overextension of federal law into the social as much as political terrain of the South: it attacked not just the legal architecture of slavery but what Sumner conceived of as the everyday distinctions of caste. The Supreme Court affirmed as much by arguing that national legislation against racial discrimination in public accommodations such as inns, transport, and theaters was an unconstitutional attack on "private rights between man and man in society."

By ruling that refusal of public accommodations on the basis of race was a private matter, unless legislated positively by the state, the Court not only protected racial discrimination, but it also made the political acts by which race was reproduced and enforced mark a vastly inflated conception of privacy. In his majority decision, Justice Joseph P. Bradley establishes this inflationary logic by analogy to the techniques of counterrevolutionary violence used to oppose Reconstruction: "An individual cannot deprive a man of his right to vote . . . he may, by force or fraud, interfere with the enjoyment of the right in a particular case; he may commit an assault against the person, or commit murder, or use ruffian violence at the polls, or slander the good name of a fellow citizen; but, unless protected in these wrongful acts by some shield of State law or State authority, he cannot destroy or injure the right."[41] By simultaneously making racial discrimination private and racializing privacy, the Court severely limited Reconstruction's legislative scope. Its decision marked the purely negative and formal character of rights possessed by Black Americans, who were now "mere citizen[s]"—a legal designation that Colin Dayan calls a "new figurative entity in American law."[42] The ruling also laid the groundwork for separate but equal in *Plessy v. Ferguson,* a legal key to the reactionary climate of the turn of the century.

Responding to the ruling, Cable intervenes in a legal debate over the distinction between public and private that made the status of everyday life in the South a site of political struggle. Accepting the constitutional situation in which the Court had "thrown the whole matter over to the States of the South," he levels his criticism at southern elites who, placed "on our honor and on the mettle of our far and peculiarly famed southern instinct," would enshrine into law a system of "arbitrary and artificial social distinctions that interfere with society's natural self-distribution" ("FCE" 409, 416–17). As Cable's sarcasm suggests, he believed that the white South's apparent "race instinct" was no basis for civil distinctions. Far from protecting privacy from nefarious legal attempts to enforce social equality, "the color line points straight in the direction of social equality by tending towards the equalization of all whites on one side of the line and of all blacks on the other" (417). Because segregation was not intended to separate white and Black people but to enforce Black menial status, Cable argued that what was at stake was a question not of "private morals" but of public equity (409). His argument seems to shift race from the terrain of the private, where it had been placed by the Court, to the public. The South's problem, after all, was a public caste system that "blunts the sensibilities of the ruling class" and prevents the formation of bourgeoise class distinctions that could stabilize civil equality (415). However, as a legal metaphor, public equity invokes the bourgeois public sphere as a terrain of individual conscience and morality, allowing Cable to play a regional theme on the Court's view of the privacy of everyday life.

Compounding the sense that the white South's response to Reconstruction held the key to a distinctive system of life and law, the *Century* printed a response to Cable's piece from the de facto leader of the New South movement, Henry Grady. Grady argued that "there is an instinct, ineradicable and positive, that will keep the races apart, that would keep the races apart if the problem were transferred to Illinois or to Maine."[43] The issue, for Grady, was that in the Reconstruction South, where the "race instinct" was apparently the locus of social life, Congress had tried to legislate into being a "social intermingling of the races" that undermined the very racial integrity that produced race instinct, thus threatening "the disorganization of society." It was this apparent situation that led Grady to claim "in perfect frankness . . . [that] if no such instinct existed, or if the South had reasonable doubt of its existence, it would, by every means in its power, so strengthen the race prejudice that it would do the work and hold the stubbornness and strength of instinct."[44] In reply, Cable picked up on Grady's tautology to hammer home his central point: conservatives failed to recognize the existence "of a boundary line between social relations and civil rights," which "for justice . . . must remain ever faithfully the same."[45] Clearly, the race instinct could not be such a line since, as Cable stressed and as Grady tacitly admitted, it was not an expression of "society's natural self-distribution" but a product of a regime that had made slavery "the corner-stone of the whole social structure" ("FCE" 409). It was, therefore, subject to change. Nevertheless, in arguing that class distinctions form a more "natural" "boundary line" than race, Cable draws on a peculiarly affective treatment of social distinction premised on a white southerner's experience of living in a caste system.[46]

What led Grady to declare segregation's bald contradictory logic was Cable's insistence that race was a matter of individual feeling. While race instinct might be "pure twaddle," Cable concedes that "of race *feeling* there is no scarcity . . . And as another man's motive of private preference no one has a right to forbid or require it." So considered, "just in degree as it is a real thing [race instinct] will take care of itself" ("FCE" 418). Its form shifted, an arbitrary political relation that threatens proper civil boundaries "takes care of itself," effecting the "natural self-distribution" Cable sees as the basis of a liberal public sphere. By making Reconstruction "each state's private affair," the Court had made race the arbiter of privacy; Cable responds that, as experts in "race feeling," cultured southerners should be particularly adept at making the kinds of affective social distinctions required to stabilize the "boundary line" of private life in the wake of emancipation.

Saidiya Hartman cites Cable's argument as an example of how, by imagining the social as private, Reconstruction-era liberals disavowed the "entanglement of state and society" required to reproduce slavery's affective modes of subjection after emancipation.[47] Similarly, Scott Romine sees Cable's affective regionalism as emblematic of the reconstruction of southern exceptionalism in nationalist ideology. Referring to Cable's second Reconstruction novel, *John March, Southerner* (1894), Romine argues that Cable constructs a regional object "comprehended in emotional terms," and criticized as a positive political postulate, but which is "never not 'the South.'"[48] These accounts demonstrate how Cable participates in the reproduction of race after Reconstruction by plotting space as feeling, but they miss the altogether more fractured conception of historical time his regionalism implies. In trying to locate a distinctively southern basis for bourgeois privacy, Cable demands a "boundary line" not just between public and private but one that "*must* remain ever faithfully the same." As his conditional language suggests, the whole reason for the argument with Grady—which boiled down to who could most legitimately claim the mantle of southern feeling—was that whatever either party may have wanted, the boundary hadn't and couldn't remain the same. The changes to the everyday social life whose meaning and basis Grady and Cable contested could not be resolved by appeals to continuity and consensus, whether in the shape of public equity or race instinct.

Cable's strained depiction of caste as both the barrier to and generator of reformist regional affect is a window onto fundamentally changed social relations. In *The Grandissimes,* less constrained by the conventions of reasonable political debate about race, Cable employs Creole genealogies and bloodlines as narrative devices in which public and private appear inseparable in troubling ways for the book's liberal protagonist, Joseph Frowenfeld. Cable makes this porousness a lens through which to allegorize Reconstruction as revolutionary process. In his fiction, Cable's critique of caste remains racially inflected. For instance, *John March, Southerner* satirizes the social conservatism of the New South movement by depicting the fictionalized county of Dixie, mired in the corruption of white Democrats rather than Black radicals. However, reclaiming a unifying regional identity from his political antagonists (hence Dixie), the novel relegates Reconstruction to a tragic racial wound in the southern psyche, symbolically manifested in the childhood scars that the liberal protagonist, March, receives at the hands of the emancipated slave (and later Republican politician) Cornelius Leggett. March's beating comes as Leggett's revenge for his own brutalization by his former master, who attempts to reassert racial dominance after emancipation.

Read in these terms, it is tempting to see Cable purely as symptomatic of the racial continuities and disavowals underpinning white liberalism: to make him an authorial forebear of Ike McCaslin or Quentin Compson. But disavowal seems a misleading concept through which to read his work, one perhaps motivated by a scholarly tendency to read the nineteenth-century South from beneath Faulkner's shadow.[49] Written following Cable's very public spat with Grady, *John March, Southerner* primarily employs Reconstruction to look forward to the emergent politics of the 1890s.[50] In *The Grandissimes,* Cable more self-consciously engages the problem of imagining Reconstruction historically. There his idiosyncratic attempt to mediate liberal politics with what he saw as regionally specific feelings does more than disavow the construction of race; it requires him to imagine versions of social change that equate neither to liberal progress nor to its arrest. Where his essays sidestep this problem, in the interests of a forward-looking political moderation, *The Grandissimes* builds out the anachronistic allegorical structure first modeled in *Old Creole Days* to work through the difficulties involved in writing (and reading) revolutionary change from the perspective of the plantation South. In doing so, it makes available a literary temporality and historical sense contrary to the disavowed continuities that link nineteenth- and twentieth-century liberalism.

This Is Not a Parable
In a sense, *The Grandissimes* exemplifies the epic pathos familiar to the classic historical novel. Through the Grandissime family, Cable narrates the decline of a New Orleans Creole dynasty shortly after the Louisiana Purchase. The novel's family conflicts track the "preposterous, apathetic, fantastic, suicidal

pride" of a planter class struggling to maintain its arcane regional manners and customs in the face of an implacable modernity, characterized by the U.S. nation-state (*G* 32). Broadly speaking, this historical narrative is also allegorical: Cable extends and develops the framework he employed in the stories of *Old Creole Days* so that the 1803 "cession" of Louisiana from French to American rule parallels the readmission of the former Confederate States to the Union after the Civil War. As Cable would go on to do in his essays, he uses the novel to criticize a caste system, exemplified by public codes of family lineage, racial purity, and honor, that his Creole characters cling to.

However, as in *Old Creole Days,* this transition can be read equally as linear and recursive: as representing either the decline of an old order or its persistence. As the narrator makes clear, stepping back from the historical action to comment on the political present, "To-day almost all the savagery that can justly be charged against Louisiana must . . . be laid at the door of the *Américain*" (*G* 329–30). The narrator's shift into a dialect usually reserved for the characters at once Creolizes the nation-state and modernizes the Creoles' seemingly prehistorical "savagery." Past and present cross over, and crucially, this crossover is embedded in the narrative voice itself. Throughout *The Grandissimes,* Cable complicates the allegory between cession and Reconstruction by building it on self-consciously unstable hermeneutic foundations. By tracing these instabilities according to their own logic, I mean to suggest that the problem of interpreting *The Grandissimes* lies less in how one emphasizes (or even resolves) the opposing facets of change and persistence in its allegorical plot than in making a novel that is so obviously intended to be read allegorically—in which the narrative voice so insistently comments on its own allegorical possibilities—amenable to allegorical interpretation. In short, Cable generates his novel's historical and political meaning by demanding that the reader make allegorical identifications between times, places, and interpretive registers that won't cohere.

More often than not, these tensions turn on the regional and temporal specificity of Creole culture. In a typical moment of allegorical commentary, the narrator criticizes an apparently Creole truism that only a white man can be considered a gentleman, explaining that "the South kept the flimsy false bottoms in its social niceties only by constant reiteration" (*G* 126). Cable makes an analogy to his contemporary moment, in which such "flimsy" appeals to tradition survive by reiteration. But he constructs the link between past and present on a separate analogy between the distinctive space of Creole New Orleans and "the South" more generally. This allegorical connection is otherwise foreclosed by Cable's treatment of Creole "social niceties" as the product of a circum-Caribbean history that resists easy incorporation into an exceptionalist South (and, by extension, the nation-state). The novel acknowledges these connections by intertwining its family histories with the history of French colonialism and the Atlantic slave trade. Cable represents the legacies of slavery through the evils of the "Code Noir," exemplified most clearly in the story of the dismemberment of the rebellious enslaved African king Bras Coupé, involvement in which unites and haunts the novel's main characters. Retold by three separate characters, the story forms an oral history (representative of Creole vernacular culture) that roots the ties that bind the novel's warring families in a Francophone intimacy with New World slave revolution. The whole point of Cable's allegory, in a sense, is to make Reconstruction synchronous with a time-space that preexists and contradicts the sectional coherence of the South.[51] He requires the reader to make the transitional move from past to present and, in spatial terms, from New Orleans to the South, but to do so, he employs a fictional time-space that resists a linear historical shift from arcane to modern and its associated spatial paradigm. In this way, he gives the reader a sense of epochal historical change in inverse proportion to the extent that this change can be understood as epic transition.

More fully than in *Old Creole Days,* Cable turns this historical structure toward political questions raised by Reconstruction. The novel follows Joseph Frowenfeld, an orphaned German American immigrant to New Orleans from Philadelphia, as he negotiates the Creole elite's attempt to come to terms with its submission to a government it sees as a threat to its culture, land, and slaves. Despite his liberal idealism, Frowenfeld partly integrates himself into Creole high society, taking it as his mission to study Creole history and family politics and to convince the elite of the evils of caste. To this end, Frowenfeld tries to right injustices underpinning a feud between two premier families, the Fusilier Grandissimes and the De Grapion Nancanous. These injustices relate to two subjects: high society's refusal to recognize Honoré Grandissime f.m.c. (free man of color), the mixed-race half-brother of the head of the Grandissime family (also called Honoré Grandissime), and the Grandissimes' possession of a plantation rightfully willed to the novel's heroines, Aurora and Clotilde Nancanous.

Through these injustices, Frowenfeld confronts Honoré with what Cable frames as an ethical-political question of "restitution" (*G* 220). Restitution clearly carries a double meaning for Honoré and Frowenfeld: familial wrongs invoke a broader reckoning with the history of slavery. This double meaning is the basis of the novel's critique of caste and its allegory of Reconstruction. However, it also encapsulates the complexity of allegory in the novel because interpreting the plot this way, as the characters do and as the narrative voice suggests readers also should, requires chains of metonymic connection (and misrecognition) that Cable frames as characteristic of Creole caste thinking. Reading *The Grandissimes* allegorically involves making private or familial dispossession interchangeable with historical dispossession by following the metonymic chains that link self, family, and race in the Creole attachment to "blood." Barbara Ladd and Bryan Wagner argue that by turning a historical novel into a family romance, Cable displaces colonial dispossession, racial violence, and slave insurrection onto a patriarchal past.[52] But the political resolutions of Cable's novel become less clear (and less easy to read as resolutions) if we follow them through the historically doubled allegorical structure that he lays out.

Honoré Grandissime, the figure on whom the question of restitution turns, encapsulates the doubled historical implications of Cable's allegory, being both a plantation owner and a city merchant. On the one hand, his "cemetery-like" countinghouse, "a den of [male] Grandissimes . . . beyond middle life and some . . . yet older," signifies a people without a future (*G* 120). He ends the novel by selling his family's most lucrative plantation, destroying the value of the Grandissime land titles, and entering into commercial partnership with his excommunicated half-brother. On the other hand, declension is not absolute. Honoré engineers a marriage between Frowenfeld and Clotilde Nancanou, whose plantation he restores. The estate remains part of the commercial future, as the reformist petit-bourgeois shopkeeper Frowenfeld becomes heir to a plantation and diversifier of its capital (shades of Cable's investment in the New Orleans Cotton Exchange). Similarly, Honoré's recognition of his brother falls short of signifying a new social order. As Honoré recognizes, "he [himself] had come out the beneficiary of this restitution, extricated from bankruptcy by an agreement which gave the f.m.c. only a public recognition of kinship which had always been his due" (279). The "f.m.c.," denied a name even in "restitution" to kinship, cannot enjoy the fruits of recognition. After murdering his revanchist uncle, Agricola Fusilier, he is forced into exile in France, where he drowns himself. With his death, the novel forecloses any association between historical change and racial progress.

The historical precarity of the novel's allegorical moment also impacts its political meaning. While the 1803 "cession" of Louisiana to American rule parallels the postbellum reunification of the nation-state during Reconstruction, *cession* also recalls *secession*. An attempt to read either a narrative of the old regime's collapse or its revivification on joining the postbellum nation is upset by the fact that both possibilities cohere in the same allegorical object, in this instance in the same word.[53] Cable plays on this idea throughout the novel. In a brief passage of Grandissime family history, readers are told how the father of both Honorés was forced to abandon his Black family to marry a white Creole. Highlighting the thinly veiled parallel between Grandissime race pride and the electoral formation of a solidly Democratic South after 1877, the narrator suggests the marriage "was necessary to save the party—nay, that was a slip; we should say to save the family; this is not a parable" (*G* 108). An instruction not to read a parable when the narrative voice is at its most parabolic grates, but in an important sense, it rings true as an account of interpreting the novel. The moments in which Cable encourages his readers to see an allegory reveal a contradiction between the novel's political critique of caste as an exotic hangover from the past that has survived Reconstruction and its historical narrative of the collapse of a social system. As the narrator comments, "This is a world which allows nothing without its obverse and reverse" (215–16). The novel is not just ambivalent (though it may well be that): the contradiction Cable establishes is more total than the suggestion that something is dying but caste remains (an arrested development). Such a reading is no doubt viable, but it involves stepping outside the allegorical dilemma on which Cable bases his imaginative universe. I am suggesting it is instructive to *read through* this dilemma. Read on its own terms, then, *The Grandissimes* is not only a historical allegory—depicting a change on a scale somewhere between stasis and transition—but also an attempt to imagine a way of reading history that the novel's narrative commentary ambivalently frames as distinctively Creole.

To interpret the novel allegorically, the reader has to follow patterns of metonymic connection modeled by Honoré. Tracing one such characteristic chain of identifications and slippages will demonstrate the hermeneutic difficulty of reading *The Grandissimes* for both its immediate and allegorical referents. When Frowenfeld demands that Honoré make restitution to his brother and the Nancanous, Honoré expounds that "there is a kind of tree not dreamed of in botany . . . that lets fall its fruit every day in the year . . . We call it—with reverence—our dead father's mistakes. I have had to eat much of that fruit; a man who has to do that must expect now and again a little fever" (G 219). Honoré appears to refer to his own father's mistakes in family matters, of the kind that require restitution of another Creole family's birthrights. However, the ambiguous collective pronoun *our* suggests an indeterminate lineage (Honoré and his brother? the Grandissime family? Louisiana? the South?). By converting the family tree into a tree of knowledge, Honoré suggests that Creole genealogy contains and reproduces "every day" an original sin, slavery, just as Cable's narrator suggests that the caste system is maintained across the contemporary South by "constant reiteration." As Frowenfeld makes explicit—channeling Cable's attack on southern conservatism—this sin is not confined to the past but is reproduced by a culture that, faced with a legitimacy crisis, "turns and asks the question which is behind it, instead of the question which is before it" (220).

Crucially, we arrive at this interpretation—which implicates nostalgia in the postbellum reconstruction of caste—by associating political injustice interchangeably with family wrongs. Honoré claims that the restitution Frowenfeld demands threatens "that old traditional principle which is the secret of our existence": namely, the metonymic chain that, for Creoles, links name, family, and race. By way of explanation, he tells Frowenfeld that "a Louisianan . . . is a Louisianan; touch him not; when you touch him you touch all Louisiana! So with us Grandissimes; we are legion, but we are one" (G 222). Honoré appeals to what Frowenfeld critically labels the "Creole 'we'" (151), a process of identification and exclusion whose logical conclusion is the Manichaean oppositions of white supremacist ideology. As Agricola Fusilier puts it, "when we say, 'we people,' we always mean we white people. The non-mention of color always implies pure white; and whatever is not pure white is to all intents and purposes black" (59). These categorical conflations are the source of that failure to distinguish between private distinctions and public ones that Cable will go on to criticize in his essays on the rise of New South segregationism. They produce a curious violence in Honoré's language. He despairs that he will "become the destroyer of my own flesh and blood," even though, as he later acknowledges, he really does no such thing. In the novel's logic, there is no "boundary line" between individual and group, no separation between private restitution (the deeding of a plantation to another Creole or the symbolic acknowledgment of a brother) and public destruction. Restitution is, as Honoré puts it, a "pure—even violent—self-sacrifice" because his self, his family, and (by implication) his race are all equally his "flesh and blood" (222).

The important point here is that the association Frowenfeld criticizes—the misidentification of public and private endemic to caste—is the same one the novel requires of readers if they are to make the novel into an allegory: whether this is a historical allegory of civilizational collapse or a political one about the backlash to Reconstruction. Hence, Creole apocalypse and recurrence are inseparable. Even if it destroys his "flesh and blood," Honoré's sacrificial act only affirms a Creole identity that is, after all, based on "apathetic, fantastic, suicidal pride." In a world in which Creole blood politics seems to be as much at stake as any specific family fortune, Cable implies that by sacrificing his family, Honoré will return to Creole genealogy its wavering authority. In Cable's allegory, the caste system is not (or, at least, is never quite) a hangover from the past. To read restitution as a question of facing up to slavery (as Cable clearly intends, in one sense) or to read the very particular locale of New Orleans as representative of a more general sense of the South, the novel suggests that readers must read like Creoles. And to do so is to understand regional particularity and difference as a response to epochal social crisis.

As Fredric Jameson notes, this tension between allegory and history is implicit in the nineteenth-century European historical novel, which balances mimetic representation of "authentic" history with the construction of a transhistorical conflict between political forces "in which everyone has to take sides."[54] Viewed from the perspective of a Reconstruction South that lacked the familiar script of an epic historical transition from ancien régime to a new order, Cable turns this implicit tension between allegory and history into a kind of metanarrative: his novel is as much a commentary on how to read revolutionary change from within plantation society as it is a historical novel in its classical form. Without the model of bourgeois revolution that guides the historical novel, Cable nonetheless pursues an epochal historical sense.

So far, I have focused on *The Grandissimes* as an allegory about historical reading, but it is also a novel about writing. If reading revolution means reading like a Creole, then the novel also suggests that the caste system produces a certain style of historical storytelling. Cable establishes this connection by metaphorically describing Frowenfeld's attempt to understand and reform New

Orleans as an act of reading that at least promises to presage one of writing. Frowenfeld undertakes the "perusal" of a "newly found book, the Community of New Orleans," a book "written in a strange tongue," "whose displaced leaves would have to be lifted tenderly, blown free of much dust, re-arranged, some torn fragments laid together again with much painstaking, and even the purport of some pages guessed out" (*G* 103). Attempting to unravel the peculiarities of a city shaped by a distinctive style of storytelling, Frowenfeld spends his evenings compiling books of notations. But sucked into the intrigues of Creole family politics, he never completes the "unwriteable volume which he had taken to con" (137–38); he never alights on a form that can resolve interpretation and writing to make the recovered, fragmented, and reassembled material of the region's distinct (and traumatic) social life into a totality. The implication is that Cable's own "volume," equally pulled between historical recovery and political critique, is the outcome of an analogous rift. Given the novel's political commitments, then, why does *The Grandissimes* so frequently treat its historical world as a "story-shaped world" whose literary style Cable compares to an antihistorical Creole obsession with genealogy and blood?[55]

History in Creole Type

Frowenfeld's guide through the world of Creole family politics, Doctor Keene, tells him "blood is a great thing here in certain odd ways" (*G* 15). Although Cable critiques the racialized obsession with blood, he insistently compares its "odd ways" to his own literary method, linking Creole genealogy and the writing of history in fiction. The link Cable draws between blood and storytelling in *The Grandissimes* is central to his attempt to mount an "indigenous" critique of southern white supremacy, even as the novel exposes the violent histories on which claims of white southern indigeneity were based in the wake of Reconstruction.

This tension defined Cable's literary reputation as both an authentic representative and critic of Creole life, a reputation built on his "discovery" by Edward King, the *Scribner's* correspondent whose serialized dispatches from his expedition to the former Confederate states during Reconstruction, *The Great South* (published as a book in 1875), did so much to shape the literary image of the Reconstruction South as an exotic colonial product.[56] The tension also shaped Cable's ambivalent entry into the American canon in the Jim Crow era. Introducing Cable for *The Library of Southern Literature* (1909), Mrs. John S. Kendall claimed that "miscegenation formed the theme" of his writing and "seemed to have taken possession of Mr. Cable's mind," so that "he wrote as though his pen had been dipped in blood."[57] Writing from the vantage point of post-*Plessy* segregationist fervor, it is unsurprising that Kendall treats Cable's "theme" as personal pathology, rather than an engagement with racialized social conditions. Nevertheless, she makes an important move between imagining "miscegenation" as Cable's "theme" (making him anathema to the segregationist South) and framing blood as the exotic and attractive materiality of his writing (making him an archetype of the white southern author). Her slippage highlights a distinction central to *The Grandissimes:* what is most important about bloodlines in the novel is not the racial authority they bestow (or undermine) but how one uses them to tell stories.

Cable approaches the ongoing histories of colonialism, slavery, and racial dominance that uphold Creole society obliquely and ironically through the telling and retelling of complex family genealogies. He does this to expose as recent inventions the seemingly long-standing traditions whose "constant reiteration" bolsters white supremacy.[58] There is something here of Michel Foucault's understanding of genealogy as a method that "opposes itself to the search for origins" and takes critique, rather than historical narrative, as its aim.[59] Cable's digressions into the "hints, allusions, faint unspoken admissions, ill-concealed antipathies, unfinished speeches, mistaken identities, and whisperings of hidden strife" that constitute Creole race thinking are deconstructive: they demonstrate how white supremacist genealogies disavow interracial kinship and colonial violence (*G* 96). Nevertheless, through Frowenfeld's fascination with Creole storytelling, Cable also frames genealogy as a model for a broader historical vision, a promise of totality.

The novel's most important family history is delivered early on, by Doctor Keene to Frowenfeld, as the young immigrant recovers from a bout of yellow fever that kills his family upon their arrival in New Orleans. As both Frowenfeld's and the reader's initiation into the city's exotic social life, the genealogy maps the tangled family connections that structure the plot by undermining the Creole elite's colonial origin myths. It is also delivered as an embedded story and a metafictional comment on a Creole style of storytelling. "Making himself especially entertaining in an old-family-history kind of way," Doctor Keene tells his story with the dual purpose of distracting a sick patient and impressing upon him the "odd ways" in which "blood is a great thing" in New Orleans (*G* 14). He offers an ironically elevated account of how the Grandissimes' "pilgrim fathers of the Mississippi Delta" expropriated a colonial patrimony from Indian territory, forging a "lily-white" heritage from the "dubious materials" of their fabled descent from a Natchez princess (22). Agricola proudly holds up this "indigenous" descent as justification for "one favorite cry, with which they greeted all strangers . . . Invaders! Invaders!" (23). But as Keene emphasizes, the Grandissimes' heritage is better traced down the maternal line, "fathers being of little account in Natchez heraldry" (17). Given that he is discussing the reproduction of a slaveholding patriarchy through "less responsible entanglements" than marriage, Keene clearly intends his maternal lineage to imply a Blackness less easily assimilable to a colonist's sense of legitimacy (22).[60] Such passages led Creole historian Charles Gayarré, on whose *History of Louisiana* (1866) Cable drew liberally, to berate the novelist for implying that Creoles were of "viciously mixed blood," possessing an "ignoble descent from the ill specimens of three races—Indian, African and French prostitutes."[61]

While establishing the novel's critique of caste, Keene's genealogy also provides Frowenfeld with a model of historical stylistics. The narrator explains that "[Keene] was a poor story-teller. To Frowenfeld—as it would have been to any one, except a Creole or the most thoroughly Creoleized Américain— his narrative, when it was done, was little more than a thick mist of strange names, places and events; yet there shone a light of romance upon it that filled it with color and populated it with phantoms. Frowenfeld's interest rose—was allured into the mist—and there was left befogged" (*G* 15). Doctor Keene is "a poor story-teller" because his history works by diversion rather than progression: it "mist[s]" and "befog[s]" what it should clarify: the totality of Creole history that Frowenfeld is left to reassemble "with much painstaking." Rather than bringing the past into the present for interpretation, it fills the present with romantic "phantoms." At the same time, this is precisely the pleasure for Frowenfeld, who aspires to become a "thoroughly Creoleized Américain" through his own literary endeavors. Cable frames Doctor Keene's storytelling in relation to his own self-fashioned reputation as the American literary scene's authentic recorder of Creole life. Keene's tale is suitably enthralling to basically become the narrative voice for three chapters, almost without interruption by the narrator (an unusual thing in a novel saturated with narratorial commentary).

This is because Keene's narrative promises to reveal something else besides a political critique of Creole caste thinking: "For in the midst of the mist Frowenfeld encountered and grappled a problem of human life in Creole type, the possible correlations of whose quantities we shall presently find him revolving in a studious and sympathetic mind, as the poet of today ponders the 'Flower in the crannied wall'" (*G* 15–16). The deferrals that highlight the constructed nature of Creole genealogy point to a "midst of the mist," a meaning to be found in the narrative process itself. As a textual allusion, *Creole type* suggests a mode of storytelling that bridges the regionally particular with a universal "problem of human life." Quoting Alfred Lord Tennyson's "Flower in the Crannied Wall," Cable suggests that Frowenfeld sees this conjunction of the particular and the universal as a way of thinking about the emergence of new life from a ruin, and—to follow the Tennyson allusion—a way of understanding his subject "roots and all, all in all."[62] An allusive, deconstructive form, Creole genealogy nevertheless inspires the representative questions of historical vision and transition that animate the historical novelist.

More problematically, the word *type* lends a quasi-racial status to this storytelling method. Frowenfeld discovers what Cable suggests is a specifically Creole and, by implication, a more generally (white) southern mode of writing that turns "type" (text) into "type" (race). By associating Frowenfeld's literary aspirations with his own novel, Cable suggests that the metonymic mode of interpretation central both to *The Grandissimes* and Creole caste thinking can be the basis for a historical style. Thinking *with* this typological style, the novel suggests, will enable Frowenfeld to link the particular and the general (the political and the historical), to create the kind of knowledge that Cable's political writing argues is fundamental to readmitting the South to the mainstream of historical progress (as well as to writing historically). As in his ambivalent treatment of race feeling in his essays, Cable suggests that social life in the South contains experiences, produced by the caste system, that can survive and even promote the transition that remains stalled in his reading of southern history (Frowenfeld is, after all, both a writer and a reformer).

Ultimately, Frowenfeld's literary aspiration never amounts to anything beyond a book of tables documenting the daily weather: the work that unites Creolized history and liberal political critique is an "unwriteable volume." In aligning Frowenfeld's immanent critique of Creole life with his own political and literary project, Cable demonstrates the ambivalence of his investments in regional particularity: is his novel the fulfillment of Frowenfeld's project or the expression of its impossibility? More importantly, the crux of *The Grandissimes'* vexed allegorical structure is that it lodges Cable's political investments in the broader interpretive dilemma I have described in the novel. By creating a strained allegorical form that provides a kind of metacommentary on the historical novel, Cable plots the tensions I have described in his politics as constitutive of a moment of historical crisis rather than an archaic social life. The mixture of symptom and self-consciousness I am describing is central to the fragile historical sense of a literary form, the historical novel of Reconstruction, which is defined by the way that writers hold together political and historical commitments that do not always cohere. As the following chapters show, it is often when writers most explicitly marshal Reconstruction to vocalize contemporary political demands that they reflect most self-consciously on how the period's historical convulsions had reshaped extant parameters for understanding politics.

This tension recalls another aspect of Foucault's account of genealogy, less obviously assimilated to the thinker's suspicion of history as a narrative form. Viewed through a genealogical lens, Foucault argues, the past is not a narrative but a record of "the hazardous play of dominations" implicit in the cultural ideas that make history meaningful. However, Foucault also insists that such ideas "must be made to appear as events on the stage of historical process."[63] Genealogy names a tension between critique and narrative, an attempt to identify the historical convulsions and transformations that shape power's transhistorical continuities. In a different and more ambivalent way, this aspiration motivates Cable's historical sense. In Cable's case, a twinned commitment to narrating the cultural particularity of the South as a product of thoroughgoing historical transformation and to critiquing caste as an anachronous system of domination produces a historical sense that fractures his liberal account of transition. Rather than imagining anachronism as something that can be wiped out by natural historical process (or political reform), Cable makes it into a means of plotting a revolution that does not cohere to a progressive historical narrative. His self-consciously textual No Souths formalize the combined and uneven development of his liberal progressivism and his historical sense of revolution.

If Cable's plotting of revolution is symptomatic of his political attempt to bend a liberal narrative to the social conditions of the plantation South, his contemporary Albion Tourgée is seemingly more direct in approaching Reconstruction as revolution. However, in the process of historicizing what he framed as Reconstruction's failed or missed revolutionary moment, Tourgée encounters his own difficulties. In the next chapter, I discuss Tourgée's use of the historical novel to negotiate the problem of imagining the state as the motive force of revolution in a plantation society. Where, for Cable, allegory provides the literary means for negotiating his political and historical visions, Tourgée uses irony to explore the radically changed capacity of republican political ideas as means of comprehending the relationship between the state and the social in the Reconstruction South.

2

Albion Tourgée and the Ironies of the Reconstruction State

In January 1865, Karl Marx wrote to Abraham Lincoln on behalf of the International Workingmen's Association to congratulate the president on his reelection and to encourage him toward an ambitious reading of the Union's war aims. Tendentiously assuming Lincoln's shared position with "the workingmen of Europe," Marx counsels him on the world historical significance of the Civil War's development into a war for emancipation. In Marx's telling, the "slaveholder's rebellion" had made "the very spots where hardly a century ago the idea of one great democratic republic had first sprung up"— and so provided "the first impulse . . . to the European revolution of the eighteenth century"—into the site for a "holy crusade of property against labor." Destroying this counterrevolutionary republic would necessitate a revolution in republicanism itself, which Marx hoped would inaugurate "true freedom of labor for all," in place of an ideology that "before the Negro, mastered and sold without his concurrence . . . boasted it the highest prerogative of the white-skinned laborer to sell himself and choose his own master." Generalized emancipation was the necessary horizon of a "matchless struggle for the rescue of an enchained race and the reconstruction of a social world."[1]

His exaggerated vanguardist hopes for the Republican Party aside, Marx exploits an ambiguity involved in imagining the republican state as a vehicle for emancipation. Drawing on classically republican principles of the dignity of labor and freedom from domination, Marx's phrasing assumes an equivalence between an act of "rescue" familiar to even conservative strands of antislavery thought—in which the nation-state negates an arbitrary political power and condition of dependence (slavery)—and a more expansive intervention in which abolition embroils the state in a "reconstruction" whose horizon is distinctly social (and implicitly revolutionary).[2]

Of course, the political development of the U.S. nation-state eventually played out very differently (and the author of the *Eighteenth Brumaire* was hardly hubristic about the possibilities of bourgeois state capture). The point is that Marx's rhetoric relies on a certain porousness of the line between the political and social horizons of state intervention; its readability—if not its prophetic accuracy—hints at the fracturing of republican civil categories easily read as continuous throughout the period. I begin this chapter about the ironies of Reconstruction state formation in Albion Tourgée's writing with Marx's letter to suggest that emancipation subjected what, in republican thought, was a boundary between the state and a "social world" to the pressures of revolutionary process. A Union army veteran, radical carpetbagger, judge, reformer, and novelist, Tourgée was a vocal critic of laissez-faire Republican Party elites, whom he saw as sacrificing and demonizing Reconstruction and the abolitionist principles that motivated it. He was no Marxist, but his Reconstruction writing tracks a flitting into and out of legibility of the revolutionary ambiguity Marx's letter exploits.

Tourgée was catapulted to literary prominence by the unexpected success of his novel *A Fool's Errand* (1879), a bitterly ironic elegy for the "magnificent failure" of a righteous cause (Reconstruction) and a historical figure (the carpetbagger) that had been besmirched in the national consciousness.[3] Published under the pseudonym "one of the Fools," before its commercial success led to its reprinting under Tourgée's own name, the novel fictionalizes Tourgée's experience as a carpetbagger abandoned by the federal government in his attempts to reconstruct North Carolina's political and legal system and to quell the state's Ku Klux Klan insurgency. The eponymous "Fool" is Comfort Servosse, a northern Union veteran who moves his family to North Carolina, buys a plantation that he divides into small lots worked by former slaves (thereby promoting the producerist aspirations of a class of "citizens in embryo"), and sets about convincing his hostile neighbors to support the Reconstruction of their community along the lines of free labor, republican government, and democratic participation (*AFE* 98). The Fool is initially optimistic about the prospect of planting his impeccable abolitionist principles in the hostile ground of the South, but despite winning local support, he and his allies are betrayed by "the Wise Men": Republican politicians and journalists in the North who fail to intervene to prevent the Klan's vigilante violence and who willfully follow southern reactionaries in depicting carpetbaggers as the villains of Reconstruction (4).

The novel parallels the nation-state's failure to enforce Reconstruction immediately after the war with the Republican Party's abdication of the South to solid Democratic rule in the era of Hayes's "New Departure" policy, in which Tourgée wrote. This requires a doubled narrative perspective, one that flits between the Fool's "pioneer work" on the ground and a detached retrospective voice that diagnoses the failures of Congressional Reconstruction (*AFE* 22). These juxtaposed perspectives create space for an ironic commentary on the plot that charts the Fool's journey toward realizing a lesson the narrator imparts early on: "that social conditions of three hundred years are not to be overthrown in a moment, and that differences which have outlasted generations . . . are never to be healed by simple victory—that the broken link can not be securely joined by mere juxtaposition of the fragments, but must be fused and hammered before its fibres will really unite" (20). "The North is simply a conqueror," the Fool learns, "and if the results she fought for are to be secured, she must rule as a conqueror" (153). While there was little prospect of this in 1879, the Fool's experience has a contemporary message: formal rights mean nothing without strong federal enforcement, a process of fusing and hammering capable of rendering the instrumental power of the nation-state organic. Tourgée thereby turns political disenchantment about the South's resistance to social change into a justification of the broad horizons of renewed federal power. By depicting the Fool's immersion in North Carolina's unreconstructed social conditions as an irresolvable conflict between sincerely held principles, Tourgée frames the South as a space of what Leigh Anne Duck calls "thick and binding regional cultures."[4] As the site of competing sincerities, this space necessitates and sustains the project of an interventionist republican state.

Both a political concept and a literary style, sincerity was Tourgée's authorial calling card. As I will argue, it has been central to his recovery as a political writer who embodies an activist tradition. My focus is on how his didactic treatment of sincerity—as a concept uniting organic and instrumental accounts of political power and social change—is expressed through, and rubs up against, an irony that resists easy political interpretation. Both in *A Fool's Errand* and its follow-up, *Bricks without Straw* (1880)—which uses the same narrative structure to narrate the grassroots political struggles of formerly enslaved people—the relationship between sincerity and irony opens up a tension between political and historical perspectives on Reconstruction. The (perhaps surprising) difficulty of reading Tourgée's seemingly didactic irony lies in the ambiguous development of the nation-state as a vehicle for revolutionary aspirations. Tourgée's Reconstruction writing plots the imaginative contradictions involved in seeing the changing, multilevel, and uneven form of the Reconstruction-era state as a motive force for social change. I will demonstrate the contingency of these imaginative investments by comparing Tourgée's depiction of organic state power in his fiction to his landmark legal argument against segregation in *Plessy v. Ferguson* (1896). There, from the twilight of Reconstruction, Tourgée attempted to make the historical ironies his fiction plotted sit still as the basis for a legally cognizable definition of national citizenship. The resultant paradoxes mark the increasing difficulty of imagining a revolutionary national power rooted in what, for very different reasons, Justice Henry Billings Brown's majority ruling in *Plessy* called "the established usages, customs, and traditions of the people."[5]

The allure of an egalitarian tradition defined by the consistency of principle that Tourgée advocated has been central both to his recovery as a writer and to the conception of Reconstruction as an unfinished revolution. In the latter case, depicted as a narrative of citizenship bestowed and denied, Reconstruction dramatizes the radical possibilities and tragic limitations of republican ideology in its dalliance with abolitionism. In Eric Foner's famous account, the failure of Reconstruction comes down in large part to the fact that Radical Republicans committed themselves to presiding over an activist state and a broadened conception of citizenship which stretched "the civic ideology" of republicanism to its breaking point.[6] What Du Bois called the "eighteenth-century accents" of "abolition-democracy" here represent the tragic flaw of the republican worldview: a kind of innate ideological limit that abolitionists and Radical Republicans could not surpass in seeing through the creation of an equitable state.[7]

If this innate limit was Radical Republicanism's hamartia, Tourgée has been of increasing interest to modern scholars because his self-fashioning as a radical outsider, on an anachronistic "fool's errand" to uphold the radical memory of abolition against an amnesiac Gilded Age culture, suggests a bridge between abolitionism and modern liberal conceptions of civil rights. Tourgée represents a what-might-have-been: a peculiarly American egalitarian lineage in which antebellum "radical individualism" is divested of its aversion to the activist state.[8] He bridges the historiographical gap, or period of arrest, represented by Reconstruction's unfinished promise to create a modern civil rights order, in that his radicalism "simultaneously harked back to the abolition movement . . . and looked forward to the NAACP."[9] This pursuit of a usable past in the lost continuities of nineteenth-century radical idealism also has a more distinctly left-wing variant. We might see Tourgée as a stepping stone on the way to a Popular Front desire to place the abolitionist generation in an American revolutionary tradition. This desire is exemplified in Howard Fast's Reconstruction novel, *Freedom Road* (1944), whose plot and penchant for set piece political dialogue shares much with Tourgée's *Bricks without Straw* and whose protagonist—the formerly enslaved Reconstruction leader Gideon Jackson—absorbs his democratic revolutionary spirit as much from the writings of the American Renaissance as from his experience of slavery.

In my reading, the relationship between Tourgée's politics and the historical sense of his writing provides no such unbroken link. The ambivalence I am identifying is not the product of ideological continuities in American republicanism (tragic or heroic). Rather, it responds to the peculiar revolutionary pressure slave emancipation exerted on the nature and boundaries of the "social question." Tourgée's work strains at a hegemonic political language; this strain provides a window onto revolutionary contingencies defined less by Marx's fully reconstructed "social world" than by what Christopher Taylor, with reference to Jamaica, calls the "shattered social" created by emancipation.[10]

The State and the Social

Tourgée imagined Reconstruction's goals through a republican model of politics (and revolution) that prizes civic virtue and self-possession. This ideology privileges normative categorical distinctions between state and society that the overlap of slavery and revolution troubles. As much is evident in perhaps the most influential modern attempt at a republican theory of revolution. In *On Revolution* (1963), Hannah Arendt argues that revolution's true novelty lies in the reinvention of the political realm (as opposed to Marx's social world) as "the space of appearances where freedom can unfold its charms." Viewed as the public space of freedom and common human action, she defines politics against the social, imagining the social realm to be the space of necessity and reproduction. Her ideas are based on a utopian reading of the American Revolution's constitutionalism, against which subsequent revolutionary movements in France and Russia "surrender[ed] . . . freedom to necessity": by politicizing the social question, she argued, these revolutions abandoned politics as a distinct sphere of action, conceding instead to an abstraction of the social will of the people (in particular the poor) that Arendt labels "the passion of compassion."[11]

The discourse surrounding Reconstruction that I examine in this chapter clings to an idea of revolution as a fundamentally political process. However, despite Arendt's attempts to the contrary, when state power is drawn so directly into the terrain of plantation slavery, the distinction between the political and the social cannot hold. A key problem of Arendt's categorical opposition is that it replicates what she identifies as the American Revolution's blindness to its particular social question: the existence of chattel slavery. While she acknowledges that for the Founders, the social question was "hidden in darkness," she does not confront its reemergence as a direct, rather than hidden, imperative in the Civil War.[12] As a contradictory attempt to imagine revolution through a republican framework, Arendt's distinction provides a usefully symptomatic model of the assumptions that frame republican theories of political revolution, such as those developed by Tourgée and other Radical Republicans. But by omission, it also highlights ideas that trouble such a theory, ideas that Tourgée, in his moment, had to face more directly than Arendt.

Tourgée's program for the revival of Reconstruction clings to the civic virtue of political life as the space of freedom. At the end of *Bricks without Straw*, the converted confederate general Hesden Le Moyne explains to a Republican congressmen that northerners have failed to see slavery as more than a social system that the nation-state could abolish. The true object of future intervention in the South, Le Moyne suggests, should be a program of federally funded and regulated public education, designed to replace centralized political authority with the New England township system, which "came over in the Mayflower" and in which "each township is in itself a miniature republic, every citizen of which exercises in its affairs equal power with every other citizen."[13] Le Moyne imagines an organic connection between grassroots politics and the national power required to "mold the minds of every class of the southern people that all should be indoctrinated with the spirit of local self-government" (*BWS* 512–13). But his program does not resolve the more stubborn question that Tourgée's novels treat as Reconstruction's revolutionary problematic: where does the instrumental force required to create this organic connection come from?

This question animated the Radical Republican constitutional theories on which Tourgée drew, exemplified by Charles Sumner and Thaddeus Stevens.[14] While Sumner and Stevens argued that emancipation redefined the civil and constitutional limits of federal power, both were ambivalent about where to locate, and how to identify, the basis of this novel power. In an 1867 lecture, "Are We a Nation?" Sumner argues that the Civil War had resolved the "constant duel between the Nation and the States," granting the nation-state "all those central, pervasive, impartial powers" required to "protect the citizen in all the rights of citizenship." However, he hesitates in locating the origin of this centralized power. Adopting a nominative metaphor, Sumner argues that "words are sometimes things . . . New capacities require a new name . . . If among us in the earlier day there was no occasion for the word Nation, there is now. A Nation is born." National consciousness was created by the centralized power required to combat secession; like the instrumental power it names, the word *nation* brings about the "new capacities" of central authority. Still, Sumner maintains that while "names may be given by sovereign power to new discoveries or settlements . . . as a general rule, they grow out of the soil, they are autochthonous." To this end, he roots the "new capacities" of nationhood in an organic genealogy that goes back to the Founding. Part autochthonous, part instrumental, what he half-ironically calls "the imperialism of the Declaration of Independence" proposes a radically altered conception of the reach of central state power as if it were a national tradition.[15]

More surprisingly, this indecision also characterizes Stevens's explicitly instrumental theory of the federal government's territorial acquisition of the defeated states. Arguing for Congress's direct control over the states, Stevens defined the positive power of Reconstruction primarily by what it would not be, "restoration." Instead, he argued, "reformation must be effected; the foundation of their institutions, both political, municipal and social, must be broken up and relaid."[16] He confronted opposition to his plan head-on: "it is revolutionary, say they. This plan would, no doubt, work a radical reorganization in Southern institutions, habits and manners. It is intended to revolutionize their principles and feelings . . . The whole fabric of Southern society must be changed."[17] Among the most uncompromising articulations of Radical Republicanism's dalliance with the state as a means of effecting social change, Stevens's speech contains important definitional hesitancies. He identifies his alternative to "restoration," respectively, as "reformation," "reorganization," and "revolution." The status of the social is also mediated; it emerges as an awkward third term in Stevens's characterization of the nation-state's impact on "*both* the political, the municipal *and* the social" institutions of the South. "The whole fabric of southern society" is clearly where an enlarged national power operates, but while it is clear *where* the social fabric is geographically, its conceptual location wavers between "institutions," "habits and manners," and "principles and feelings."

What is at issue for Stevens is not the scope of Congress's authority—unlike many of his colleagues, he believed this was to be as expansive as was required to destroy the Slave Power—but how to imagine the terrain into which the state intervenes and through which it attains the organic, shaping power of a revolutionary force. Is the social made of political institutions, communal customs, or personal principles? In their attempt to represent the organic character of an explicitly instrumental power, Sumner and Stevens waver over how to imagine a constitutional or political revolution (from above) affecting and harmonizing with a social revolution (from below). Neither wholly conceivable as a top-down act of the nation-state nor as a revolt against the state, emancipation was, as Du Bois pointed out, "the logical result of a crazy attempt to wage war in the midst of four million black slaves," whose refusal to remain enslaved in effect made social revolutionaries of Radical Republicans who were much more given to seeing revolution as a political and constitutional process.[18] Could this contradictory, contingent struggle be imagined as having form and direction (as something like a revolutionary project)?

Tourgée's depiction of Reconstruction as just such a project, betrayed and possibly redeemable, shares much of Stevens's and Sumner's ambivalence about the source and direction of historical change. Articulating the lesson that events will later teach the Fool, his mentor, Enos Martin, explains that "these States must be rebuilt from the very ground-sill" because "such exhaustive revolutions as we have had" require "a thorough change in the tone and bent of the people" (*AFE* 22). Echoing Stevens, Tourgée locates the reach of state power in an image of communal everyday life, "tone and bent," peculiar to the conquered territories of the former Confederacy. The novel's repeated scenes of dialogue and failed conversion depict this "tone and bent" as at once the sign of an everyday life that has to be changed and as a model for the organic force required to change it. Writing barely a decade after Sumner and Stevens, Tourgée very self-consciously historicizes the opening up (and possible closing off) of a moment in which this tension was legible as an image of the nation-state's revolutionary potential.

Toward the end of the novel, the narrator casts a summative eye over the collapse of Reconstruction, recounting that the Fool "could not bring himself to see that race, color, or previous condition of servitude, had anything to do with the doctrine of inherent right . . . because he regarded slavery as simply an unnatural and wrongful accident—a state of society which had been imposed on the rightful and natural one" (*AFE* 301). Without contradicting this conviction, we are told that Servosse "felt that ignorance, poverty, and an ebon skin were each of them terrible afflictions" and "that they might all of them be classed as public evils in our American democracy" (302). The shift into passive voice characterizes the didactic irony of Tourgée's juxtaposed narrative perspectives: the idealistic Fool now sees that "the doctrine of inherent right" requires the revolutionary transformation of the "tone and bent of the people." The Fool's tragic failure validates his principles because it is carried out heroically, against the grain of history, thereby justifying by its very failure the instrumental force required to dislodge "the social conditions of two hundred years."

But Tourgée's irony is precarious. The narrator recounts that "without abandoning his principles . . . [the Fool] had come almost to believe that what are termed principles are only ingrained habits of thought and hereditary systems of belief" (*AFE* 303). The very shift into a historical voice that creates an ironic perspective—such as is required to read the novel as a validation of the Fool's anachronistic consistency of principle—questions "principle" itself as a motive force of social change. Despite his political investment in and chronological closeness to Radical Reconstruction, Tourgée's narrative perspective creates a precarious historical distance, a temporal double bind that strains the continuity of the radical tradition, and the account of the activist state, that his novel constructs.

Practicing What You Preach

The locus of this double bind—and of the historical ambiguity underpinning the novel's apparently didactic politics—is Tourgée's valorization of sincerity. The preface of *A Fool's Errand* outlines sincere folly as the novel's activist ideal. "The real Fool," it explains, "is the most sincere of mortals," and it is "only in the element of simple undoubting faith that the kinship of genius and folly consists." However, the sincere fool is the counterpoint to a more ironic, Shakespearean manifestation of the role. Laying out this opposition, Tourgée signs his preface with the ambiguous moniker under which he first published the novel: "*one* OF THE FOOLS" (*AFE* 3, 4; emphasis added). As an authorial persona and conduit for political consistency, sincerity might not be what it seems.

On the one hand, sincerity is a relativistic concept through which to allegorize historical conditioning. Two central chapters of the novel plot a schematic history of the Civil War and Reconstruction in which North and South are "divergent civilizations" that "played at cross purposes, each thinking that he knew the other's heart far better than he sought to know his own" (*AFE* 123, 121). A two-page diagram divides the pages into two columns, with headings that lay out, across "the line of demarcation," "the Northern idea of the situation" / "the Southern idea of the situation" and "the Northern idea of the Southern idea" / "the Southern idea of the Northern idea" (122–23). Of this schema, the narrator claims, "the South, as a mass, was honest in its belief of the righteousness of slavery . . . The North, in like manner, was equally honest in its conviction with regard to the wickedness of slavery . . . yet neither credited the other with honesty" (123). Sincerity marks a political impasse whose only solution is federal intervention into southern social relations. The narrator endorses a version of Stevens's and Sumner's ideas that would have seen the South "divided up into territories without regard to former statal lines . . . under national control . . . until time should naturally and thoroughly have healed the breaches of the past" (116).

On the other hand, sincerity represents a politics in and of itself, a model of what the activist state should be like. Tourgée presents the failure to overcome sincerity's allegorical impasse as a failure to be sincere. Congressional Reconstruction was an "abortion, or, rather, [a] monster, doomed to parricide in the hour of its birth," because it was born "from the womb of party necessity and political insincerity" (*AFE* 117). At once abortion and parricide, the legislative compromises that substitute for Tourgée's radical plan not only abort Reconstruction, but they also kill the dream of an abolitionist state. Sincerity here hangs between a model for the politics required to bring life back to Reconstruction and a vision of the activist state as an irrecoverable legacy.

This tension is crucial to Tourgée's "elegiac tone," which Jennifer Rae Greeson argues "registered—quite earlier than did the political discourse of his day—the extent to which the Reconstruction South had been the site of an irresolvable collision between national ideals and national reality."[19] I say this is a tension because Reconstruction's outcome was not unambiguously resolved in 1879. The novel's very appeal was founded on the fact that after the 1877 Compromise, fears of a Democrat majority across former Confederate states led, in James McPherson's words, to "the reconversion of most abolitionists to a hard-line attitude on the South," in which "many former defenders of Hayes' policy began to talk like Garrison," or—accounting for *A Fool's Errand*'s surprising popularity—like Tourgée.[20] Tourgée's representation of the tragic (and anachronistic) pathos of a political tradition seeks out the fragile signs of life and the potential continuity of a political constituency.

To do this, he reworks a popular stylistic representation of the Reconstruction South, common to travel accounts of the period, which depicts the region as poised between history and politics. In claiming to depict events unfolding according to their own logic, such accounts foreground their instrumental role in shaping an ongoing process.[21] This narrative instrumentalism took different forms. In *The Prostrate State: South Carolina under Negro Government* (1874), James S. Pike presents his sensationalized account of "the spectacle of a society turned bottom side up" by the barbarism and corruption of Black legislators as detached journalism, even as he predicts that the shock caused by his apparently neutral portrayal of Reconstruction's inverted reality will motivate a political "method by which [the state's] Africanization can be prevented."[22] In a less polemic tone, Edward King's travel account, *The Great South,* promises "the reading public a truthful picture of life in a section which has, since the close of a devastating war, been overwhelmed by a variety of misfortunes." King's studiously apolitical developmentalism highlights the "rich field for investment" revealed to South watchers who are willing to see past the superficial glamor of politics. Yet in his chapter on South Carolina, he endorses Pike's "excellent book" as evidence that such natural historical progress requires the active uprooting of the "frightful incubus" of Black self-government.[23]

With very different aims, Tourgée framed his novel as a literary heir to the urtext for politically instrumental fiction, *Uncle Tom's Cabin* (1852), but he also drew on Harriet Beecher Stowe's reputation as a documentarian. Imitating *A Key to Uncle Tom's Cabin,* Tourgée published an expanded edition of his novel in 1880, retitled *The Invisible Empire,* in which his "Famous Historical Romance of Life since the War" is supplemented by a second part that quotes extensively from congressional reports on the Klan to prove the veracity of the events in the novel and to demonstrate that "never before in literature has an apparent romance linked together so many facts."[24] Ploughing this dual furrow, the marketing for *A Fool's Errand* in the back matter of *Bricks without Straw* proclaims the former novel to be "the marked book of this generation" because it is the heir to Walter Scott's invention of "the historical novel" as much as to Stowe's perfection of "the novel with a purpose" (n.p.). Tourgée's fleeting encapsulation of the literary zeitgeist rested on a sense of the South's fragile historicity. Memorializing Reconstruction's failure just as life seemed to have been returned to the possibility of federal intervention in the South, he uses the idea of sincerity to question what political writing—and the idea of a continuous Radical Republican state project to which he attaches it—can *do* in such a moment.

This questioning plays out most prominently in the Fool's dialogues with his unreconstructed neighbors, scenes Tourgée uses to conceptualize his novel's own literary-political intervention. Across two such discourses between the Fool, his wife (Metta), and a local magistrate (Squire Hyman), sincerity and the potential of political conversion become topics of conversation. Meeting in the Fool's library, the group discusses some abolitionist books Hyman has borrowed. Hyman's recognition that "the people who wrote those books believed what they were writing" leads him to understand that his ideas have been historically conditioned and may be subject to change (*AFE* 76). He tells Metta: "I've heard the colonel [Servosse] talk, and what he says looks mighty plausible too. I think it's that has had a good deal to do with unsettlin' my faith" (74). The Fool's ideas appear plausible because, like the books Hyman loans, they are sincere. Responding to Metta's observation that "we practice what we preach," Hyman replies, "I believe you're very much in earnest, both in preachin' and in practicin'" (76).

While the mutual recognition of sincerity opens a space for reconciliation, it unsurprisingly reverts to a model of cultural relativity: equally sincere, each character can only reflect their historical conditions. Exasperated, the Fool exclaims that "it is useless to discuss the matter" (*AFE* 81). Between equally sincere views, force decides. However, while the Fool claims he can't go on, Tourgée goes on: he revises the same problem, through the same Socratic dialogue, across numerous chapters, across a series of books. As his characteristic mode of fictional-political argument, the technique led the Black feminist author Anna Julia Cooper to quip, in affectionate recognition of Tourgée's literary service to the neglected cause of Reconstruction, "all his offspring are little Tourgée's—they preach his sermons and pray his prayers."[25] Over time, this quality garnered him a reputation as more of a pamphleteer than a litterateur. After reading Cable's manuscript for *John March, Southerner*, Richard Watson Gilder defended the bounds of good taste by warning Cable away from the "shades of Tourgée" implicit in his own more didactic moments.[26] But as in Cable's fiction, it is in such moments that Tourgée submits the interventionist capacities of his own writing to self-conscious historical scrutiny.

The impasse of sincerity is an allegory for political writing. The book Hyman and the Fool discuss—a narrative by a northern abolitionist who is whipped for decrying slavery in the community in which the Fool now lives—is modeled on *A Fool's Errand* (itself a fictionalization of Tourgée's similar experience). Hyman reveals that he is one of the people depicted in the book and commences to speak his own instrumentality, telling the Fool, "I have still a greater reason for being angry, after reading one of those books on my own, personal, individual account . . . I, Nathaniel Hyman." When the Fool identifies him as one of the characters, Hyman replies, "That's exactly what I am" (*AFE* 78): namely, an allegory for historical conditioning who speaks with exaggerated self-awareness about being an allegory. Hyman's strained individuation aligns being what one is with being rooted in one's social conditions; paradoxically, it also makes this rootedness into a model for the instrumental capacities of politically sincere writing.

This paradox shapes Tourgée's depiction of sincerity as a noble failure. Describing the Fool's attempts to convert his neighbors, the narrator says that the Fool's words "seemed to have touched a deep chord in their hearts, not so much from what he said perhaps, as from the fact that he had dared to say it" (*AFE* 129). The affective capacity of the Fool's words is premised on their failure: where they fail as political conversion, their sincerity immerses him in the community he seeks to convert. From the opposing standpoint, Hyman tells Metta: "My son, Jessie, he's heard the colonel speak once or twice, an' he's clean carried away with him . . . He's quite took up with the notion you spoke of a while ago,—that freein' the slaves is the best thing that's ever happened for the white folks of the South. Maybe he's right, but it sounds right queer to hear him talk so. He's like you say though—practicin' what he preaches, an' is going in to work as if he'd been raised to it all his life. It looks hard and sounds queer; but maybe he's right" (75). The Squire's dialect is overtaken by figures for the material force of speech's affective power. "Carried away" and "took up" by the sound of Servosse's words, Jesse embodies the Fool's language ("he's like you say"), but he does so only because of the syntactical peculiarities of Hyman's parochial dialect and, in his own peculiar way, "as if he'd been raised to it all his life." Ultimately, this does no good: like the Fool, Jessie is exiled in the absence of the political power to back up his ideas. At the end of the novel, in death, the Fool comes to embody the contradictions of Tourgée's model of sincerity. He is described by a local Unionist as "an earnest man" whose "ideas wasn't calkilated [sic] for this meridian" (361). The epitaph on his gravestone—"our Carpetbagger" (360)—renders his out-of-place politics (and their failure) into an image of sincerity as regional belonging.

Somewhere between political principle and a historical measure, sincerity enables Tourgée to grapple with the problem of how to characterize Reconstruction-era social change. As a model for political writing, sincerity "sounds queer" and "looks hard" because it articulates competing notions of change—one organic and one instrumental—as if they are embodied by a singular political language, capable of reviving a consistent political tradition. By sticking with, and reading through, Tourgée's ironies, rather than treating them as the vehicle for a singular "message," I am asking what representing Reconstruction historically *does* to his politics. This is a different emphasis to critics who (in something of an analogue to seeing Tourgée as the embodiment of American egalitarian tradition) argue that his literary dialogues formally model a republican polity.[27] Rather than reflecting a stable republican position on Reconstruction's revolutionary legacy, Tourgée's surprisingly elusive literary form negotiates the crisis of such a position.

To see how sincerity charts a historical idea of "the political" in crisis, it is useful to read Tourgée against Lionel Trilling's twentieth-century distinction between sincerity and authenticity. Trilling conceived sincerity as an ethical concept that "does not propose being true to one's self as an end but as a means."[28] Reacting to New Left radicals—whose theories of social alienation he believed valorized a retreat from public life into private authenticity—Trilling argued that sincerity was not an identity but a "rhetoric avowal": a participatory, broadly consensual, and increasingly anachronistic negotiation of a public selfhood not subsumed by the alienated social experience of modernity.[29] Responding to the breakdown of Cold War liberal consensus, Trilling posits a republican model of selfhood that, similar to Arendt's of revolution, mediates between political participation and an alienated social world.[30] As with my account of Arendt, I am not suggesting an identity between Tourgée and Trilling's concepts. Nor is it necessary to share Trilling's conclusions to note that sincerity becomes especially meaningful as a way of negotiating the boundaries of political life in moments of crisis for a republican distinction between the political and the social.

The distinction between sincerity and authenticity was not historically available to Tourgée. Instead, he uses sincerity to juggle concepts for measuring entrenched social difference specific to his era. As Michael Elliott argues, the postbellum tendency to see literary representation as an ethnographic medium for documenting cultural types reflects "the epistemological confusion" of a realist moment in which discourses of culture did not clearly distinguish between relativistic and essential ideas of difference.[31] Tourgée's idea of the politically activist (and universalist) potential of sincerity is rooted in his hostility to what he saw as the morally evasive "false standard of truth" established by realism's emergent literary episteme.[32] In that sense, we might see his attachment to sincerity as opposed to Henry James's portrayal of the concept in *The Bostonians,* as the misguidedly feminine idealism of "the heroic Age of New England life—the age of plain living and high thinking, of pure ideals and earnest effort, of moral passion and noble experiment," which has abolished its own political reason for being and become an anachronistic (if attractive) cultural type.[33]

But Tourgée's ironizing of sincerity is more like a mirror image of James's than its opposite. For James, in *The Bostonians,* the problem with sincerity, as it characterizes the feminist idealism of Olive Chancellor, is that it assumes a transparency of personality that leaves no place for the distinctly literary act of exploring the gap between ideality and reality, surface and depth, exterior and (perhaps his novel's favorite concept) interior. In a novel in which no one says what they mean, sincerity leaves no room for the discerning reader of character (or literature), who is better modeled by the unreconstructed southerner, and relentless ironist, Basil Ransom. Nevertheless, through Basil's obsession with the beguiling voice of Olive's protégé, the young orator Verena Tarrant, James clings to the affective power of sincerity and commitment, once they are detached from politics and rendered into an aesthetic performance.[34] Unlike James's characters, Tourgée's *only* say what they mean; he celebrates the political power of sincerity to keep a dying "heroic Age" alive.[35] Yet like James, he makes sincerity the counterpoint to an evasive narrative irony that renders the object of political commitment behind the affective power of sincere language particularly difficult to read.[36]

Though it would not be right to call it Jamesian, Tourgée's irony mobilizes cultural "confusion" about the mutability of social conditions, and the source of the power that intervenes in them, a confusion concerning the relationship between the state and the social. It does so to question the temporality and origins of social change. The explicit playfulness with which he converts his tragic historical sense into a model for politically interventionist language captures a fundamental historical division in what the state has come to mean for Tourgée and in how it relates to the social life that is both its interventionist object and its organic basis. This novelistic contradiction plots the contradictory dynamics of state and revolution played out in Reconstruction.

The Stalemated State

To put all this in the form of the question that motivates Tourgée's historical sense: where did revolution come from, and why, for a time, did it seem to be embodied by so unlikely an institution as the American nation-state? This ambiguity is also key to Du Bois's concept of "abolition-democracy," of which Tourgée seems an apt representative and which has become a commonplace description of Reconstruction's unfinished radical tradition.

Du Bois argued that through a combination of military exigency and the system-shattering actions of enslaved people, who refused to work and flooded the Union lines in a "general strike against slavery," the state (however fleetingly) was made revolutionary.[37] His account of the slaves' collective role in forcing emancipation transformed the modern historiography of Reconstruction. But its contingencies are sometimes too easily limned as a celebration of the "agency" of enslaved people or a transhistorical ideal of "abolition-democracy."[38] As he made clear, the moment's combination of military power and "bottom-up" social force is difficult to define politically. The Confederacy's existential commitment to a total war for slavery made possible and effective a general strike that, combined with the military power and interests of the Union, meant "abolition came in as a determining factor and was transformed to a new democratic movement."[39] The upheaval Du Bois depicts is defined by its hybrid status as a revolution from below enacted by a transforming capitalist nation-state: abolition-democracy describes less as a discrete ideology than a conjuncture.

When Du Bois asks of this conflation of forces, "Can we imagine this spectacular revolution?" he is both challenging readers to consider the enslaved as historical actors and asking a genuine question about the source of revolutionary action.[40] The tendency to make emancipation into to an either-or moral question about who freed the slaves blunts the generative imaginative problematic that Du Bois raises and that Tourgée's novel, and the historical novel of Reconstruction more generally, also take up.[41] This was neither revolution from below nor above but a process in which the state—and perhaps more importantly, the militias and civil society institutions through which the coalition of groups allied to the Republican Party exercised an uneven quasi–state power on the ground in the Reconstruction South—became mediums for the grassroots political action and aspirations of enslaved people.[42]

What Tourgée abstracts into narrative form is a concrete problem of the state's abstraction. Both the ambiguous role and uneven reach of the state in Reconstruction resulted from its indeterminate class character. Contrary to Lost Cause myths of the North's "bayonet rule," what Gregory Downs and Kate Masur call "the stockade state," was a body that could enforce its power only in concentrated locales.[43] Following an early demobilization of most of the wartime machinery of the Union army—especially in Tourgée's North Carolina—state power was outsourced to civilian organizations, political clubs, militias, and networks of patronage and dependence that became sites of local (often violent) struggle.[44] This contradictory expansion (and the early demobilization that conditioned it) reflected a national political struggle between a fragile coalition of interests—abolitionists, Free-Soilers, industrialists, and a newly unified financial class created by Union bond issues—that held together Republican rule and set limits on the state's activist horizons. By funding the war through a huge increase in national debt, premised on the elimination of the gold standard, the federal government in effect "mortgaged a radical reconstruction of the South even before the war ended"; advocates of "sound finance" required the government machinery that enforced Radical Republican legislation to also maintain the extractive export industries capable of funding a return to specie repayments. When the formerly enslaved and their allies vied for control of the dispersed mechanisms of state power, then, they became the radical flank of a "stalemated American state" that was dependent on the simultaneous reconstruction and revival of the plantation economy.[45]

However compromised this institutional power was (whether it represents a "Yankee Leviathan" or a "Stockade state"), it mediated new conditions of struggle and a new balance of forces in a radically transformed social terrain. This balance of forces also reflected a new relationship between the plantocracy and the nation. The systems of racial and economic domination that emerged from Reconstruction in the plantation South represent a novel situation as much as a retrenchment of slavery. Planters traded control of the national government—which had previously been an instrument for enforcing their distinct legal and property regime—for local control of labor repression.[46] The postbellum South's intensely violent racial regime was enabled by limitations on federal enforcement of protections established during Reconstruction; but what, from one perspective, seems like a rolling away of the state was, viewed from another, part of a nationwide "new era of state organized violence in defense of private property and respectable property holders."[47] The *indirectness* of state power as a revolutionary force was mirrored by its *indirectness* as a counterrevolutionary one: plantation elites were forced into a defensive relationship to the federal government even as "important parts of national modernization and state expansion . . . became associated with the underdeveloped South."[48]

In an important sense, then, the Reconstruction state was not one thing; its uneven revolutionary extension into areas of life that exceeded republican demarcations of the political and the social was difficult to imagine as a unitary "project."[49] This political ambiguity is registered in the tensions and anachronisms that constitute Tourgée's depiction of the possibilities of abolition-democracy. His ironic narrative form provides a way of thinking about this conjuncture as it constitutes a revolutionary moment in the recent past as much as a tradition to be revived. The interpretive difficulty of Tourgée's irony lies in questions that are at once familiar and alienating to modern readers: how does one imagine the revolutionary potential of a "stalemated state"? Can the state remain an object of revolutionary attachment in the absence of a revolutionary project?

This interpretive difficulty is keenest when Tourgée self-consciously adopts the guise of the historian, most notably when he ironically praises the Ku Klux Klan's counterrevolution as an antidote to the insincere "sickly sentimentalism" of Republican politicians (*AFE* 305). The narrator locates the Klan's success in its recognition that "the whole South must be fused into one homogeneous mass, having one common thought, one imperial purpose, one relentless will. It was a magnificent conception and in a sense deserved success!" (289). Recalling the need for Reconstruction to shape the "tone and bent of the people," Tourgée's narrator imagines the Klan resolving the antinomies of sincerity. White southerners "most sincerely believed there resided [in their race] the inherent right to rule," and therefore, "all else was lost in this one thought . . . [which] gave tone and color to the whole intellectual and moral life of this people" (292). He frames the Klan as at once a revolutionary and a national body. Condemning its counterrevolutionary terror, he nevertheless calls it "the most brilliant revolution ever accomplished," a provocation he emphasizes by insisting, "for revolution it was" (290, 289).[50] While it seems to represent a communal social life impervious to change, then, in Tourgée's intentionally provocative framing, the Klan constitutes a reactionary mirror image of the revolutionary union of state power and the social glimpsed as the radical promise of Reconstruction. By framing resistance to the state as a state-making force, Tourgée imagines the continued possibility that an organic conception of state power might have survived Reconstruction's failure.

His depiction is, of course, ironic, but the irony is stubbornly difficult to decipher. As Tourgée well knew, the Klan was not a pseudo-state. Its decentralized, localized brand of terrorism was effective precisely because it exploited the indirect nature of the federal government's expanded rule without challenging the wider balance of power.[51] By elevating the Klan into an "Invisible Empire, with a trained and disciplined army of masked midnight marauders making war upon the weakling 'powers' which the Wise Men had set up in the lately rebellious territory," Tourgée took aim at the national Republican Party as administrators of a failed state (*AFE* 226).[52] However, his didactic purpose does not completely explain away Edmund Wilson's reading of his "self-identification . . . with the disqualified and dispossessed planters . . . with whom [he] had so much in common."[53] Wilson aligned Tourgée's and the Confederacy's Lost Causes in a tragic narrative about the disenchantment of a mid-nineteenth-century American radical generation that was supplanted by the modern bureaucratic state.[54] It is a misinterpretation, but it is one that Tourgée requires his readers to flirt with. And he does so in the process of questioning the pastness of Reconstruction's revolutionary conjuncture.

Crucially, as with Tourgée's allegorization of his own political language, his ironic memorialization of the Klan acknowledges its historically tendentious character. It is only possible when the Fool steps into the guise of the historian. The narrative perspective here is split between the Fool and the didactic narrator who glosses the protagonist's changing views over time, claiming that previously "the object-plate on which [the Fool] gazed had been too near the retina to be clearly pictured thereon" (*AFE* 286). In adopting a historical perspective, the narrative voice is poised, like the novel itself, somewhere between political events that still have a purchase on the present and a retrospective account of a political moment slipping into the past. The Fool's identification with the Klan is "a solution [that] answered every condition of the problem" of analyzing Reconstruction's failure (292).

This is one of many moments in which the novel comments on its own precariously historical character. For Tourgée, imagining a form of political power embedded in the everyday life of the South means confronting a broader "problem" of perspective: is this power confined to the past, or can it be remade in the present? The question of the location of state power is also a question of the pastness of Reconstruction's revolutionary horizon, and it remains unresolved not simply because Reconstruction is unfinished but because Tourgée depicts a moment in which the state seemed both the subject and object of revolutionary change. Immersed in the history from which he attempts to draw political conclusions, Tourgée's narrative form grapples with two contradictory accounts of Reconstruction as revolution: one in which revolution is something that states do and another in which revolution is something done to the state.

A Fool's Errand doesn't resolve these ambivalences, but it does take them up as the problem of imagining Reconstruction as revolution. The question of the political *legacies* of this moment is dealt with more concretely in Tourgée's second novel, *Bricks without Straw*. There he shifts focus from the tragic historical figure of the carpetbagger to represent the everyday lives and political aspirations of formerly enslaved people. By depicting the struggles of Black characters abandoned by the state, Tourgée attempts to humanize a conception of citizenship drawn from Reconstruction, one whose scope exceeds the formal rights that were being hollowed out as he wrote. Three years after Tourgée published *Bricks without Straw,* Justice Bradley identified the racialized legal figure of the "mere citizen" as Reconstruction's legislative legacy. As I detailed in the previous chapter, the decision in the *Civil Rights Cases* set the stage for the Court's ruling in *Plessy v. Ferguson,* the landmark legal case that helped usher in the intensified legislative reaction of the turn of the century and which Tourgée used to refight the constitutional battles of Reconstruction.

In the next section, I trace how Tourgée thinks with and up against the racialized limits of republican ideas of possessive individualism in *Bricks without Straw* to imagine the positive and prospective force of a citizenship rooted in the South's social fabric (something that could be inherited rather than imposed). This lays the basis for an account of how Tourgée attempted to make abolition-democracy's revolutionary conjuncture legally cognizable from the increasingly reactionary horizon of the 1890s. Together, his novel and his legal argument negotiate notions of race, time, and property that stretch the ideological underpinnings of republican ideas. This ideological stretching helps us to see the revolutionary contingencies beneath the racial continuities that republican ideas of citizenship, in particular of possessive individualism, express.

The Strange Career of Possessive Individualism

Bricks without Straw humanizes the problem, pursued in *A Fool's Errand*, of how an interventionist politics of "principle" and "inherent right" can become "ingrained" and "hereditary." Tourgée used the unexpected public attention brought by his previous novel's commercial success to outline an explicit political program, advocating a scheme of federally funded and regulated public education as the means for rooting freedom in slavery's social terrain. The novel represents the efforts of the former slave Nimbus and the disabled Black preacher Eliab Hill to exercise their newly acquired political and contractual rights, educate themselves, and establish a community of free agricultural laborers. When the self-sufficient community of Red Wing—built by Nimbus and Eliab with the help of a New England schoolteacher, Mollie Ainslee—is destroyed by white paramilitaries, Tourgée supplements the action of the novel with a programmatic account of his scheme to "make the spelling book the sceptre of the national power" (*BWS* 346).

That Tourgée sees public education as a means of extending the Reconstruction state's forceful imposition of new social relations is enshrined by the image that closes the novel: a "spelling book" bearing the Latin inscription "In Hoc Signo Vinces," with these words you conquer (*BWS* 521). In a lengthy dialogue between the Confederate grandee Hesden Le Moyne—converted to Red Wing's cause by his love of Mollie—and a skeptical Republican congressman, Tourgée lays out an educational plan to "mold the minds of every class of Southern people [so] that all should be indoctrinated with the spirit of self-government." Tourgée would later advance this plan himself in his political tract *An Appeal to Caesar* (1884), a book intended to steer James Garfield's presidential campaign toward a renewed interventionist policy on the South.

Tourgée poses Le Moyne's plan as both the political solution to the historical problem of revolutionary force posed in his previous novel and a long-term process that questions the sufficiency of formal rights as the emancipatory horizon promised by the state (515).

However, having "forecast[ed] the future of the country after a consideration of its past," Le Moyne reproduces a familiar impasse: "There we are," the congressman replies, "at the very point we started from. Like the poet of the Western bar-room, you may well say, my friend, 'And so I end as I did begin'" (*BWS* 513). Despite providing a formal and political response to the dilemmas laid out in *A Fool's Errand*, by humanizing the pathos of the revolutionary state and suggesting a programmatic means for its extension, the novel does almost literally end where the previous one began: "Day by day the irrepressible conflict is renewed. The Past bequeaths to the Present its wondrous legacy of good and ill. Names are changed but truths remain . . . On the trestle-board of the Present, Liberty forever sets before the future some new query. The Wise-man sweats drops of blood. The Greatheart abides in his strength. The King makes commandment. The Fool laughs" (521). Tourgée's epigraph makes "the Fool" represent a comic as much as tragic historical conundrum. The temporal riddle frames his literary struggle to seize renewed political hopes from the past as a wry and fatalistic reflection on the "irrepressible" workings of historical time, analogized to the "irrepressible conflict" between the nation-state and the ideals of state sovereignty that Tourgée attacks. But now the impasse is framed as a problem of political temporality: how to embrace long-term social change as a radical legacy without conceding to the gradualism that defined reconciliationist politics (and the position of the Republican Party) after Congressional Reconstruction?

Le Moyne presents the revolutionary credentials of his educational program through a comparison of national revolutionary traditions that foregrounds this tension: "The French may shout over a red cap, and overturn existing systems for a vague idea," he explains, "but American conservatism consists in doing nothing until it is absolutely necessary. We never move until the fifty-ninth minute of the eleventh hour" (*BWS* 513). Acting as an authorial mouthpiece, Le Moyne expresses, as an American virtue and a tenet of his "realistic" political program, what Tourgée would describe as a mortal danger four years later, in *An Appeal to Caesar*. There he complains that "we refuse until the fifty-ninth minute of the eleventh hour to recognize the presence of danger . . . The nation suffered in the War of the Rebellion because it would not listen to the words of warning . . . It is the same inclination to trifle with the danger which lies before us that makes the problem of the African in the United States a terrible one to-day."[55] While Tourgée intended his educational ideas to be a response to such political inactivity (and his novel to be a means of building support for the response), aligning a peculiarly American Revolutionary tradition with organic long-term social change necessarily raises an anxiety about lost revolutionary time. This dilemma permeates Tourgée's depiction of Black experience during Reconstruction, which he turns into a parable for the development of a model of citizenship that could retain something of the social force of the activist state.

As Tourgée presents it, making the citizenship bestowed by the nation-state socially effective involves passing a contractual right that is shallow and vulnerable to expropriation across generations, so that it is not just given by law but taught, learned, and in a neo-Lamarckian sense, inherited.[56] The opening chapters of the novel describe the successive legal "transformations of the slave" through which Nimbus passes in contracting his freedom with the state: he joins the Union army as contraband, next he enters into a marriage contract, then he registers to vote (BWS 41). This acquisition of freedom takes place as drama of naming and property. Nimbus's singular moniker is bestowed by a slave master powerful in "der way ob names," who specializes in "rearing slaves for market" (5, 16). Colonel Desmit gives each of his slaves a single, unique name so that "in a moment he could ascertain every element of the value" (17–18). Marking Nimbus's prior status as chattel, this vestige of slavery also renders him a "pure *nullius filius*—nobody's son," enshrining his inability to pass on a legacy (46). Nimbus's name poses a problem for the various agents of the state who contract with him, each of whom attempts to give Nimbus a patronymic conferring legal personhood through the ability to inherit. Rendering the transition from property to personhood into a series of contracts, the state struggles to overcome the social abjection according to which whatever Nimbus "had acquired in slavery was the master's" because "husband and wife there was not one in four millions . . . Uncle and aunt and cousin, home, family—none of these words had any place in the freedman's vocabulary" (34–35).

These opening scenes model a freedom at once in excess of the law's formal mechanisms and, at the same time, subjected to the state. Nimbus initially refuses his master's surname, declining "ter brand my children wid no sech slave mark" (BWS 54). He questions the contractual order of freedom.

Claiming that a "nigger got no use for two names," he demands that the legal order bend to the social world of the enslaved: the forms of kinship familiar to the "*nullius filius*" and beyond the cognition of legal possession (45).[57] Leaning heavily on tropes for representing marriage and contract in the slave narrative, Tourgée has Nimbus demand a different kind of recognition to that offered by a contractual order that "threw the responsibility of illegitimacy where it did not belong" (37).[58]

Ultimately, though, it is Nimbus who recognizes the centrality of inheritance to freedom. He tells Eliab that his children "must hev a name, an' I must hev one ter gib 'em" (*BWS* 55). While Tourgée suggests that contract freedoms recapitulate the master's sovereignty, he is in no doubt as to the direction of travel, describing the marriage contract in particular as "the first step in the progress from the prison-house of bondage to the citadel of liberty" (35). In an ambivalent moment, Nimbus chooses the name of his former overseer to adorn his marriage contract. Unable to pass an inheritance with a name that designates him a former article of property, he can do so as an exploited laborer. Tourgée suggests the continued exploitation involved in the contract relation; he identifies Reconstruction as a period in which vernacular understandings of freedom, not limited to contract, were vital political desires. At the same time, he clings to a conception of freedom as a process of generational development embodied in a legally cognizable conception of inheritance.

These opening scenes constitute a parabolic miniature of a novel in which Tourgée imagines the acquisition of citizenship through "the freedman's vocabulary." He constructs this vernacular into a historically particular version of what Hortense Spillers calls the "American grammar," in which Black social life is overdetermined by the contradictions of inherited kinlessness.[59] Tourgée imagines the process by which a flimsy "inherent right," easily overturned in the absence of state protection, becomes a socially ingrained, inheritable possession: a legacy of the promise of the Reconstruction state. No doubt, the novel swings between representing Black attempts to dictate the terms of freedom and a paternal invocation of the need to educate Black southerners in the rudiments of a republican political order dependent on what Saidiya Hartman calls "the burdened individuality of the responsible and encumbered freedperson."[60] Tourgée's parabolic narrative ultimately "affirms possession as the fundamental premise of relations," but he is alive to this tension.[61] As much is suggested by his own authorial act of naming. Nimbus was the name Tourgée gave to a real fugitive slave whom he employed during his time as a Union soldier in occupied Kentucky. In a distinctly ambivalent fictionalization, he parallels his own authorial role in affixing meaning to Black freedom with the power of his fictional slave owner, Colonel Desmit.[62] Expressing the parabolic transition from slavery to freedom as a nameable political category, Tourgée wrestles self-consciously with racialized concepts of possession that are not fixed but in flux.

Like Cable's more genteel ideals, Tourgée's politics are symptomatic of a "civic ideology" rooted in notions of possession derived from chattel slavery. The point is that his unconventional form of the historical novel dramatizes the disjunction involved in trying to think slavery's upheaval through a political language rooted in that system. This fragile relationship of historical and political representation can be inverted by tracing what happened when Tourgée tried to make the revolutionary dilemmas outlined in his novels into the basis for a real-world positive legal category in his defense of Homer Plessy. Tourgée's legal argument in the *Plessy* case looks back on the relationship between state power and social custom from the horizon of Reconstruction's failure as a state-sanctioned political project. What emerges is a curiously unstable framing of race and property as possession and inheritance that captures the antinomies of Reconstruction-era state formation at the moment they became legally unimaginable to the segregationist state.

Seeing how Tourgée historicizes this moment requires us to rethink slavery's relationship to the cultural and legal language of possessive individualism. The other side of the scholarly tendency I have questioned, which sees Tourgée as an activist bridge between the abolitionist and civil rights traditions, is a critique of the republican ideas he held as a historically continuous cultural language for "preserving and reproducing the episteme of chattel slavery": namely, an understanding of selfhood as property that wedded Blackness to social death.[63] This critique follows Hartman in arguing that the "proprietorial notions of the self" underpinning Reconstruction-era debates about citizenship secured "the identity of race as property, whether evidenced in the corporeal inscriptions of slavery and its badges or in the bounded bodily integrity of whiteness secured by the abjection of others."[64] I have argued that Tourgée's ideas of citizenship were steeped in racialized notions of property, even as he rejected citizenship as the prerogative of whiteness, but it is worth questioning whether the only "vantage point" such a language provides is one in which "emancipation appears less the grand event of liberation than a point of transition between modes of servitude and racial subjection."[65] The tendency to frame emancipation's formal limits through a changeless legal language for inscribing race as property risks downplaying the cultural significance of "transition[s] between" (or more appropriately to the argument here, transformations of) social forms that Reconstruction's circumscribed language of citizenship makes visible.

By conceiving of the social as a creation of legal (and legalistic) language, this critique of legal formalism also risks making slavery and freedom into primarily discursive categories. Slavery's continuities become, per Frank Wilderson, "a scandal at the level of discourse"; and, as Stephen Best puts it, "revolution (even that which would dispense with slavery) promises to remain largely inefficacious at the level of the semiotic" (and, we might add, invisible at the level of culture).[66] The limits of emancipation become a collective failure of a cultural and legal language of freedom born with slavery.[67] This scholarship draws important connections between new world slavery and modern citizenship, foregrounding the way that race serves alternately to interpolate and subject the individual to the state, but it risks conflating the social with the legal, capitalism with the ideology of possessive individualism.[68] When the movement between novel and distinct forms of racial domination is described as the persistence of a singular and inadequate legal language of freedom—and that language made into a cultural-legal synecdoche for a contingent social system—slavery becomes an original sin that the law repeats ad infinitum.[69]

In slavery's revolutionary afterlife, the boundary between the state and the social is contested and contingent. Such contestation underpins C. B. MacPherson's original conceptualization of possessive individualism in early modern political theory. MacPherson argued that the Lockean proprietary notion of personhood—in which an inalienable property in oneself is subject to the ability to alienate the property of others—reflected social and political conditions not attributable to the market per se (conceived as a transhistorical synecdoche for capitalism), but a nascent capitalist society in which the existence of a nonrational laboring class "in but not of civil society" was an "implicit assumption."[70] This was the social common sense of the seventeenth-century Atlantic mercantile economy. The emergence of the proletariat as a cognizable political force fractured the status of this common sense as an "assurance of cohesion" and "moral justification" of the political order, even as possessive individualism persisted as an idea in political theory.[71] Perceptions of emancipated slaves as beyond political rationality were common in nineteenth-century American thought (and beyond). However, the significance of Reconstruction is precisely that such conceptions could no longer form an "implicit assumption." Given the period's social and political upheavals, the connection between legal personhood and chattel slavery looks less like a "social ontology" than a contested, unstable relationship.[72]

It is through this compromised legal and cultural language that Tourgée thematizes revolutionary crisis.[73] In the *Plessy* case, Tourgée pursued legal categories that could positively express the relationship between state power and everyday social life that Reconstruction threw into question: he attempted to make the shifting terrain of the Reconstruction-era social sit still in the eyes of the state. The ironies he employs in his legal argument demonstrate the (contested) waning from view of an imagined revolutionary conjuncture resistant to the continuities of a language of legal personhood.

Homer Plessy's Property

The *Plessy* case is a landmark in the history of segregation. With regard to the questions of narrative periodicity discussed here, it also forms a moment of historical punctuation: a death knell for a conception of citizenship that defined the promise of the Reconstruction state. The Supreme Court's ruling gave constitutional assent to an understanding of the Reconstruction Acts as a positive mandate for racially segregated citizenship. The Court confirmed the constitutional legitimacy of de jure segregation, finding that the formula of separate but equal neither contravened the right to equality before the law outlined in the Fourteenth Amendment nor constituted a badge of servitude as described in the Thirteenth. The Louisiana Separate Car Act, which the defense challenged, mandated segregated carriages for white and "colored" passengers on intrastate travel so long as the separate facilities were of equal standard. This equality clause was a legal nicety designed to elide the Reconstruction Amendments and masked the fact that the very nature of separate accommodations marked the second-class status and more fundamentally, as a number of scholars have credited Tourgée with arguing, *the race* of passengers consigned to the "Jim Crow" car.[74]

Tourgée's attack on the race-making powers of segregation also opens up a historical contest over the narrative of Reconstruction. In particular, his argument that Homer Plessy possessed a legally defensible property in his reputation as a white man ironically roots the state power that protects citizens from racial discrimination in the local, everyday communal life that Justice Brown uses to justify segregation and that Tourgée saw it as the nation-state's revolutionary duty to reconstruct. This union of organic and instrumental power, familiar from Tourgée's novels, was less easy to fix in the positive formal terms demanded by the law (even in so intentionally political a test case as this). What results is a framing of possession, race, and rights that sits uneasily with the category of national citizenship that Tourgée tries to convince the Court is Reconstruction's legacy.

A summary of the case is necessary. Tourgée's brief surveys the outcome of Reconstruction seventeen years after *A Fool's Errand,* when the emancipatory state appeared to have been replaced by the racial police state. The Louisiana Separate Car Act was justified constitutionally on the basis that it was a "police power," in which an individual state of the union acted to protect the social health of its citizens. According to the Court's ruling in *The Slaughterhouse Cases* (1873), this power justified a state government intervening directly in private life, thereby enabling Louisiana to circumvent restrictions on government power that had elsewhere been used to blunt the Fourteenth Amendment (most notably in *Cruikshank v. United States* [1875] and the *Civil Rights Cases*). Tourgée's case was premised on the idea that these readings of the Fourteenth Amendment had enabled the states to pursue segregationist policies by fundamentally eroding the primacy of national citizenship, which upheld equality of rights.

Justice Brown's ruling refuted Tourgée's argument by rendering segregation an expression of local "established usages, customs, and traditions of the people," which dual citizenship (state and national) was designed to protect. Arguing that "in the nature of things," the Fourteenth Amendment "could not have been intended to abolish distinctions based upon color," he solidifies Justice Bradley's implicit racialization of citizenship in the *Civil Rights Cases* and elides the role of state power in policing the racialized "nature" of custom.[75] Tourgée preempted the spuriousness of this instrumentalized concept of custom by showing how it had been created by law. He cites the Fugitive Slave Act and *Dred Scott* as precedents for the primacy of national (rather than state) citizenship. By highlighting the national character of slave law, he dismisses the states' rights doctrine used to justify segregation as "a curious fetish in our legal and political thought," one that hides the primacy of the nation-state and the instrumentality of state power more generally.[76] Quoting Justice John Marshall Harlan's minority decision in the *Civil Rights Cases,* he asks, "Shall this court which was so ready to commit the government to the perpetuation of wrong, hesitate to apply the same rule to secure the rights of its citizens?" ("BPE" 318).

A national slave law justified the creation of an equally national citizenship to overcome it. Given that the Civil War had destroyed slavery and strengthened federal power, Tourgée argued it was paradoxical to revert to a parochial concept of citizenship. The Fourteenth Amendment had created "a new citizenship—new in character, new in extent, new in method of determination, [and] new in essential incident" ("BPE" 261). By turning segregation into a narrative about the scope of the central state power created by Reconstruction, Tourgée probably harmed his chances of winning the case.[77] He could have argued that the Separate Car Act enforced racial inequality without requiring the Court to overturn its legal interpretation of the Fourteenth Amendment. Instead, in a political move, the case was designed to force the Court's assent for "the revolutionary nature of the Reconstruction Amendments."[78]

Tourgée's contention that social custom was less an object to be protected by law than a field shaped by law raises the question of how to account for his famous argument that "the reputation of belonging to the dominant race, in this instance the white race, is property," possession of which the Fourteenth Amendment protected from state interference ("BPE" 247). In an influential reading, historian C. Vann Woodward argues that this argument constitutes the irony of a case that attacked segregation by defending the rights of members of a mixed-race Creole elite to pass for white.[79] Where more recent responses have moved away from Woodward's reading, they retain his focus on irony to explain Tourgée's idiosyncratic argument either as symptomatic or deconstructive of segregationist ideology.[80] Read against Tourgée's fictional irony, though, his idiosyncratic treatment of race is better seen as a defensive attempt to freeze the disappearing social horizons of the Reconstruction-era state into a singular (and so historically continuous) legal property. His argument about race speaks more to the waning context of Reconstruction than to the waxing, and now more familiar, paradoxes of segregationist racial ideology.

Tourgée argued that the Separate Car Act had invested train conductors with a spurious legislative power through which to determine race in the absence of legal and genealogical precedent. This quasi–state power violated a curiously communal property held by Homer Plessy. Crucially, this property is not quite race (which Tourgée, like Cable before him, argues is necessarily unknowable and which, unlike Cable, he identifies explicitly as a product of misplaced state power). What Tourgée concretized into a single property was Plessy's specific place in the social life of New Orleans. On Tourgée's suggestion, the Comité des Citoyens, which brought the case, chose a light-skinned Creole as plaintiff, in whom "the mixture of colored blood is not discernable" ("BPE" 264). Rather than challenging the reality of race, Tourgée stressed the conventional nature of its indeterminacy in a particular location.[81] He generalized this local experience into a universal principle, arguing that "in any mixed community the reputation of belonging to the dominant race, in this instance the white race, is property, in the same sense that a right of action or of inheritance is property" (247). This idiosyncratic formula allowed him to frame a specific idea of the relationship between custom and the state. He did not hold that Plessy was either white or Black; as a key point of strategy, Plessy declared himself on arrest to be "of mixed Caucasian and African descent, in the proportion of seven-eighths Caucasian and one-eighth African blood" (264). Tourgée exploited the fact that "there is no law of the United States, or of the State of Louisiana defining the limits of race" ("BPE" 249).

The specific terms of Plessy's property take their shape from the paradox of a man claiming both that he was and was not white (Plessy had to identify himself to the train conductor as not white to be removed from the car) and of a law that both fixed race and refused to legislate what it was. The property that Plessy holds in his reputation as white consists of two terms: *action* and *inheritance*. This property, violated by the law, balances self-identification with heredity and self-creation with communal determination.[82] By insisting on the paradoxical contingencies that make up Plessy's reputation as a single concrete property, Tourgée held together two notions of identity and social relations familiar from his novels: one organic, the other instrumental. More significantly, he abstracted (and universalized) a notion of custom from the specific social life of Creole New Orleans, in which Plessy could apparently be both passing and declaring his heritage.

Tourgée appeals to this regional specificity by raising a hypothetical scenario, in which Plessy traveled with a wife and children "belonging to the other race." In this case, the racial distinctions that the act "not only permits but requires and commands" would have "interfere[d] with natural domestic rights of the most sacred character." The power of Tourgée's argument, here, lies in its treatment of interracial contact as an archetype of the everyday: "Has a State power to compel husband and wife, to ride in separate coaches," he asks, "because they *happen* the one to be colored and the other white?" ("BPE" 248; emphasis added). Tourgée summons an image of a particular milieu—New Orleans—in which such potentially transgressive relations are quotidian.[83] As he presents this milieu, social custom balances the transgressive and quotidian possibilities attached to interracial "domestic rights," providing a regionally particular sense of the social that legitimizes an expanded conception of citizenship.

Tourgée recasts citizenship rights, which he insists come from a positive grant of state power, as a defense of custom from the impositions of the state. As police power, the activist state becomes a segregationist threat to organic social life; the Fourteenth Amendment becomes a bulwark against using the state as "a machine to effect the compulsory assortment of passengers on the line of color" ("BPE" 270). Tourgée even imagines the segregationist state as a bastardized image of reactionary accounts of Reconstruction; the theft of Plessy's customary property constitutes "*pro tanto* an act of legalized spoliation—an act of forcible confiscation . . . under legalized forms and statutory methods" (248). Turning to the language of eminent domain, he frames segregation as a reckless extension of state power into a regionally specific social life that embodies the disappearing unity of national power and organic experience that Tourgée glimpsed in Reconstruction. As in *A Fool's Errand,* there is a kind of excess to Tourgée's irony. His necessarily tendentious notion of a communal property that is racial but not quite race struggles, like his idea of sincerity, to fix a new relationship between the state and the social. As in his account of sincerity and inheritance, Tourgée attempts to narrate the character of a citizenship that appears equally to be lodged in a revolutionary state power and in a social life that resists the state.

My point in closely reading Tourgée's legal language is not to suggest an identity with his Reconstruction novels. From the horizon of Reconstruction's collapse—and most importantly, in the legal terms cognizable to the state—the indeterminacy of his irony reads differently. Reading the *Plessy* case against Tourgée's fiction, one can see the difficulty he had in imagining Reconstruction's revolutionary character as it intersected with a nation-state that, if it had never quite been the subject of a revolutionary project, was increasingly becoming the subject of a segregationist one. Nevertheless, Tourgée's idiosyncratic legal categories contain traces of a revolutionary historical sense, visible at the moment that its political horizon disappeared from view. These traces constitute the end of a process conceived more fully in Tourgée's fiction: an attempt to narrate a revolutionary situation in which the radical potential of the state became increasingly derelict but in which the state seemed the only game in town for inaugurating "the reconstruction of a social world."

As my account of *Plessy* and possessive individualism suggests, the 1890s was an important moment in the changing historical sense of Reconstruction. This historical sense was shaped by shifting cultural understandings of the relationship between race, property, and social custom. In the next chapter, I pursue the historical perspectives on revolution that are opened up and foreclosed by imagining historical time through race. Addressing the fragile historicist capacities of racial representation in turn-of-the-century passing novels, I argue that Frances Harper's *Iola Leroy* (1892) and Charles Chesnutt's *The House behind the Cedars* (1900) make racial sentiment into an anachronistic lens for viewing Reconstruction's revolutionary event from the changed political horizon of the 1890s.

3

Charles Chesnutt, Frances Harper, and Passing's Revolutionary Event

In the last chapter, I read Tourgée's account of Homer Plessy's ambiguously raced body as an awkward measure of the temporality of Reconstruction social change—awkward because racial logic traffics in the unchanging. This embodied temporality captures several features of the racialized poetics of the late-century passing genre, despite passing fiction's focus on racial fluidity: an interest in the inevitable return of disavowed heredity; a metaphoric yoking of economic to racial value; subjection of specificities of time, place, and experience to transhistorical determinations of identity; and the recycling of abolitionist sentimental conventions that render chattel bondage a touchstone for social injustice. Through these well-worn tropes, writers in the 1890s made passing into a fictional medium for representing "the problem of the color line" as the political "problem of the Twentieth Century."[1] But as Du Bois's doubly problematized phrasing of racial segregation as a novel epochal period marker suggests, the phenomenon also implied a retroactive lens onto a more contingently historical problem of the nineteenth century.

Through passing, writers approached Reconstruction as a moment of revolutionary breakage—of a change in the nature, if not the existence, of racial embodiment—and true to the obliqueness and disavowal that characterizes the genre, in passing they often turned away from this breakage. In this chapter, I argue that Frances Harper's *Iola Leroy* (1892) and Charles Chesnutt's *The House behind the Cedars* (1900), passing novels set during Reconstruction, dwell on the temporal implications of this late-century tendency; in doing so, they shape the contradictions involved in using racial embodiment to tell the time of Reconstruction's revolutionary event into something like a period discourse.

In trying to make Reconstruction inheritable in the *Plessy* case, Tourgée drew on ideas he rehearsed in his own passing novel, *Pactolus Prime* (1890).

Eva Saks notes that the 1890s inaugurated a profusion of legal decisions about race and inheritance that "allegorize[d] the body" as the site on which courts relitigated (and evaded) Reconstruction. Through the "embodiment of political issues as miscegenous figures," courts turned contingent historical disputes over rights and property into fixed biological questions about race: narrating Reconstruction historically was subsumed into the act of reading the body racially.[2] Saks argues that this phenomena indicates a "crisis of representation" implicit in segregation's logic of racial identity.[3] A critical sense that "passing is about identities" has similarly led critics to read the era's passing fictions for the way they either disrupt or confirm a continuous racial logic that made segregation into a "second slavery."[4] By contrast, I treat racial embodiment as a precarious temporal lens for representing Reconstruction from the horizon of the 1890s and ask how a racial crisis of representation makes legible revolutionary crisis.[5] The crisis in question is the abolition of slavery as a distinct system of property that gave rise to, and socially anchored, the meaning of race. The precarious place of Reconstruction in turn-of-the-century fictions of the color line, I suggest, foregrounds the problem of how to narrate a revolutionary event when the change it inaugurates does not map onto racial progress.

This problem was particularly acute in the liminal decade of the 1890s, when, buoyed by the Supreme Court's decision in the *Civil Rights Cases* and the federal government's failure to quash the beginnings of formal disfranchisement (signaled by the Mississippi Constitution of 1890), reactionary Democratic regimes began to formalize the color line as the new "cornerstone" of the South's social and political life. The elision of Reconstruction in late-century passing fiction reflects this context. Prior to this late-century moment, in the immediate aftermath of the Civil War, Lydia Maria Child's *A Romance of the Republic* (1867) and Rebecca Harding Davis's *Waiting for the Verdict* (1868) use passing to invoke a change in what race is asked to signify. Whatever conclusion one draws about each writer's racial politics, in the wake of emancipation they use familiar antebellum passing plots—which, by revealing a character's hidden Blackness, turn an abstract question about interracial sympathy into a concrete one about the willingness to acknowledge direct kinship—to mark Reconstruction as the scene of a similar qualitative shift in the abolitionist imagination: could the same racialized affect that helped people to feel chattel bondage was a universal scandal against humanity constitute a positive constituency in support of a racially equal body politic?

By contrast, in the reactionary political climate that motivated the late-century resurgence of the passing genre, the specificity of Reconstruction as a moment that shapes the meaning of racial embodiment gives way to a representation of the color line as slavery's pernicious legacy. Tourgée's *Pactolus Prime,* William Dean Howells's *An Imperative Duty* (1891), Twain's *Pudd'nhead Wilson* (1893), and Pauline Hopkins's *Contending Forces* (1900) all employ the strategies of passing fiction to foreground the color line as a social experience (and way of reading history) that tragically joins the present to slavery. This is perhaps most starkly figured in Hopkins's novel, in which to produce a sense of the contemporary—"a romance illustrative of negro life north and south," as her subtitle has it—she deletes the years between the Civil War and her present moment, thereby turning Reconstruction into an axial absence between her novel's first section (on the antebellum South) and its second (on the contemporary North).

The elision is not always so complete, and as I will argue, it is constitutive. In various ways—and with various different attitudes toward the sentimental poetics they employ—these writers make claims on their present that depend on a sense of emancipation's unfinished business. Nevertheless, they all read segregation's logic backward as a metaphor for historical continuity. By contrast, Harper and Chesnutt pick up on this symptomatic elision. Setting their passing novels during Reconstruction and conspicuously writing out the historical scene that structures their fictions, they thematize a tension that faced writers seeking to intervene in the era's racial politics through the emergent narrative lens of segregation. Both novels use the sentimental tropes of abolitionist fiction to metaphorize race through slavery and to protest the color line. However, set against the disappearing backdrop of Reconstruction, the metaphoricity of each writer's abolitionist poetics becomes increasingly fragile, opening up a divide between the historical and political perspectives of their novels.

To be clear, I am not suggesting that Reconstruction and segregation are easily separated eras or phenomena nor that Harper's and Chesnutt's novels are somehow more politically committed (or radical) than, for example, Tourgée's or Hopkins's because they reflect on Reconstruction as a moment of revolution in the past. These problems of periodization and politics are inextricable. When the historian Rayford Logan memorably argued that "the last decade of the nineteenth century and the opening of the twentieth century marked the nadir of the Negro's status in American society," he did not refer to a simple supplanting of Reconstruction.[6] The organized movements to legally codify disfranchisement and segregation were a backlash against the federal government's attempt to renew Reconstruction policies after the Republicans returned to national power in 1888, most notably through federal oversight of national elections and aid to public education in the South.[7] Similarly, this moment saw the emergence of the ideology of race relations as the static, depoliticized, and racially segregated category for understanding social conflict in the South. As Judith Stein argues, this worldview—the hallmark of Booker T. Washington's rise to prominence—was not an accommodation to political defeat but an ideological intervention (the "moderate" flank of a violent political campaign) to contain populist agrarian agitation and interracial fusion politics.[8]

"The nadir," then, was driven by resurgent popular and party-political campaigns that fueled new segregationist responses. This dialectic motivated Tourgée and Harper, in particular, to use their passing novels to advocate for a renewal of Reconstruction's goals in the early years of the decade. That said, the reactionary currents that characterized the period (and that found constitutional sanction in *Plessy*, in 1896) did represent an important *ideological* shift, with implications for the literary depiction and political deployment of the color line. Through the 1890s, the color line—which, as complex and contingent social practice shaped life and politics across the United States before and after the Civil War—came to signify a totalizing social logic that not only defined the present but, as C. Vann Woodward famously argued, colonized the ability to see the past as anything other than a procession of apparently ancient racial "folkways."[9] Reconstruction was not, as Woodward more erroneously suggested (and as I will discuss later in this chapter), a moment of racial egalitarianism, but, the idea of the color line as it developed at the end of the nineteenth century, and as it shaped twentieth-century racial discourse, created an anachronistic language for reading the past. As such, it provides Harper and Chesnutt with the "necessary anachronism" required to depict Reconstruction's social fabric as the scene of revolution.

Passing through Reconstruction

In outlining the temporality that passing lends to race, literary scholarship has generally described the melodramatic, gothic, or parodic resurfacing of slavery, as a return of the repressed, after emancipation.[10] As a way of telling the time through race, this uncanny continuity overlooks revolution as a form of social change that race, as both historical idea and structure of domination, was made to measure. In Tourgée's *Pactolus Prime* and Howells's *An Imperative Duty*—passing fictions to which Harper's and Chesnutt's novels responded—the racial drama is defined by a fleeting sense of Reconstruction's alterity that ultimately gets subsumed into an unbroken timeline of race relations.

Tourgée's polemical novel follows the fictional structure outlined in his Reconstruction novels. *Pactolus Prime* is dominated by schematic dialogues between its eponymous protagonist—a formerly enslaved bootblack who, having escaped slavery and passed as white to fight in the Union army, lives as a Black man in Washington, DC—and his elite white customers. In these dialogues, Pactolus outreasons his interlocutors to articulate a series of political measures, including support for education, that Tourgée intended to influence a new Republican regime toward more interventionist policies on the South.[11] Unlike in his previous novels, however, Tourgée frames his political moment as an era determined by the tragic continuities of slavery rather than by Reconstruction. He displaces the political struggles of Reconstruction onto Pactolus's mysterious past, which Pactolus hides from the other characters and which, for most of the novel, Tourgée hides from the reader. In this way, Tourgée subsumes the specific history of Reconstruction into a more general temporal sense of slavery's presence in a present defined by the race problem.

In DC, Pactolus employs the son of his estranged wife and former master (himself Pactolus's half-brother), Benny. Benny has no knowledge of his relationship to Pactolus, who advises him to pass because "as a white man you can do more than a thousand colored men" to reform "*white* sentiment, white civilisation, white Christianity."[12] "Forget your mother's side of the family-tree," Pactolus advises, "the slave had no family . . . [and] generations of bondage might as well be forgotten: there is no honor in them" (*PP* 136). Whereas in *Bricks without Straw,* this abject history is the basis for political community, *Pactolus Prime* offers no such counterpoint. Despite protesting the social ostracism faced by Black Americans, Tourgée uses Pactolus's account of race as the marker of an abject past to invoke the contemporary racial crisis his novel protests. At the end of the novel, Pactolus's doctor and lawyer discuss a theory of history that sums up Tourgée's warning to his readership: "It would seem strange," the lawyer summarizes, "if the climacteric sin of the centuries—American slavery—should have left behind it a mysterious spore which should breed a scourge similar in character to itself. Yet it is not impossible" (346). Like Blackness in the law of slavery, Tourgée depicts racism as a genealogical taint linking past and present in continuum.

This timeline obscures an easily missed feature of *Pactolus Prime:* Tourgée displaces the drama of passing that determines his plot onto an elliptical history of Reconstruction, a history he reports belatedly and at second hand, rather than representing directly. Pactolus's autobiography, discovered by his lawyer in the act of executing his will, recounts a sensational plot in which the reader learns that Pactolus was enslaved before escaping and passing as white so that he could join the Union army. After the war, he purchases a plantation in South Carolina and, continuing to pass as white, takes "an active part in the political events of the time" (*PP* 312). When he is shot by his former master—an act of personal revenge recalling Reconstruction's widespread political violence—he undergoes an operation that blackens his skin and prevents him from passing. Condemned to live under the social ban of Blackness, Pactolus moves to Washington, DC, masquerading as the servant of his daughter, Eva. There he amasses a fortune under a pseudonym to protect Eva from discovering her lineage. On his death, Pactolus's secret is revealed. Faced with the choice between denying her paternity and social ostracism, Eva disappears into a convent.

By turning what might have been a political narrative of Reconstruction (from the perspective of a fugitive slave) into a racial inheritance plot concerning Pactolus's implausible body, Tourgée frames the kind of novel he had previously written as untenable in his present moment. Pactolus's wound is such "an injury as stops a watch when the pivots are worn out" (*PP* 266); it makes the social injury of Blackness into a symbolic shorthand for the more contingent history it conceals. The significance of his life story, "an o'er true tale of some dark age brought suddenly into juxtaposition with ours" (280), is that it is recorded but not narrated. Pactolus's lawyer can find "traces enough" of his life, "the records are full of him," but its significance boils down to its relevance in determining Pactolus's, and his child's, racial identity (184). Using Pactolus's body to highlight the mutability of identity and dispute segregationist logic requires Tourgée to turn Reconstruction into a historical trace.

By contrast with Tourgée, Howells's anti-segregationist leanings in *An Imperative Duty* are studiously restrained. Nevertheless, he, too, employs a temporal schema in which Reconstruction fleetingly appears as a moment of alterity only to disappear into the continuities of American race relations. The novel is largely devoid of historical markers. Howells constructs his historical moment allusively by relating the action to a Reconstruction past that enters the narrative as a racial crisis for its protagonist, Rhoda Aldgate. Rhoda is thrown into turmoil when she is informed by her aunt, Mrs. Meredith, that her mother was a mixed-race slave. Correcting Rhoda's assumption that she was born illegitimately, Mrs. Meredith explains that Rhoda's mother "was your father's wife. Slavery was past then, and he was too good a man for anything else, though he knew his marriage would ruin him."[13] Howells quietly places Rhoda's birth during Reconstruction; in discovering the scandal of Blackness, she discovers a Reconstruction scene on which Howells chooses not to dwell.

Despite the fact that interracial marriage was still technically legal in Louisiana when Howells wrote, he uses the public acknowledgment, and subsequent cover-up, of the marriage to invoke Reconstruction as a racially exotic and temporally distant moment whose otherness his critique of racial melodrama requires him to disavow. According to the meticulously reasonable Dr. Olney, Rhoda's sudden sense of duty to a race she does not know constitutes melodramatic (and segregationist) race thinking: a "dutiolatry" in which "right affected her as a body of positive color, sharply distinguished from wrong, and not shading into and out of it by gradations of tint, as we find it doing in reality" (*ID* 132, 34). Modeling his novel's opposition to segregated and gendered extremes of feeling through Olney, Howells abandons the complex question of Reconstruction's radical difference from the present. Rhoda's identity crisis splits past from present: she imagines that "there are two selves of her, one that lived before that awful knowledge, and one that had lived as long since" (87). Olney relieves her of this "desperate retrospect," and her dutiolatry, by teaching her to disavow the past (136).

Howells profits from the racialized melodrama whose disavowal his novel performs.[14] For Olney, "the remote taint of [Rhoda's] servile and savage origin gave her a kind of fascination which refuses to let itself be put in words" (*ID* 133). Rewriting a complex primal scene in conventionally racialized terms, Howells avoids explicit discussion of Reconstruction (or politics at all) in favor of a criticism of racial melodrama that takes pleasure in seeing a homogeneous past precisely in melodramatic terms. When Rhoda and Olney marry, the narrator announces that "as tragedy the whole affair had fallen to ruin. It could be reconstructed, if at all, only upon an octave much below the operatic pitch" (139). Treating reconstruction as a metaphor for realist representation (and trying to reconstruct the race problem on terms other than politics), Howells abandons its homonym as an atavistic scene indicative of the sensationalized racism his novel condemns. In the end, he can only deal with the past through the lens of segregation, even as he satirizes race thinking. Like Tourgée's politically contrasting critique of segregation, Howells raises but cannot extend the constitutive sense that narrating Reconstruction requires a radically different timeline than the history of race relations.

In Harper and Chesnutt's novels, a similarly elliptical treatment of Reconstruction functions very differently. Both writers set their novels, at least in significant part, during moments that fracture the meaning of racial embodiment and of the literary tropes used to invoke it. Reconstruction's disappearance, therefore, comes to signify the difficulty of narrating a moment of revolutionary crisis in a racialized language that speaks to the present.

Sleeping through Revolution

In key moments of *The House behind the Cedars* and *Iola Leroy*, a character is lulled by an act of reading into sleeping through telltale signs of epochal social change. As scenes of reading and historical scene setting, these moments capture and comment upon a literary treatment of time that makes important aspects of historical specificity (almost) unreadable. Chesnutt's narrative takes place over the course of 1868–69, in the wake of the military reoccupation of North Carolina designed to enforce the Reconstruction Amendments and overturn President Johnson's conservative Reconstruction plan. The main action of Harper's narrative runs from around the time of the Emancipation Proclamation through Reconstruction and into the present. Both novels date their action elliptically, through references to political events.

While neither book is a traditional historical novel in the sense that it pursues "the authenticity of the historical psychology" of a distinct past, they both make Reconstruction's symptomatic elision from an emergent segregationist discourse into the basis for a historical sense.[15] These scenes of disrupted sleep constitute what Mikhail Bakhtin called a "chronotope," an archetype of the way that each novel's "indices for measuring space and time" makes "the epoch . . . not only graphically visible, but narratively visible."[16] In a miniature of the novels themselves, narrative time and historical time come apart in these scenes, bringing a moment of revolutionary change into view *in tension* with the generic sense of time that characterizes passing and the emergent racial discourse of the 1890s.

Chesnutt's version of the scene occurs soon after the Civil War in the fictional town of Patesville, North Carolina, where the visiting aristocrat George

Tryon inadvertently stumbles upon the secret identity of his fiancé, known to him as a white woman, Rowena Warwick. Tryon does not realize that his betrothed is actually named Rena Walden and is the unacknowledged daughter of an elite white man who maintained a secret family with Rena's mother, "a free colored woman," named Molly Walden.[17] Tryon and Rena are engaged after Rena follows her brother (Tryon's lawyer), known publicly as John Warwick, to South Carolina to pass as white and live on a plantation John acquired after the war from his deceased wife. Visiting Patesville to pursue an uncollected prewar debt at the same time as Rena secretly returns to visit her sick mother, Tryon nearly uncovers Rena's secret when their paths converge in a doctor's office. Conveniently, Tryon delays the convergence by falling asleep.

Chesnutt uses this scene to foreshadow the inevitable discovery of Rena's racial identity and to invoke the tragic determinations of the color line that negate the lived contingency of interracial contact. Eventually discovered and rejected, Rena dedicates herself to a career teaching in a freed people's school. Having refused Rena as his fiancée, Tryon pursues her as his lover; Chesnutt suggests that, in this event, Rena would follow the condition of her mother. By refusing to "give his name to Mis' Molly's children,—to whom it would have been a valuable heritage," Rena's father had reflected "the growing tyranny of the slave power," which Chesnutt tells readers began in the 1830s to close off a previous era "when race lines were not so closely drawn" in North Carolina (*HBC* 108–9). At another moment of potential flux in the state's racial order, Rena would be forced into the same position. Escaping this fate, she dies when she contracts a fever after running into a swamp to evade the advances of Tryon and the Black plantation owner, Jeff Wain.

Along with foreshadowing the novel's tragic ending, with its overtones of antebellum melodrama, Tryon's sleep dates the novel. He is lulled by "the air of Patesville [which] was conducive to slumber. A visitor from some bustling city might have rubbed his eyes, on any but market day, and imagined the whole town asleep—that the people were somnambulists and did not know it" (*HBC* 112). From the opening of the novel, Chesnutt associates the temporal (non)specificity of his story, which takes place "a few years after the Civil War," with a spatial location in which time appears to accrete rather than to pass (3). This spatially specific time sense is embodied in Patesville's town clock, which John imagines being "so irreconcilable . . . as still to peel out the curfew bell" for slaves and free Black residents, "as though the land had never been subjugated" (4). Though Tryon's "state of somnolence" seems to reflect this stasis, it is brought on by period markers that suggest a different kind of scene altogether, indicating that this "visitor['s]" sense of a town unconsciously sleepwalking through history is an "imagined" one that elides the historical particularity crucial to the novel (75).

To invoke "the air of Patesville" that lulls Tryon, the narrator lists a seemingly dispassionate inventory of local everyday occurrences, culminating in "a dozen two-wheeled carts, loaded with lightwood and drawn by diminutive steers, or superannuated army mules branded on the flank with the letters 'C.S.A.,' which represented a vanished dream, or 'U.S.A.,' which as any negro about the market-house would have borne witness, signified a very concrete fact" (*HBC* 74). Tryon's misrecognition of a changed scene as a static one replays the novel's opening, in which John—returned to Patesville after an absence of "ten years," like Tryon, in the guise of "a stranger from South Carolina"—ruminates on a town in which "time seems to linger lovingly long after youth has departed, and to which he seems loath to bring the evil day" promised by time's "destroying hand." Chesnutt's narrator warns that John's observations are "trite reflection[s]—as apposite to the subject as most random reflections are" (3–4). Having noted the "irreconcilable clock" that confirms the town's immunity to change, John is immediately struck by the sight of a "colored policeman," who serves as "a stronger reminder than even the burned buildings that war had left its mark upon the old town with which time had dealt so gently" (5). That mark—noted, if not (quite) narrated—is Radical Reconstruction: the scene around which time and history fracture in Patesville.

By replaying these opening misrecognitions, Chesnutt connects his novel's location to a form of reading. Tryon interprets his surroundings with the "mental acquisitiveness" Richard Broadhead argues was characteristic of late-nineteenth-century readers of regionalist fiction; he mistakes the signs of a "concrete" history for the timeless aesthetic details of a "mildly interesting view."[18] Continuing his reading, Tryon "idly" takes up a magazine, in which he stumbles on "an article by a Southern writer, upon the perennial race problem that has vexed the country for a century" (*HBC* 74). Cast like the town as temporally static, "the perennial race problem" shadows a more epochal sense of history. The sensationalist article frames racial intermixture as a threat posed by "the abhorrent tide of radicalism," which in 1868 had so recently overcome Presidential Reconstruction.[19] In response, the article argues simultaneously for the impossibility of racial amalgamation and the suddenly pressing necessity for a segregated body politic to prevent it: "The writer maintained that owing to a special tendency of the negro blood, however diluted, to revert to the African type, any future amalgamation of the white and Black races, which foolish and wicked Northern negrophiles predicted as the ultimate result of the new conditions confronting the South, would therefore be an ethnological impossibility; for the smallest trace of Negro blood would drag down the superior race to the level of the inferior, and reduce the fair Southland, already devastated by the hand of the invader, to the frightful level of Hayti, the awful example of Negro incapacity" (74). Highlighting Tryon's failure to notice that his fiancé is just such an "ethnological impossibility," Chesnutt's irony also acts as a reflection on reading a revolutionary moment (for which *Hayti* and *amalgamation* are synonyms) through the lens of passing. To interpret the plot as Chesnutt's critique of a racial logic that proceeds, like his novel's setting, "as if the land had never been subjugated," one must observe the history of Reconstruction—the "concrete" political ground of race, to which "any negro about the market-house would have borne witness"—fading into the background, becoming detail.

In a sense, Chesnutt requires readers to treat Reconstruction this way. The "visitor from some bustling city," for whom these telltale signs are scenic background is more an image of Chesnutt's presumed cosmopolitan reader than of the country boy, Tryon. If such details are not central to the plot, they are stylistically central to the allusive free indirect narrative voice that structures Chesnutt's ironies. The dramatic irony that allows readers to sense the inevitable force of racial custom—always about to impinge on the characters—relies on things happening in the background, and Chesnutt gives this background mimetic density through references to a social crisis so embedded in everyday life as to appear quotidian. Readers might spot such seemingly throwaway details as Molly's aside, in a letter to Rena that includes, among routine updates of births and illnesses, the news that "Old man Tom Johnson was killed last week while trying to whip black Jim Brown, who lived down on the Wilmington Road" (*HBC* 66). Similarly attuned to textual allusion, they can preempt the tragedy that the color line dictates will befall Rena. Still, Chesnutt refuses to disclose anything about Reconstruction as such. By unfolding the ironies, inversions, and misrecognitions of his passing plot through a thick narrative and social fabric, he requires a studious misprision of Reconstruction as mimetic detail.[20] As he frames it, for Reconstruction to become the context of a racial plot, it must disappear as an event.

Harper's version of this scene also dates a plot light on temporal markers by self-consciously invoking the kind of reading her novel requires. Harper's sleep scene occurs when Harry, the brother of the protagonist, Iola, receives a letter from Iola informing him of their father's death and disclosing the family's secret history. Harry and Iola are children of a wealthy Mississippi slaveholder, Eugene Leroy. Sent to the North for their education, they believe themselves to be white. However, in the letter, Iola informs Harry that their mother, Marie, is Eugene's former slave. Having "manumitted, educated, and married" Marie, Eugene believes that freedom, like slavery, will pass along the maternal line; he tells her, "I have manumitted you, and the children will follow your condition."[21] Doubting his certainty, Marie convinces Eugene to send the children North to pass as white. On Eugene's death, his cousin discovers "a flaw" in Marie's manumission papers, rendering the marriage illegal. The family is "remanded . . . to slavery" and "instead of heirs . . . are chattels" (*IL* 122). While Harry remains at school in Maine, Iola is kidnapped, separated from her mother, and sold into slavery in North Carolina. After being rescued by the Union army, Iola works as a field nurse and is reunited with Harry when he is wounded fighting in a Black regiment.

After the war, Harry and Iola dedicate themselves to reuniting with their mother. Throughout the novel, which associates family reunification with the act of "lasting service for the race" (*IL* 262), they each reject the opportunity to pass. Returning to North Carolina to find her mother, Iola teaches in a settlement project before moving North with her mother and brother, where she is barred from respectable employment by the color line and joins a "conversazione" of socially engaged Black professionals (243). There she meets the reformer Dr. Latimer, who encourages her to write a book about her experience. After refusing the proposal of the white abolitionist Dr. Gresham, she marries Latimer and returns to North Carolina, where she, he, and Harry run a school, Sunday school, and medical practice to teach the "sentiments of good citizenship" to freed people living in "lowly homes and windowless cabins" (279).

Harper makes her own sentimental literary strategies, and the racial discoveries that propel her plot, contingent on a political moment that she treats only allusively. On receiving news of "the terrible misfortune which had suddenly overshadowed his life," Harry falls into a "swoon," rendering him catatonic for several months (*IL* 123, 120). His catatonia results from an act of sentimental reading; generated by Iola's letter, "all tear-blotted and written with a trembling hand" (122), it demonstrates the power of sentiment as, in

Karen Sanchez-Eppler's words, "a bodily act" capable of uprooting prejudice.[22] Previously unsympathetic to abolition as an abstract political question, Harry suffers an emotional shock that changes everything. On returning to consciousness, he realizes "there is a difference between looking on a man as an object of pity and protecting him as such, and being identified with him and forced to share his lot" (126). Swayed into a new understanding of kinship, he joins the army, "not so much for the sake of fighting for the Government, as with the hope of finding my mother and sister" (125). Rather than casting the racist sympathies of white bourgeois readers for the "Tragic Mulatta" into a universal moral standard, Harper repurposes sentimental tropes for a Black audience. The novel suggests that sentimental writing can generate a Black political public: specifically, as critics have argued, it makes testimony to slavery's ongoing racial and sexual violence central to the formation of a new Black women's movement in the 1890s.[23]

However, Harry's sentimental political awakening literally puts him to sleep, dating the action according to an absent history. Roused from catatonia, Harry asks the doctor: "was it a dream or was it a reality? It could not have been a dream, for when I fell asleep the grass was green and the birds were singing, but now the winds are howling and the frost is on the ground . . . How long have I been here?" (*IL* 123). The doctor informs him, "you have been sick for several months, and much has taken place of which you were unaware" (125). Harry's decision to join a Black regiment fighting in Grant's Mississippi campaign indicates that he awakens in the winter of 1863, having slept, Rip Van Winkle like, through the Emancipation Proclamation. Until this point, the novel's action proceeds against the background of a war whose progress is curiously undifferentiated. Harry's discovery is recounted secondhand in a flashback that departs from the novel's focus on Iola's rescue from slavery and service in an army hospital. The flashback retroactively dates "the harrowing scenes through which they were constantly passing," explicitly placing those scenes on the front line of a conflict that, in 1863, had become a war for emancipation (59). Harper is able to make the act of following the condition of your mother into the novel's political imperative because Harry's and Iola's avowal of their racial identity, and literal pursuit of their mother across the South, is given transformative political power by an absent moment.[24] Becoming Black at the moment of emancipation, their racial identity is attached to a broader political purpose and constituency, rendering it inseparable from the political imperative to fight for freedom.

Harper employs the same technique when Iola, Harry, and their mother are reunited and tell each other their stories. Harry remarks on how much Iola has changed from the girl he "recognized as sister a half dozen years ago"; this rare temporal marker situates the family's reunion, like most of Chesnutt's novel, in 1868, that key year of Radical Reconstruction (195).

The novel's ability to connect the sentimental, the racial, and the political relies on both the specificity of the historical moment it depicts and on a general foreshortening of time that for the most part elides historical specificity. The sensational reunions and personal flashbacks through which the characters realize their shared kinship and experience emotional transformation bring into view personal histories shaped by slavery that perforate an otherwise flat present tense. Harry's conversion into a sentimental reader occurs in a long flashback of several inset chapters that takes the reader back to slavery (largely without dates). Similarly, when, in a flashback preceding Harry's, Iola reports the secret history that bursts into her life and converts her to a racial loyalty that means she will never pass, she explains that racial kinship feels like lost time, "feels as if years had been compressed into a few short months" (*IL* 114). The sense of immediacy that makes sentimental (and racial) subjects in the novel—the sudden incursion of slavery's legacies into the present—requires the elision of the specific political moment that shapes that present and gives newfound racial kinship meaning: the years of Reconstruction. In this way, Harper presents sentimental narrative as a contradictory form of timekeeping.

Chesnutt's and Harper's scenes of somnolent reading imagine Reconstruction as it becomes historical background. In the process, both authors comment on the form of reading engendered by their passing novels. They suggest that to read for Reconstruction is to read anachronistically because it means to read in tension with the more evident political aim of critiquing segregation. At the center of this dichotomy is a question about how to narrate a historical moment in which the abolition of slavery as a system of property fundamentally transforms the material constitution of race, at the same time as protesting the contemporary violent enforcement of the color line. This representational problem confronted writers of racial fiction at the turn of the twentieth century, when the social and political practices of segregation, racial violence, and disfranchisement transformed the color line into a totalizing social logic (one that colonized the ability to think about the past as much as the present).

In Howells's and Tourgée's novels, the tension disappears from view in the creation of a fictional present defined by the race problem. Harper and Chesnutt offer counternarratives to Tourgée's and Howells's treatment of the Tragic Mulatta figure by creating heroines for whom living as Black is a concrete experience rather than an abstract emotional quandary.[25] But they also do something more; they use the emergent discourse of the color line to formalize questions that I have been arguing are fundamental to the historical novel of Reconstruction: how can one read a revolution in the past that seems to leave unfinished the political work of Reconstruction? How does narrating Reconstruction's revolutionary dynamics problematize the political frameworks through which change and stasis came to be understood after emancipation? In relation to this second question, their treatment of the allusive tropes of passing as an elusive poetics of historical time helps us to rethink how the legacies of the 1890s made invisible the cultural afterlives of revolution, even as those legacies shaped what we have come to understand as the afterlife of slavery.

Race and/as Anachronism

The House behind the Cedars and *Iola Leroy* have not generally been treated as historical novels (or novels about Reconstruction). This tendency indicates more about the literary and historical narratives made available by the period marker "post-Reconstruction" than any interpretive error. Both novels have been important to the formation of a canon representing the rise of the African American novel; as such, they have been treated as being about the period that witnessed this emergence. As documents of a burgeoning imaginative and political response to the nadir of American race relations, their sense of history has been conveyed in terms of a problem more familiar to twentieth-century Black writing: that of "reclaiming" the history of slavery as a workable cultural resource.

Iola Leroy has been a key novel through which feminist critics have reconstructed the conditions and concerns of the early Black women's movement ever since Hazel Carby used it to frame the cultural resources that a new Black intellectual leadership forged in the 1890s to respond to Black women's violent exclusion from the public sphere.[26] The novel has, therefore, interested scholars because it "reclaims antebellum, Civil War, and Reconstruction history from a Black point of view"; this recovery describes a usable past or tradition significant because it countered (rather than expressed) a historical

rupture.[27] Carla L. Peterson argues that the historical sense of the "New Negro Novel of the Nadir" (in which category she includes *Iola Leroy* and *The
House behind the Cedars*) recovers usable "group traditions" from slavery to
"establish continuity with a ruptured past" under "'the pressure of the present' of Post-Reconstruction policies."[28] In these terms, *Iola Leroy*'s historical
recovery of Black women's experience is defined by a post-Reconstruction
memorial turn to slavery.[29]

This slippage was also central to Chesnutt's canonization as representative of the limits that the literary marketplace imposed on Black writers
seeking to make art from slavery. Richard Broadhead's and Eric Sundquist's
influential readings of his career argue convincingly that the nostalgic and
racist limitations imposed by the commercial demand for dialect writing
led Chesnutt to turn, in protest, toward a starker (and less commercially
lucrative) political representation of racial violence in the present.[30] These
readings frame Chesnutt's account of the underrepresented social lives and
culture of mixed-race southerners, in *The House behind the Cedars* and *The
Wife of His Youth* (1898), as a way-station between his early conjure stories
about slavery's legacies and his mature contemporary novel, *The Marrow of
Tradition* (1901). If Chesnutt is "the historian of an unrecorded phase of Black
experience," then the experience in question is the formulation of the color
line, not Reconstruction.[31] In another vein, critics of law and literature have
read *The House behind the Cedars* as an imaginative response to the legal
culture of segregation. Stacey Margolis, Brook Thomas, Gregg D. Crane, and
William E. Moddelmog all acknowledge the novel's Reconstruction setting
but only insofar as it enables a critique of the legal ideology underpinning
"the decimation of civil rights *after* Reconstruction and [at] the beginning
of the Jim Crow South."[32]

I am not suggesting that critics have misrepresented *The House behind the
Cedars* and *Iola Leroy* by arguing they rewrite the history of slavery for the
era of Jim Crow. That critical slippage is symptomatic of an idea of history
employed in the texts themselves; it is one side of the dialectic that structures
the simultaneously diachronic and synchronic representative mode of the
historical novel of Reconstruction (both a political and historical genre).
The incorporation of Harper's and Chesnutt's novels into a novelistic tradition that stresses the synchronic pole of this dialectic makes sense from the
horizon of the world Jim Crow made. Their treatment of Reconstruction's
vanishing revolutionary horizon interests me here precisely because it reads

this disappearance through an emergent segregationist language of racial custom that came to define not only literary-historical narratives but also what it was possible to think about Reconstruction when conceived through the prism of the color line.

This problem also faced C. Vann Woodward when, from the opposite end of legal segregation's historical life span, he presented Reconstruction as a moment that had become unthinkable to a segregated present. Woodward's landmark book *The Strange Career of Jim Crow* (1955) was perhaps the most influential historical work of the segregationist era to challenge what he called the system's "illusion of permanency."[33] In opposition to the reactionary common sense of a historical profession that still routinely saw Reconstruction as a period of revolutionary disaster, Woodward generally stressed its politically moderate character. Nonetheless, his book represents an early and important twentieth-century attempt to use Reconstruction's epochal character as evidence for the historical contingency of segregation. Its idiosyncrasies, therefore, help us to track the difficulties of giving narrative form to Reconstruction's social upheavals through the category of race.

The Strange Career of Jim Crow was as much about its present as the past. Woodward originally published his book the year after *Brown v. Board*'s challenge to a key pillar of segregation's legal edifice and updated it in 1966, in the wake of the civil rights movement, to include an increased focus on Reconstruction. In the original, Woodward argued that the emergence of legally codified and institutionally rigid segregation was a political and cultural construction of the last ten years of the nineteenth century. More than this, he detailed how the creation of de jure segregation normalized a cultural and political discourse that framed an emergent practice as the transhistorical essence of southern life, making it difficult for subsequent generations to see the past in any other terms.[34] With increased force in the 1966 edition, he contrasted this period with a Reconstruction moment shaped by the collapse of slavery as the social institution regulating interracial contact. He stressed that in the vacuum created by this institutional fracture, the color line was unevenly drawn across different areas of the South. Local struggles over resources and political power conditioned landscapes in which contingent forms of racial separation existed alongside new arenas of public contact. "There were," he contested, "too many cross currents and contradictions, revolutionary innovations and violent reactions," for segregation to emerge in what he insisted was its defining—and by 1966, when he added these words, tottering—image, as an all-encompassing and state-enforced social logic that made racial oppression coterminous with ostracism.[35]

Woodward's narrative demonstrates how Reconstruction troubles the models segregation handed down for understanding the relationship between race and social crisis because, in using Reconstruction to dispute the anachronistic idea of segregation's permanence, he struggles with his own anachronism. Woodward attempted to describe the social world instigated by slavery's collapse without making segregation into history's telos. Yet employing race relations as his interpretive lens, he ultimately restricted the conceptual means for understanding what changed during Reconstruction to a binary opposition between integration and segregation. Reconstruction appears anachronistically as a record of "forgotten alternatives" and experiments for an interracial society conceived specifically in the mold of Woodward's liberal hopes for a later era.[36] Even as he disrupted the historical ubiquity of the color line, it remained his conceptual frame of reference.

As a result, identifying patterns of racial separation before the Civil War and during Reconstruction became something of a cottage industry for American historians challenging Woodward's suggestion that Reconstruction was a forgotten moment of integrationist possibility. But importantly, where "the Woodward thesis" became untenable was not in its assertion of a significant difference between Reconstruction and a codified system of legal segregation and racial distinction from the 1890s.[37] Rather, as Michael O'Brien argues, Woodward's difficulty lay in trying to account for this difference as a precursor to specifically *liberal* political and civil relations. The issue was his (strained) faith that the civil rights movement's "second Reconstruction" could find a usable past and political base in an indigenous, embattled (and too often troublingly illiberal) tradition of white southern liberalism.[38] To view the South historically, Woodward contended, required that one understand race as a measure of social relations changed irrevocably by the abolition of slavery. Nevertheless, in reading backward to Reconstruction from the pressing political need to find a usable past for white southerners, facing what he predicted would be "the end of an era of Southern history," he implied that race relations were a continuous field that structured events across time.[39]

Woodward retreats from one anachronism to another as he attempts narrate the color line both historically and politically. Though his anachronisms are shaped by twentieth-century imperatives, they are instructive regarding the attempt to periodize revolution through the idea of race that I am tracking in Harper's and Chesnutt's novels. These are opposite ends of segregation's historical arc: at two comparable moments—when segregation is emergent but not yet dominant and when that dominance shows the first signs of collapse—Reconstruction's revolutionary social crisis makes itself felt as a crisis in what race represents, a crisis in which race comes to be perceived as a kind of necessary anachronism.

Chesnutt models this perspective in the opening scene of *The House behind the Cedars,* when, on returning to Patesville, John remembers the shooting of "a manacled free negro" awaiting "examination under a criminal charge" and the subsequent pardon of the murderer in the town in his childhood. Looking forward from 1868 to Chesnutt's contemporary moment, the narrator adds that "as Warwick was neither the prophet nor the son of a prophet, he could not foresee that, thirty years later, even this would seem an excessive punishment for so slight a misdemeanor" (*HBC* 5). Chesnutt recalls Twain's (anti-)prophetic authorial intervention at the end of *Pudd'nhead Wilson,* when the narrator avoids describing the "curious fate" that befalls the wrongfully enslaved Tom Driscoll after his manumission (and, by implication, befell emancipated slaves after the antebellum moment Twain's novel narrates) because it would be "a long story."[40] Twain's performative blindness to Reconstruction as the future of his plot foregrounds the continuity between the enslaved past and the segregated present that his analogical parody of segregation requires. Chesnutt invokes something of the same tragedy, but by comparison, John's prophetic vision is clouded by the very moment Twain disavows. Speaking through this moment—and using John's backward look in 1868 to write forward to the present—Chesnutt aligns his anachronistic historical dilemma with John's speculative one: he draws attention to the problem of imagining Reconstruction through the color line and imagining the color line through Reconstruction.

As I argue in the following sections, Harper's and Chesnutt's elliptical treatments of Reconstruction allow us to read this tension—between narrating race historically and using the color line as a political analogy—as their moment's period discourse. The sense of this tension as a period one is raised obliquely by Du Bois's famous turn-of-the-century contention that "the problem of the twentieth century is the problem of the color line." Du Bois's simultaneously signal and doubly problematized phrasing raises a question about using race as a periodizing medium, a question that belies the prophetic rhetorical force that has made his statement into scholarly shorthand. In his 1940 autobiography, *Dusk of Dawn,* he elaborates on this question from the horizon of an era in which segregation was more entrenched. Subtitling the book "The Autobiography of a Race Concept," Du Bois uses his own life as a "a digressive illustration and exemplification of what race has meant in the world in the nineteenth and twentieth centuries."[41] The method is "digressive" because he uses autobiography as a way to chart the *changing* meaning of the "race concept" over time while also treating the color line as a unifying experience that makes his life politically representative.

Race is a category Du Bois can "feel better than [he] can explain." For him, the tension between narrating it historically and making its phenomenology into a political tool is the problem of the Black political intellectual. He imagines himself "crucified on the vast wheel of time," flying "round and round with the Zeitgeist, waving my pen and lifting faint voices to explain, expound and exhort; to see, foresee and prophesy."[42] To be both a historian of race's mutability and a race leader is to live anachronistically, as a symptom of the age one wants to supplant. This dilemma is familiar to twentieth-century Black intellectual history; but what interests me here is the way that Du Bois uses the particular span of his own life to root the anachronism in the problem of understanding the nineteenth century's relationship to the twentieth through race.[43] Du Bois is able to make his autobiography into a record of a mutable but increasingly naturalized concept because he treats "the problem of the color line" as the problem of tracking race's changing meaning between specific moments: his birth in 1868—that key year of Radical Reconstruction again—and the height of segregation in 1940.

More than a model of the problems that race's ideological ambivalences posed to Black intellectuals, Du Bois's self-conscious symptomizing is enabled by his attempt to plot an epoch defined by the relationship between Reconstruction and segregation. Harper and Chesnutt open up a similarly fragile distance on the symptomatic deployment of the color line as a political metaphor. The rest of this chapter explores how they use the changing significance of sentimental literary tropes—tropes that tie racial embodiment to chattel slavery's embodied system of economic value—as a conduit for this anachronism. In different ways, the racial strategies of abolitionist sentimental fiction, dependent on the emotional and political critique of the abjection involved in making a person into property, enable Harper and Chesnutt to reflect on sentiment's strained capacity to make race mean, in the context of slavery's destruction as a system of property.

Chesnutt's Debts

Chesnutt's novel presents slavery's legacy as a matter of racial custom. The liberal-minded white lawyer Judge Straight speaks in something like an authorial voice when he advises John not to divulge his racial identity on returning from South Carolina because, despite emancipation, "custom is stronger than law—in these matters custom *is* law" (*HBC* 26). Mirroring the language of the *Plessy* case, the judge's warning renders racial division a facet of everyday life that resists the legal changes brought by emancipation. In a flashback, readers are told that Straight convinced John to move to South Carolina before the war to take advantage of the state's more liberally drawn designation of whiteness, according to which he might "assume the place and exercise the privileges of a white man" by virtue of "reputation" and "reception into society": those forms of reputational property *Plessy* had recently denied were constitutionally protected (116–17).[44] The obvious irony is that both before and after the war, John's "reception into society" relies on the law's authority only hypothetically. By passing, he "sink[s] . . . [his] past into oblivion," which he "might, of course do . . . anywhere, as long as no one knew . . . [his] origin" (118). Chesnutt suggests that custom supplants slave law as a means of enforcing racial dominance. "We make our customs lightly," Straight elaborates, but "once made they grip us in bands of steel; we become the creatures of our creations" (26). As the image of being chained to history implies, Chesnutt relates the privations of the color line to chattel slavery, in particular its commodification of people.

The concept of custom does a lot of work in the book. Borrowing tropes from sentimental fiction, Chesnutt uses conventional abolitionist-tinged language to tie together three different meanings of custom: racial tradition, economic exchange, and literary convention. He repeatedly describes Rena's passing, her marriage, and her eventual decision not to pass in language reminiscent of the slave trade. The novel begins with John returning as a rich plantation owner to violate his "mother's claim upon her child," taking Rena "down the river" to live on his plantation (*HBC* 19, 27). Similarly, Tryon proposes marriage with the hope of transporting Rena to his plantation to gain "the certainty of possession" (52). By treating Rena as a chattel slave, possessed both as an article of property and a sexual object, Chesnutt draws on abolitionist sensation fiction by depicting (metaphorical) chattel slavery as a system of legalized concubinage that debases familial and domestic relationships. In this imaginary, chattel bondage's corruption of moral and sentimental ties is a perversion analogous to incest.[45] John's objectification of Rena is implicitly incestuous, a "feeling for her [that] was something more than brotherly love" (46). It prefigures Tryon and Jeff Wain's ultimately deadly sexual desire to possess Rena absolutely.[46]

These parallels between passing and slave sale are so ubiquitous that Chesnutt even renders Rena's decision *not* to pass in such terms. After committing to a career teaching freed people, Rena moves away with Wain, who seeks to make her "a lady of proputty" (*HBC* 197). Her final, fatal escape into the swamp, as she flees Wain and Tryon, recalls the sensationalized flights from captivity in *Uncle Tom's Cabin* and *Clotel* (1853). Each of Rena's moves through the marriage economy and across the color line constitutes an act of sale or failed escape from a pernicious logic of commodification. That these transitions are metaphorical and allusive is precisely the point. Cast in the familiar language of abolitionist sentimental fiction and structured by conventional allusions to Blackness as an abjection conditioned by ownership, the novel's poetics do not need to name race as the force that returns to haunt Rena. Chesnutt encourages readers to understand racial segregation as the fabric of a social life that connects past and present by analogizing the continuities of racial custom with the familiarity of literary convention.

And yet, when John convinces his mother to give up her "claim" on her daughter, conventionality signifies differently. John reminds Molly that "the war has wrought great changes, has put the bottom rail on top, and all that— but it hasn't wiped *that* out" (*HBC* 19). The italicized shift of the pronoun's allusive meaning aligns the unspoken pervasiveness of racial discrimination ("*that*") with an upturning of property relations and a euphemism for revolution ("that") so fundamental as to also escape naming. Similarly, Judge Straight's formulation "custom is law" contains a double meaning that disrupts the sense of continuity it invokes. As Thomas and Margolis argue, it references the *Plessy* Court's instrumentalization of the "usages, customs, and traditions of the people," which made the apparent imperviousness of custom to legal intervention into a paradoxical justification for state-mandated segregation.[47] As a civil rights activist, lawyer, and correspondent of Tourgée, Chesnutt was familiar with the intricacies of the case. He treats this notion of custom anachronistically, reading it backward so as to invoke the social life of a period in which custom *was not,* in the same ubiquitous way at least, law: specifically, the moment of the ratification of the Fourteenth Amendment (1868), which the *Plessy* decision subsequently undermined.

This anachronism impinges directly on the legibility of the novel's self-consciously sentimental deployment of language relating race to human commodification. The date of the novel's setting is doubly significant because in addition to securing the constitutionality of equal rights before the law, the Fourteenth Amendment also nullified the Confederate debt and made it unconstitutional to "claim for the loss or emancipation of any slave."[48] It institutionalized an uncompensated emancipation that crippled the plantation economy's credit system, a system based on the ability of planters to leverage the perennial debts required for ever-expanded cotton production on the potential liquidity represented in the commodity value of their chattel slaves.[49] Chesnutt's allusions to slave property are set against a fundamental transformation in the relationship between race and property, a fact that he nods to with his other most prevalent metaphor for Rena's passing: the circulation of defaulted debt and devalued currency.

Chesnutt's accumulation of debt images has a plot function. Michael Germana argues that "each turn of the plot . . . is precipitated by circulating inflated paper money."[50] Tryon discovers Rena's identity during an attempt to collect on "one of old Duncan McSwayne's notes" (*HBC* 76). Chesnutt reinforces the connection between debt and slave sale by recycling the debtor's name from his dialect story "Marse Jeems' Nightmare," in which McSwayne features as an indebted slave owner who twice tries to sell a slave "fer to pay a bet."[51] Judge Straight also discovers Rena's secret when he finds a letter she has written to Tryon among papers concerning Tryon's claim on McSwayne's estate. Straight's intervention is foiled when his "note" (a debt pun that Chesnutt employs liberally) warning Rena's mother of Tryon's presence in Patesville is delivered too late. Straight pays a young boy to deliver the message using a devalued greenback, a "soiled paper by which the United States government acknowledged its indebtedness to the bearer in the sum of ten cents" (84). The boy delays his task by spending his "unearned increment" on sweets (85).

Germana reads the link between racial identity and money analogously, arguing that Chesnutt (and other passing novels of the era) draw together racial and currency debates at the turn of the century, as twin conflicts between essentialist and constructivist understandings of value; like paper money, passing here is a matter "not of being other than one seems, but of circulating nonetheless." He argues that Chesnutt "critique[s] essentialist social practice" by aligning Tryon's attempt to realize on his debts (to fix monetary value) with his discovery of Rena's heritage, which leads him to root her racial identity in her body (just as hard money advocates rooted economic value in specie).[52] For Germana, the tragedy of the passing plot reveals racism and the gold standard to be shared essentialisms.[53]

This thought-provoking reading doesn't account for the problem of Chesnutt's disappearing historical setting or his related refusal to emplot his debt imagery allegorically. Like his incorporation of Reconstruction's social upheaval into the discursive fabric of his free indirect style, Chesnutt's debts serve a mimetic as much as a plot function. Debts hang persistently at the descriptive margins of the novel, constituting Chesnutt's most prevalent period markers for Radical Reconstruction. They frame a historical moment defined less by circulation (and the monetary questions that characterized the 1890s) than by circulation's arrest in the wake of emancipation. In Chesnutt's historical landscape, liquidity has been sucked out of a slave economy; his period scene is characterized by a collapsed credit system and a crisis of southern value production.

A narrative aside during a conversation between Tryon and his cousin Dr. Green constructs this milieu. Awaiting Straight's verdict on Tryon's claim, they discuss "family connections and their varying fortunes in the late War," turning specifically to those who have been "financially ruined by their faith in the 'lost cause,' having invested their all in the securities of the Confederate Government." The narrator elaborates that "few had anything left but land, and land without slaves to work it is a drug in the market." Green identifies uncompensated emancipation as the source of the indebtedness that accompanies the novel's action. He tells Tryon that "they have taken our negroes and our liberties. It may be better for our grandchildren that the negroes are free, but it's confoundedly hard on us to take them without paying for them" (*HBC* 94–95). Abolition underpins a broken logic of exchange that characterizes both Reconstruction's social crisis and the failed correspondences of the novel's plot. This breakdown of exchange comes to the fore when Tryon discovers Rena's identity in the process of attempting to "realize on some of ... [his] securities" (70). Like the market, whose credit mechanism has been eradicated by emancipation, he ends the affair in a drugged stupor, sedated by Dr. Green and forgetting the matter of the note (which he never recovers).

As implied acts of sale, Rena's racial transformations take place against the background of a credit and labor crisis that ruptures the continuity between antebellum property relations and postbellum race relations, the continuous field of allusion created by Chesnutt's abolitionist tropes. As images of failed exchange and possession, Chesnutt's signs of slavery's collapsed value function almost like Roland Barthes's "reality effect," thickening the novel's historical sense without "participating at first glance in the order of the notable."[54] In a parallel to the decorative features Barthes records in Gustave Flaubert's domestic scenery, Chesnutt develops his opening account of "the air of Patesville" by describing Molly Walden's parlor, a room dominated by a "screen standing before the fireplace . . . covered with Confederate bank-notes of various denominations and designs, in which the heads of Jefferson Davis and other Confederate leaders were conspicuous." Withdrawn from circulation, this currency—whose value was backed by confidence in a future state built on the legitimacy of the slave trade—figures as a degraded materiality. Seeing the notes, John quotes *Hamlet*, muttering, "Imperious Caesar, dead, and turned to clay, / Might stop a hole to keep the wind away" (*HBC* 14).[55]

In their repurposed function, however, the notes do have significance. They sit alongside other recycled objects that memorialize a past defined by slavery and sentimental culture, in the shape of "a steel engraving of Andrew Jackson at the battle of New Orleans" and "a framed fashion-plate from 'Godey's Lady's Book'" (*HBC* 13). As innocuous background to a domestic scene, the bills are the first indication of the pervasive impact of a collapsed value system. Against this backdrop, readers learn that during the war, John managed a plantation "in default of older and more experienced men" and, in its aftermath, married an orphan of a Confederate soldier, inheriting the estate, again "in default of a better man" (17). John personifies the collapsed economic system against which the drama unfolds. When he convinces Rena to pass, he does so as a defaulted widower and plantation owner, seeking to shore up a perilous domestic economy by possessing his sister as a substitute for a wife and slaves.

Replaying this pattern, Tryon discovers Rena's identity in a chapter called "The Bottom Falls Out." Even though his claim on McSwayne's note turns out to be recoverable, "the first effect of his discovery was, figuratively speaking, to knock the bottom out of things for him," robbing him of "the certainty of possession" offered by marriage to Rena and his capacity to reclaim value against an indebted plantation (*HBC* 99). Similarly, Wain's attempt to make Rena "a lady of proputty" turns out to be a failed design by the "nominal owner of a large plantation" whose "pretensions to wealth were a sham" and whose plantation "was worn out and mortgaged to the limit of its security value" (172). Wain's attempt to possess Rena is aligned with John's earlier incestuous designs; he seeks to make her a plantation mistress following the apparent death (but actual escape) of his abused wife. Like the defaulted John, having "passed into the town" as a rich man, Wain fails to substitute Rena's symbolic value for the exchange value (and liquidity) destroyed by uncompensated emancipation (198). What allows Wain to pass as a "nominal" plantation owner is the same destruction of slave property that makes Rena's passing ambivalent as a metaphor for racial value judgments.

Chesnutt constructs John's, Tryon's, and Wain's attempts to possess Rena (and affix her racial identity) as failed attempts by indebted plantation own-ers to possess a slave absent the conditions for possession. The sentimental poetics that structure the novel's racial narrative and its critique of the color line sit alongside—without fully mediating—this historical crisis. Chesnutt's debts are too significant to his plot to properly be called reality effects, but their liminality shares something with Barthes's account of realism's turn to detail. Barthes explains that this turn responded to a tension between historical "order[s] of the notable": caught between an eighteenth-century attachment to neoclassical aesthetic systems and the emergent "regnum of objective history," realism was the literary mode of an era that, lacking a distinct *aesthetic* language for reality, "must seek a new reason to describe."[56] Chesnutt's references to chattel bondage contain two similarly competing approaches to the representational and historical possibilities inherent in abolitionist sentiment. His overdetermined period markers disrupt the sense of historical continuity required to read his sentimental poetics as an allegory connecting slavery to segregation. By holding the two different temporalities together, he offers readers two alternative ways of reading his novel's historical scene. *The House behind the Cedars* is both a historical and a political novel, but in the way he combines these narrative planes, Chesnutt refuses to allow readers to pass over a problem that was symptomatic of the period: namely, the tendency to elide a fundamental transformation in the relationship be-tween racial embodiment and embodied value when narrating the color line.

Rena embodies sentiment's time sense. The narrator explains that "Rena's life since her great awakening had been that of the emotions, and her tem-perament made of it a continuous life. Her successive states of consciousness were not detachable, but united to form a single if not entirely harmonious whole. To her sensitive spirit to-day was born of yesterday, to-morrow would be but the offspring of to-day" (*HBC* 134). The time of sentiment (the temporality of the novel's political register) is continuous. This temporality stands in opposition to the one Chesnutt sets up in the historical reflections of the novel's opening. Unlike Rena, John is unable to see the future when he looks out from Radical Reconstruction. I have been less concerned with whether or not *The House behind the Cedars* constitutes sentimental fiction than with understanding the way it grapples with sentiment's anachronistic character.[57] Chesnutt's characters are driven by sentiment to pursue justice, but Chesnutt describes this impulse as anachronistic. In helping Rena, Judge Straight is driven by "sentimental weakness and . . . quixotic loyalty" to her father (83). Even the novel's moral voice, the poor, formerly enslaved dark-skinned cooper Frank Fowler, rescues Rena because of a quixotic sense of himself as her servant. "One of those rare souls that can give with small hope of receiving," Frank's chivalry aligns him with the affected feudalism Chesnutt satirizes in the novel's faux aristocrats. His love for Rena has "branded him her slave forever" (121). A loyal slave in the shadow of an abolished chattel relation, Frank embodies an untimely morality encapsulated by a broken logic of exchange. His attempt to intervene on Rena's behalf comes literally too late: she dies despite his efforts.

The point is not that Chesnutt satirizes sentiment. Unlike Howells or Twain, he refuses to do so. For Chesnutt, sentiment marks a necessary political imperative: a temporality that aligns the color line with slave property offers one way of reading the novel. But by situating his historical scene between temporal visions that he refuses to resolve, Chesnutt suggests that the revolutionary crisis of emancipation and the racial crisis of the 1890s form a "single if not entirely harmonious whole." His problem of the color line is that of accounting for race as an afterlife of slavery *without* eliding the revolutionary afterlife of Reconstruction.

Merely Circulating in *Iola Leroy*

Chesnutt's novel plots the strain a sentimental poetics that related racial embodiment and slave property came under in the 1890s. This strain was a condition of abolition's afterlives. Sanchez-Eppler argues that the struggle over voting rights for Black men and white women replaced sentimental culture's embodied political language with a disembodied conception of rights focused not on "corporeal oppression but . . . juridical exclusion."[58] Complicating this diachronic argument, Amy Dru Stanley demonstrates how, after emancipation, feminists and campaigners for Black rights turned the figure of the chattel slave into a flexible "icon of American culture," so as to metaphorize forms of corporeal dependency preserved by the apparently contractual world of marriage and the market.[59] Slavery's abstraction of people into property was always a legal-political metaphor, one that Tim Armstrong argues produced a "culture of slavery" explicitly concerned with the relationship between metaphor and materiality, a "tropology" that had "narrative consequences" beyond emancipation.[60] I am drawing attention to the specific historical implications of a moment when the terms of that cultural abstraction, and its consequences for understanding racial embodiment, became doubly and more ambivalently metaphorical.

Iola Leroy uses the belatedness of sentiment to explore how emancipation impacts the ability to embody politics. The book's sentimental impact is based on its narrative of familial separation and reunion, experiences that Harper uses to express a sense of political belonging. This narrative is structured by the repeated telling and retelling of Iola's experience of enslavement and emancipation, which foregrounds the sentimental impact of her story on other characters, and its ability to act as the substance of persuasive political writing. Toward the end of the book, Iola's soon-to-be-husband, Dr. Latimer, articulates Harper's aspirations for the political potential of sentimental narrative when he advises Iola to "write out of the fullness of your heart a book to inspire men and women with a deeper sense of justice and humanity" (*IL* 262). This imperative caps the treatment of Iola's life as the kind of political fiction whose "mission," as Harper puts it in a "note" at the end of the novel, is to "awaken in the hearts of our countrymen a stronger sense of justice and a more Christlike humanity in behalf of those whom the fortunes of war threw homeless, ignorant and poor on the threshold of a new era" (282). But these repeated retellings of Iola's experience also act as a form of disappearing testimony that complicates a direct translation between the historical experience of slavery and the conditions for political writing at "the threshold of a new era." As Harper (re)tells Iola's story, she opens up a gap between experience and its conversion into narrative form: Iola's experience comes to seem less material and more metaphorical. At the same time as she dematerializes Iola's experiences, Harper foregrounds the figural nature of Iola's body, questioning whether Iola can embody a political constituency in the changed social conditions of the 1890s.

As indicated earlier, one reason *Iola Leroy* has received so much literary-critical attention since the 1980s is that Harper places an embodied history of racial violence, familial separation, and sexual abuse at the center of her figuration of a Black female readership and political community. She turns illegitimacy and severed kinship—the "dynamics of naming and valuation," through which Spillers argues slavery's abjections of Black communal life were reproduced across time (and which Tourgée struggled with in his conception of Black citizenship)—from an abstract "symbolic order" into concrete experience.[61] Iola is a model of Black women's authorship because her racial allegiance is not an abstract question of justice: she has "bound her heart to the mast of duty" because duty is inseparable from her experience of bondage (*IL* 263). Unlike in Tourgée's and Howells's novels, Harper's heroine acknowledges her lineage because she experiences racial identification directly as enslavement, sexual violence, and separation from her mother.[62] Harper imagines that the book Iola would write (and the one she herself has written) will transform sympathies because it rearticulates racial embodiment as a shared experience of sexual precarity and family separation, as a basis for political community.[63]

However, the alignment between racial embodiment and political belonging is complicated by what Geoffrey Sanborn identifies as "the nearly total absence of the body" as a descriptive presence in *Iola Leroy*.[64] What is striking about Harper's representation of the body is not that she eschews it entirely. Her corporeal reticence and recourse to euphemism reflect what Darlene Clark Hine calls a "culture of dissemblance," through which Black women cultivated a "self-imposed invisibility" in a public sphere in which they continued to be treated as sexual objects.[65] But, euphemism aside, Harper *does* focus on Iola's body as an object of fascination and scrutiny, and she does so as part of a broader tendency to lodge sympathetic attachment in what she figures as Iola's strangeness. This strangeness emerges from Harper's treatment of Iola as simultaneously embodying a representative and an unrepresentative experience.[66] In Iola, embodiment and sympathetic attachment come apart. This is especially true of the way that Harper manipulates the conventions of the Tragic Mulatta plot, which relies on a character's whiteness to elicit sympathy. In Dr. Latimer's words, Iola is "not one who can't be white and won't be black" (*IL* 278); Harper creates a mixed-race protagonist whose appeal is not ultimately dependent on tragedy. Nonetheless, she uses the convention more broadly to depict the disbelief Iola elicits.

Tom Anderson, the fugitive slave who pleads for his battalion to free Iola, is attracted to her because she is "jis' ez white es anybody's in this place" (*IL* 38). Echoing Tom, the sympathetic physician Dr. Gresham and the Union general who take Iola into their camp exchange statements of disbelief: "A woman as white as she a slave?"; "Could it be possible that this young and beautiful girl had been a chattel?" (58, 39). Such expressions of disbelief or implausibility—originally but not exclusively located in Iola's whiteness—are the predominant feature of the sympathy she elicits. Iola's mother exclaims, "Can it be possible!" on being reunited with her (196). For Tom, Iola's implausibility is characterized not just by her color but by the fact that she is a slave who has not labored; he specifies that "her han's look ez ef she neber did a day's work in her life." Despite Harper euphemizing Iola's experience of sexual violence at the hand of her masters, Iola fascinates Tom because she has avoided the fate of the so-called fancy slave: "they say she war sole seben times in six weeks, 'cause she's so putty, but dat she war game to de las'" (42). Through such expressions, Harper critiques abolitionist fiction's often lurid fascination with "concubinage," but by emphasizing disbelief itself, she has her characters voice the conventional responses of abolitionist readers as expressions of sympathy for an impossible slave. Despite Iola not being a Tragic Mulatta, the pathos she embodies is still somehow that of a woman subject "to the fate of Tantalus . . . without his crimes" (118). Iola is overdetermined by a peculiar kind of pathos. Her nonrepresentative body is complemented by her voice, which is "strangely sympathetic as if some great sorrow had bound her heart in loving compassion to every sufferer who needed her gentle ministrations" (40). The sympathy she elicits is strange because it conveys a universality that fails to match the particular (and unlikely) "great sorrow" she experiences. "Strangely sympathetic" as well as "strangely beautiful," her affect is rooted in an experience that she doesn't embody (257).

Iola's strange capacities for embodiment dramatize a relationship between sentimental politics and history. An object of fascination and comment early in the novel, Iola's body vanishes from view to the same degree as the historical specificity of her experiences. As her story gets told and retold, those experiences disappear into the expressions of pathos and disbelief her story generates. In the penultimate chapter, Iola begins the last of many rehearsals of her "mournful past" by telling Dr. Latimer: "Oh, Doctor, you cannot conceive what it must have been to be hurled from a home of love and light into the dark abyss of slavery; to be compelled to take your place among a people you have learned to look upon as inferiors and social outcasts; to be in the power of men whose presence would fill you with horror and loathing and to know that there is no earthly power to protect you from the highest insults which brutal cowardice could shower upon you" (*IL* 273). Neatly and didactically, this passage reiterates Iola's capacity to transform public opinion by bearing witness to slavery's crimes. Except, she no longer seems able to testify to her own experiences. Iola's experience bleeds into a conditional expression; it is not that Latimer "cannot comprehend" her experience but that he "cannot comprehend what it *must have been*." Even in her own words, she is a conditional figure.

Harper conveys a sentimental appeal under strain. Iola's strange (dis)embodiment registers the difficulty of embodying political claims in the absence of the chattel relation that linked embodiment to politics in the abolitionist imagination. Her statement to Latimer is a trope of slave narrative; it expresses a sensation Harriet Jacobs memorably described as being "pained by the retrospect."[67] For Jacobs, the phrase connotes the combined political necessity and compulsion involved in making personal experiences of sexual abuse and exploitation part of a public abolitionist discourse. Amy Post's appendix to *Incidents in the Life of a Slave Girl* (1861) suggests that for Jacobs, "consent[ing] to the publication of her narrative" recalls her coerced "consent" to the sexual relationships of her enslavement. What makes Jacobs's public "retrospect" necessary is the continued alienation of enslaved people from their bodies, conditioned by the chattel relationship. Jacobs ends her narrative by declaring that despite being (reluctantly) purchased by her abolitionist comrades, her freedom is incomplete. As long as "a human being [can be] *sold* in the free city of New York," she feels impelled to put her experience, like her bill of sale, "on record" for "future generations . . . [to] learn from it."[68] The tension between personal trauma and political necessity can be overcome insofar as an abolitionist constituency is united by a shared understanding of where to locate slavery's evil: in the scandal of human property.

Harper borrows liberally from Jacobs's skillful manipulations of sentimental culture and, as her appendix attests, blurs the "threads of fact and fiction" (*IL* 282). But *Iola Leroy* remains a novel concerned with its own fictional processes. By representing historical experience as it becomes figural, Harper depicts an abolitionist sentiment of embodiment becoming uncoupled from its political-economic context. Her conversation with Latimer culminates a long process. The first of the novel's extended flashbacks (which itself narrates information readers are in part already aware of) begins a chain of retellings: the action of the plot is recounted a further seven times.[69] Repetition is a structural principle of nineteenth-century sentimental fiction, which Jane Tompkins argues privileges the unfolding of "paradigmatic situations" over individuality or novelty. What Tompkins calls "the importance of merely circulating" characterized sentimental fiction's attempt to square mimetic and didactic purposes by encouraging readers to see narrating the world morally as akin to changing it.[70] But Harper strains the paradigm (or the feasibility of the paradigmatic). By directly representing these retellings, she emphasizes their increasingly anachronistic textuality as the narrative progresses in time away from the moment of emancipation. The first flashback and its retelling are representative. Not only does Harper have Iola tell Gresham a story that both he and readers already know, but she also makes Iola's story into an abolitionist text. Gresham is the very image of an abolitionist reader: attracted to Iola by "the deep pathos of her story," he studies her "as if a whole volume were depicted on her countenance"; his pity turns to love at the thought of a slave "rescued by the strong arm of his government" (57, 58). Iola's first account of her life in her own words is framed through conventions an abolitionist reader would expect to consume. When she informs Gresham that "the intense horror and agony I felt when I was first told the story are over," she even suggests that the capacity of such a narrative to shock readers is on the wane (114).

Harper redeploys such sentimental conventions specifically for a Black readership. Having published regularly in the Black periodical press, she assumes her readers' concrete familiarity with the experiences she describes.[71] Yet she never allows readers to detach Iola's capacity to be representative from the sentimental reading Gresham embodies. It is Gresham, in this moment, who first suggests that Iola's life could be the stuff of successful political fiction. He preempts Latimer's and Iola's opinions at the end of the novel when, having read the pathos of her countenance, he tells her: "out of the race must come its own defenders. With them the pen must be mightier than the sword" (*IL* 115–16). By the time she becomes an archetype for politically efficacious narrative at the end of the novel, Iola is already an abolitionist text, told and retold in new circumstances. This narrative device captures something critics have tended to miss in *Iola Leroy*. In reading the novel as part of the cultural formation of a Black women's movement, to which it looks forward, critics sideline the specific tensions animating the novel's backward look.

The Black abolitionist William Still's introduction to the first edition captures something of the book's historical concern. He frames Harper's novel as a synthesis of an extensive activist career, "the crowning effort of [her] long and valuable services" (*IL* 3). Harper, having published political poetry, speeches, and magazine fiction, Still suggests, has lighted on the form that allows her to narrate her age historically. In many ways, Harper's novel is not so decisive a break with her work in other forms, through which she brought abolitionist strategies to bear on Reconstruction, the women's movement, and temperance reform. She lifted the plot largely from her earlier magazine novel, *Minnie's Sacrifice* (1869), which was published in installments in the African American periodical the *Christian Recorder* as Reconstruction unfolded. In *Minnie's Sacrifice,* Harper employs the plot of a mixed-race heroine rejecting her tragic fate and embracing her racial identity so as to encourage educated Black readers to join the Reconstruction effort. Carla L. Peterson argues that serial publication allowed Harper to deliver a didactic story simultaneously with the news from the Reconstruction South, thereby staging the work as a contemporaneous report on political events on the ground.[72] After moving to Louisiana to educate and organize formerly enslaved people, Minnie is murdered by the Klan and bestowed with "the fiery crown of martyrdom."[73] Harper ends by turning the narrative into an appeal for the *Recorder*'s middle-class readers to become educators in support of Reconstruction. She parallels "the generous loving diffusion" required to create "live men, and earnest, lovely women, whose lives shall represent not a 'stagnant mass, but a living force'" with the magazine's diffusion of print.[74]

Harper's literary-political intervention assumes an audience united by social and temporal closeness to slavery. The narrator tells how Minnie's formerly enslaved compatriots "were learning the power of combination, and having no political past they were radical by position."[75] What being "radical by position" meant was no longer so clear by 1892, and while *Iola Leroy* makes a similar appeal in conclusion, its political constituency is not self-evident. Rather than suggesting print culture's ability to generate a political community, Harper asks more synoptically for men and women of "good character" to turn the social experience of their race into print, asking for "some hand to bring into the literature of this country" the "mournful tragedies and mirth provoking comedies" represented in African American life and history (*IL*

282). The unity of political activism and historical fiction is not so clearly linked as during Reconstruction. *Iola Leroy* is still a political intervention, but by turning to historical fiction as her medium "at the threshold of a new era," Harper identifies an epochal shift. Figuring a renewed political movement against the emergent racial crisis of the 1890s, the novel tracks the uneasy passing of abolitionist sentiment from a political into a historical language. This uneven relationship between the mimetic and the didactic turns on Harper's elliptical treatment of Reconstruction. Iola's experiences become conditional and conventional as an accompaniment to the disappearance of Reconstruction from the text. The sentimental logic of the plot becomes conventional alongside the disappearance of the history that anchors Iola's and Harry's racial experience in a political community. The politics of Reconstruction are not absent in the novel, then; the story takes place in parallel to them. This structure gives Harper's sentimental poetics a doubled form: as a method of protesting the racial crisis of the 1890s, it uses anachronism to depict historical conditions of racial domination as they passed from chattel slavery into a "new era."

In a sense, Harper and Chesnutt treat sentiment similarly to the way that Tourgée treats appeals to the state. For Tourgée, in the immediate aftermath of Radical Reconstruction, the state was a problematic political form, and yet it was seemingly the only legitimate body of political appeal. For Harper and Chesnutt, sentiment is both a political methodology and an out-of-date language. With passing as a chronotope, both writers identify key symptoms of their historical moment—the color line's colonization of the historical imagination and the waning of sentimental politics' social grounding—and use them to pose questions about how to narrate Reconstruction's revolutionary event. In the next chapter, I address a related question: that of how (and whether) imagining such an event implies a coherent political subject. Where Harper and Chesnutt trace the seismic effects of the destruction of slave property elliptically, Du Bois turns to the novel form to imagine the subject at the center of Reconstruction's revolutionary moment directly. In doing so, he parses the problems of putting Reconstruction's revolutionary history into the active voice.[76]

4

W. E. B. Du Bois's Counterfactual Peasantry

In chapter 2, I suggested that Du Bois poses a thought experiment when, analyzing the revolutionary character of emancipation in *Black Reconstruction*, he asks, "Can we imagine this spectacular revolution?" I framed Du Bois's question as an attempt to articulate the character and contingency of a revolution from below that was imbricated in, and enabled by, a nonrevolutionary state power. In one sense, his is a question of agency and determination: to what extent does the balance of slave self-activity and top-down emancipation constitute a revolutionary moment?[1] But Du Bois's ambiguous tone, pitched between the rhetorical and the interrogatory, contains another kind of question about narrative perspective—more specifically, about how to imagine the subject whose perspective he seeks to adopt.

Black Reconstruction returns the emancipated slave to history as a revolutionary subject. Du Bois's pathbreaking account of emancipation as a "general strike" of the slaves and of "the black worker [as] the founding stone of a new economic system in the nineteenth century and for the modern world" institutes two major historical revisions.[2] He asks readers to reconsider the period simultaneously from the perspective of the grassroots action of the enslaved and from the horizon of the plantation's imbrication in the capitalist world-system. It is perhaps unsurprising that in so drastically upending established historical and political perceptions, Du Bois comes to a question about narrative perspective. Taken literally, the inquiry appears strange, given that over more than seven hundred pages, the book seems to answer emphatically in the affirmative. Moreover, the question follows Du Bois's account of the general strike, through which he makes the revolutionary agency of the enslaved conceivable for the American Left.[3] Nevertheless, I want to suggest that the question's ambiguously rhetorical tone frames *Black Reconstruction*'s genuine problematic. Questioning the utility of speculative thought in framing emancipated slaves as revolutionary subjects, Du Bois considers revolution in a plantation society a challenge to representation. Attending to this problematic, I will trace a neglected literary genealogy of Du Bois's speculative treatment of the plantation's revolutionary subject, stretching back to his first, and still unpublished, (historical) novel, *Scorn: A Romance* (1905).

The speculative, expressive, and, we might even say, literary character of Du Bois's recovery of the enslaved subject has been central to *Black Reconstruction*'s canonization as part of what Cedric Robinson calls "the Black radical tradition."[4] Nikhil Pal Singh, for example, argues that in imagining "the unprecedented situation of slave freedom," Du Bois faced the limits of a political language shaped by New Deal institutions based, even on the Left, on the exclusion of all but the most truncated forms of Black participation. Singh contends that to transcend this racialized empiricism, Du Bois employed a kind of writing more akin to literature than history in its capacity to "make the unthinkable thinkable."[5] Singh's argument recalls Robinson's account of a radical tradition that supplements materialist analysis with expressive cultural forms recovered from the Black past to shape "a historical antilogic to racism, slavery, and capitalism" that "preserve[s] the collective being, the ontological totality" of "a revolutionary consciousness that proceeded from the whole historical experience of Black people and not merely from the social formations of capitalist slavery or the relations of production of colonialism."[6] Reading *Black Reconstruction* alongside *Scorn*, a speculative history of emancipation and Reconstruction, reveals a speculative impulse that functions less triumphantly.

In *Black Reconstruction,* Du Bois adopts a peculiarly abortive but persistent form of counterfactual narrative he developed first in *Scorn* to narrate a social class whose historical trajectory and political legacy following emancipation he struggled to define, a precarious class that in the novel he names "a new world peasantry."[7] *Scorn* is an ambitious speculative historical novel that moves outward from the locality of the South Carolina Sea Islands to situate emancipation and Reconstruction as world historical dramas arising from a messianic conspiracy by southern slave owners to construct a slaveholding, white supremacist empire across the American continent, the Caribbean, and the South Pacific. The novel combines realistic sociological depictions of Black life and labor in the plantation South with the sensationalist conventions of the romance to advance a prophetic narrative about the emergence of a new Black political subject. By hinging his expansive, nonlinear history on the central event of Reconstruction, Du Bois built on his ethnographic studies of the Black Belt in *The Souls of Black Folk*, in which he depicted the formation of a class of peasant proprietors as Reconstruction's lost opportunity (and utopian legacy).

At the same time as he was writing *Scorn*—a section of whose plot turns on the foundation of a Black settlement community of sharecroppers—Du Bois was planning a historical and statistical study of Black life in Lowndes County, Alabama, for the U.S. Department of Labor, based on a similar project, the Calhoun School (which eventually became the basis for his first published novel, *The Quest of the Silver Fleece* [1911]).[8] Much to Du Bois's annoyance, political sensitivities led the Department of Labor not to publish the study, but Du Bois carried his interest into a 1907 Atlanta University report, *Economic Co-operation among Negro Americans*. There Du Bois argues that Black economic development is defined by a broadly cooperative approach to "earning a living" (a phrase intended to signify something broader than mere economic accumulation) conditioned by the experiences of slavery and emancipation.[9] While the study is generally progressivist in its treatment of "co-operation in capital and labor" as a response to social ills, it complicates Du Bois's commitment to a simple Talented Tenth conception of Black politics by placing the cooperative impulse in a genealogy of Black insurrection rather than uplift: cooperation, he argues, is rooted in a "spirit of revolt which tried to co-operate by means of insurrection," a spirit that takes in slave rebellions, Black abolitionist organizing in the Underground Railroad and John Brown's raid, the waves of fugitivity during the Civil War that forced emancipation, and Black demands for land that conditioned experiments with free labor in the early years of Reconstruction.[10] His account of Black economic development in the early twentieth century is determined by the foreclosed promise of the Black peasantry.

While I draw lines forward from *Scorn* to Du Bois's Marxist history, I am not focused on the biographical question of when he became a socialist.[11] Rather, I am interested in how his treatment of the Black peasantry as Reconstruction's political subject influenced his development of a method of historical analysis that produced a broadly materialist account of Reconstruction as a revolutionary moment. As in previous chapters, I see the historical novel of Reconstruction as a form through which Du Bois placed his political hopes in productive tension with the historical changes wrought by emancipation. Rather than adopting "a positivist construct of the subject of insurgency," an abstraction Brent Hayes Edwards argues some proponents of Black radicalism (including, on occasion, Robinson) retain from developmentalist formulations of the universal progression of the working class, Du Bois's speculations are productively and necessarily uneven.[12] He imagines the creation of the new world peasantry as Reconstruction's fragile what-if moment, a counterfactual hinge for his conception of the plantation's revolutionary subject. This emergence acts as a frustrated horizon, or limit point, to which he returns reflexively (both within and across these texts). The precarity at the center of Du Bois's account of Reconstruction indicates an ongoing attempt to theorize the changing relationship between the plantation and global capitalism.

For Du Bois, the transition between imagining a new world peasantry as a historical class and celebrating it as a political subject—whether in a Marxist sense or as a vanguard of Black uplift—is a "horizon [that] remains a horizon."[13] This political-historical tension defines Du Bois's version of the Reconstruction historical novel. His speculations generate a narrative form that shares much with the literary approach to revolution identified in previous chapters, even as Du Bois's more explicit dedication to theorizing the plantation as the site of revolutionary class struggle preempts aspects of his revision of historical materialism.

The idiosyncrasies of the narrative Du Bois created led his publisher, A. C. McClurg, to reject *Scorn*. McClurg claimed Du Bois sullied a potentially "notable contribution to the great race problem in America" with a narrative whose anachronistic temporality and instabilities of perspective meant readers could not fathom "the central thought of the story."[14] In my reading of Du Bois's process of experimentation and revision, the way that he complicates the "central thought," or subject perspective, of his story constitutes his primary artistic and intellectual achievement. His anachronistic treatment of this subject frames the epistemic, political, and representational contradictions he faced in rearticulating the history of capital and revolution from the perspective of the emancipated slave. By returning to this narrative form in *Black Reconstruction,* Du Bois complicates a recuperative aspiration that often attracts modern readers to that book: namely, his attempt to re-narrate the development of capitalist modernity from the perspective of "the philosophy of life and action which slavery bred in the souls of black folk" (14). Nevertheless, the aporia at the heart of Du Bois's narrative of Reconstruction was both politically and artistically generative.

If Du Bois treated Reconstruction historically as revolution, his political statements on revolution more generally are notoriously ambivalent.[15] After completing *Scorn,* he began work on a biography of John Brown, published in 1909. Assessing Brown's legacy, he wrote, "revolution is not a test of capacity; it is always a loss and a lowering of ideals."[16] However, this aphorism culminates a book that treats revolution as historical necessity. For Du Bois, Brown confronted the "present temporizing" of moderates—a phrase clearly meant to parallel contemporary responses to the race question—and proved slavery "had to die by revolution, not by milder means."[17] This contradiction between revolution as a vital historical crisis generated by slavery (a crisis with unresolved permutations) and as a question of political strategy underpinned Du Bois's thought on the subject. These tensions also characterize his engagement with Marxism. Attacking what he judged to be the Communist Party USA's naïveté about the white supremacist violence that divided the American proletariat, Du Bois affirmed in 1931 that "American negroes do not propose to be the shock troops of the communist revolution."[18] Yet only two years later, reflecting on the centrality of Marx's thought to any analysis of "the Negro problem," he optimistically predicted that "whether it be violent, as in France or Russia, or peaceful, as seems just as possible . . . Revolution seems bound to come."[19]

Even this brief selection indicates that Du Bois understood revolution as the decisive historical fact that inaugurated a post-slavery world whose conditions (and contradictions) were still in formation. I follow Du Bois's lead here. Treating revolution as his central historical topic, I trace the hesitations and revisions that constitute his counterfactual narrative mode to argue that his historical analysis of the plantation economy forced him to reimagine the revolutionary subject as a materialist problematic, rather than a definitive class or racial identity. Addressing Du Bois's revolutionary thought, Bill Mullen argues that in response to the Russian Revolution, Du Bois reread American history (in particular Reconstruction) retroactively, through the lens of the Third International's hopes for a global revolutionary subject. This "revolutionary typology" (which Mullen traces back to Du Bois's 1928 "Comintern novel," *Dark Princess*) enabled Du Bois to develop an anachronistic historical materialist method, through which he "discovered in *Black Reconstruction* the historical subject—or historiographical method—of world revolution."[20] While he usefully highlights the pairing of anachronism and revolution central to Du Bois's counterfactual impulse (and to the historical novel of Reconstruction), Mullen's Benjaminian account of Du Bois's speculative presentism frames revolution (and its subject) as a latent theme always awaiting discovery in history and reactivation in the present.

My approach to the relationship between Du Bois's fictional and historical writing pays attention to the strains in his revolutionary narrative, strains that center on how to narrate Reconstruction as a revolutionary moment. To borrow Paul Ricoeur's account of the elliptical relationship between literary form and historical emplotment, the aporia in Du Bois's speculative approach to the new world peasantry is "a gap that is historical enquiry as such."[21] His refusal to separate a structural account of the contradictions of the plantation's changing relationship to capitalism from the human struggles and aspirations of the formerly enslaved led him to pursue a narrative form whose imaginative idiosyncrasies, as much as its ingenuities, shape his materialist analysis of Reconstruction.

Scorn: An Overview

Since *Scorn* remains unpublished, I will describe its plot, form, and history to clarify my claims. Set on the cotton plantations of the South Carolina Sea Islands, the novel spans the annexation of Texas to the turn of the twentieth century. *Scorn* has received almost no scholarly attention.[22] Du Bois's biographers have treated the novel less as a literary project in its own right than a trial run for *The Quest of the Silver Fleece,* a tendency that reads Du Bois's fictional development forward from the nadir, ignoring how it arose in tandem with his historical interest in Reconstruction. David Levering Lewis describes *Scorn* as a failed draft of *Quest,* while Manning Marable also conflates the texts, assuming that Du Bois was drafting the later novel between 1904 and 1906, even though attention to *Scorn* might have sharpened the terms in which Marable frames Du Bois's turn from social science toward a fusion of art and political engagement after 1903.[23] The nature of this fusion has been an important question for critics addressing Du Bois's imaginative writing. Paul Gilroy and Susan Gillman both argue that Du Bois's juxtaposition of visionary lyricism with social science addresses a problem of disciplinarity, allowing him to overcome the positivist limits of his early historicist thought.[24] This sense of imaginative writing as a utopian supplement to social analysis has also influenced critical readers of Du Bois's novels. Mullen, Alys Eve Weinbaum, Lily Wiatrowski Phillips, and Jarvis C. McInnis all consider

Du Bois's embrace of the speculative tendencies of the romance as a means through which he added a utopian thrust to his otherwise didactic treatment of literature as social analysis. Arguing that Du Bois "imagine[s] a new relationship between blackness, cotton, and the plantation," in *The Quest of the Silver Fleece*, McInnis describes this fusion as a means of imagining alternative "cotton futures."[25] I turn to the productive dislocation between Du Bois's speculative and historical thought rather than the complementarity of art and politics. This dislocation is expressed in his adoption of counterfactual narrative to think through the disjunctions involved in narrating Reconstruction as revolution.

Attention to *Scorn*'s editorial history and its differences from *The Quest of the Silver Fleece* help to clarify this dislocation. *Scorn* exists in Du Bois's archive as two manuscripts from 1905: an initial, heavily amended draft, and a more complete revised version that was rejected by McClurg. Alongside these manuscripts sit several undated plot outlines and abandoned fragments: some seem to have been written at the same time as the novel; others, which stretch the plot further into the twentieth century, were written at some point after World War I.[26] That Du Bois returned to an apparently abandoned work suggests its importance to his literary and, I will argue, his historical and political imagination. It also indicates that Lewis's and Marable's reduction of *Scorn* to a draft of *Quest* is incorrect.[27]

Scorn shares some thematic concerns with Du Bois's first published novel. Both texts explore the socioeconomic, racial, and political dynamics of life on a cotton plantation, fusing literary writing with social analysis. In fact, before reading *Scorn*, McClurg envisioned it as a social problem novel; he suggested the "story" might "almost become a campaign document" for an election in which "the color question" was likely to feature prominently.[28] Du Bois seems to have been keen to pursue the popular political and educational possibilities of the novel form. In this vein, *Scorn* preempts *Quest*'s focus on the role of education in Black economic and political empowerment. Like the published novel, *Scorn* depicts a cooperative settlement community of sharecroppers, based around a school, and engages with questions of educational reform in the South. However, this narrative strand forms only a portion of *Scorn*'s more elaborate plot. In *Scorn*, Du Bois roots his educational focus squarely within the political and social history of slavery and Reconstruction. Formerly enslaved siblings Robert and Mary Calhoun found the school after their father, Tom Calhoun—a Civil War veteran and Reconstruction political leader—is lynched by the Klan. Recognizing, as his lover Hilda puts it, that "the negro problem is simply the labor problem masked," Robert makes the school a site of interracial labor politics, leading destitute sharecroppers in support of a mill strike by Italian laborers (S 299). This radicalization of Du Bois's educational concerns forms the political denouement to the novel, building on a narrative that is vastly different from *Quest*. *Scorn*'s long historical scope and nonlinear temporal structure mark the novel as an ambitious literary project in its own right.

Faced with his publisher's desire to cash in on the commercial success of *The Souls of Black Folk* by marketing *Scorn* as a programmatic political statement by a prominent race leader, Du Bois emphatically refused to offer a representative Black perspective on the color question. Rather, the political and literary inventiveness of *Scorn* resides in the way that Du Bois splits his narrative, and with it the novel's central thought, between class and racial perspectives, often occupying the psychology of white supremacists. Underpinning this multi-vocal structure, Du Bois employs an anachronistic temporal framework that moves backward and forward across the period between the 1840s and the turn of the twentieth century, in pursuit of the underlying forces that constitute the long history of his emergent political subject: the new world peasantry.

Scorn comprises three books, each of which narrates the period from the perspective of a different class: first, expansionist slaveholders (the Lloyd-Jones family); then corrupt carpetbaggers (the Reynolds family); and only belatedly, emancipated slaves (the Calhoun family). Together, the books chart the fates of these families as they intersect with a conspiracy to reopen the international slave trade and establish a hemispheric slaveholding empire. This conspiracy is led by a secretive fraternal order, the Knights of the Golden Circle, which Du Bois's counterfactual plot converts from a minor real-world antebellum secret society into a conspiratorial network whose imperial aspirations directly cause the Civil War and force slavery to crisis, before the group secretly resurfaces in the guise of the Klan to crush Reconstruction. The novel's dizzying plot resists easy summary, taking in a voodoo curse that foreshadows the collapse of slavery; an interracial baby swap narrative; Robert's impossible heritage, as one of two differently raced twins, born to an enslaved mother apparently by different fathers (which triggers genealogical links of baffling complexity); and a counterfactual reworking of several real political events and figures. I will focus on how Du Bois uses the Calhoun family to trace the emergence of a new political subject, in the process developing a recursive treatment of time that ruptures the novel's apocalyptic impulse.[29]

Robert and Hilda Calhoun are the children of Tom and Juno. The slave of John Calhoun (who figures prominently as an architect of American imperialism), Tom is sold and marries Juno, the enslaved half-sister of the plantation heiress, Irma Lloyd. After Juno is raped by Irma's husband, a nouveau riche filibusterer, Henry Jones, Tom murders an overseer and flees to the North. During the Civil War, he returns to South Carolina as a Union soldier, is reunited with Juno, and becomes a radical political leader, advocating land redistribution during Reconstruction. Book 1 focuses on Henry and Irma's marriage and the beginnings of the imperial conspiracy. Irma's realization of her father's and husband's sexual relations with their slaves imbues her with a pathological hatred for Black people, which she displaces onto a fantasy of a slaveholding empire capable of regenerating a decadent master class. Her shame is compacted by her half-acknowledged realization that her child may in fact be Juno's. Juno's rape by Henry leads to a fantastical plotline in which Juno gives birth to twins, one of whom appears white and the other Black. Du Bois has Juno's mother, a conjure woman named Mom Bett, swap Juno's white twin with Irma's newborn baby. In a farcical scene that the novel repeats three times, without ever providing a clear perspective, Henry and Irma foil the plot, but readers are left unsure whether the twins have been successfully swapped. Irma's disavowal of her interracial family mirrors her refusal to acknowledge her husband's involvement in the Golden Circle, and by extension the international slave trade, even as she pushes him toward a career in the radical southern wing of the Democratic Party. Henry's involvement in the secessionist conspiracy inadvertently contributes to the collapse of slavery and causes the family's ruin. Under Irma's guidance, he briefly rallies his secret order to lynch Tom Calhoun but ultimately dies mad, ruined, and ashamed.

Book 2 follows the similar fate of the Reynolds family, northerners from abolitionist stock who become embroiled in Henry's slave trading and the Golden Circle, before becoming corrupt carpetbaggers. Du Bois's account of Irma's "quiet yet bitter scorn" and the collapse of her family is mirrored by the Reynolds's experience (S 5). In turn, the fate of both families acts as a counterpoint to the emergence and redemption of the Calhouns in book 3. Du Bois uses each book to retrace the events of the last from a new perspective. As a result, the white characters' dawning realization of the genealogical links between the families (the Reynolds adopt a boy who may also be Juno and Henry's child) and of their doomed fortunes foreshadows the epochal emergence of a new people, (literally) born from the political and racial entanglements of the plantation class structure.

As this circuitous plot suggests, Du Bois's publishers did not receive the novel they expected. Unable to fathom "the central thought of the story," as the fabled tale of America's "great race problem," his editor complained that its "teaching" was not "definite and tangible enough."[30] The correspondence ironically makes Du Bois perhaps the only Black novelist of the nadir period to be chastised by a white literary editor for not writing about race and the South in a sufficiently political manner. The youngest of the writers treated in this book, Du Bois was writing when the mainstream editorial consensus that Reconstruction was a relic of the sectional past prevented writers of fiction from expressing avowedly radical views about racial politics. In 1901, the liberally minded Howells publicly criticized Chesnutt's *The Marrow of Tradition* as a "bitter, bitter" book, whose stark depiction of white supremacist violence and Black resistance was evidence that "Mr. Chesnutt . . . has lost literary quality" (this despite Howells being a patron of Chesnutt's early work).[31] Even Cable's self-professedly moderate criticism of the New South in *John March, Southerner* was deemed by Richard Watson Gilder to have veered too close to the didactic stylings of the no longer commercially popular Tourgée.[32]

Du Bois's views on Reconstruction had been shaped in part by his early reading of Tourgée's novels, and *Scorn* certainly shares Tourgée's commitment, in *A Fool's Errand* and *Bricks without Straw,* to using a fictionalized history of Reconstruction to expose the persistence of white supremacist violence in the South (if not Tourgée's sympathetic depiction of carpetbaggers).[33] Du Bois was also likely informed by Chesnutt's difficulties. The two corresponded over Du Bois's desire to start a national political weekly, and in a 1903 portrait of "the advanced guard of the race," Du Bois celebrated Chesnutt's literary achievement in resisting the "temptation of money making" by writing about race, noting that this required Chesnutt to write "powerfully but with great reserve and suggestiveness."[34]

In this context, Du Bois's inability to publish *Scorn* is striking for the fact that his editor's attempt to hold him to recognized aesthetic dictates was also a demand that he emphasize (rather than erase) his political position, to the extent of turning his novel into a "campaign document." The novel's composition history suggests that Du Bois did not depart from literary convention in favor of what we might now call counter-history because speculative fiction allowed him to express a utopian subjectivity otherwise barred from representation.[35] The relationship between art and politics here is more formative. Du Bois uses the form of the historical novel to question what constitutes a narrative, and a political, subject. In this sense, his experimentation should be viewed less as a political act, insufficient in the sense indicated by McClurg, than an attempt to work through questions that underpinned his politics. While McClurg saw artistic and political immaturity in *Scorn,* he inadvertently hit on the significance of the novel's counterfactual impulse when he questioned "the central thought of the story." Du Bois's temporal experimentation requires readers to question the identity of the class subject from whose perspective the novel speculates (to question whose thought is central to the novel). In turn, it instigates a complex rethinking of the political and historical forces that constitute the plantation's revolutionary subject.

Such rethinking was not the "teaching" McClurg had in mind. A 1910 reader's report for *The Quest of the Silver Fleece* suggests the kind of political novel his publisher sought. The reader identified the way that *Quest* afforded "white readers" an opportunity to see "things through the other end of the glass" as its greatest virtue. By offering "the point of view of the soul of the black man," the reader argued that Du Bois captured the subjective other side of a supposedly balanced perspective on "the 'problem' which confronts us in our negro population."[36] It must have been a comfort to McClurg (and suggests a lingering memory of *Scorn*) that the reader could see "nothing seditious or revolutionary in it."[37] By contrast, *Scorn* rejects a balanced race relations narrative. The experiments with time and perspective that rendered the novel unpublishable for McClurg were a necessary component of Du Bois's ambitious attempt to combine the situated conditions of plantation life with something approaching a wider theory of history, a theory with Reconstruction at its center. In what follows, I place *Scorn* as a significant literary project in relation to the development of Du Bois's historical thought. Explaining how the novel's anachronistic treatment of time (both apocalyptic and recursive) prefigures *Black Reconstruction* requires some anachronism of my own, as I move backward from the more familiar *Black Reconstruction* to *Scorn,* identifying their shared counterfactual treatment of the peasant political subject.

General Strikes and Impossible Histories

In *Black Reconstruction,* a series of agrarian counterfactual propositions ask readers to imagine what the impact on history would have been, and what the capitalist world economy would have looked like, had Reconstruction succeeded in creating a radical peasantry in the South. "A new vista opened," Du Bois argues in one such instance: "Here was a chance to establish an agrarian democracy in the South," based on "peasant holders of small properties" (*BR* 67). Repeating the phrase he used to integrate social life and labor in his 1907 study of economic cooperation, he suggests that a radical agrarian peasantry, engaged in "a tremendous series of efforts to *earn a living in new and untried ways*," could have acted as more than a petit bourgeoisie; disrupting the plantation's subsumption by a new "dictatorship of capital" (346; emphasis added), they might have established what, with deliberate provocation, he calls "a dictatorship of the proletariat" (345). "If it had been done," he argues, "the result would have been fateful for the nation and the world" (368).

This counterfactual proposition peppers the book, structuring the injunction to imagine Reconstruction as revolution. But just as frequently, Du Bois's speculations generate an account of their own failure to occur; more tellingly, they foreground the necessity of this failure as dictated by the capitalist logic of the plantation. His agrarian vista competes with his assertion that "it was inconceivable . . . that the masters of Northern industry through their growing control of American government, were going to allow the laborers of the South any more real control of wealth and industry than was necessary to control the political power of the planters and their successors" (*BR* 345). What interests me is how Du Bois's apparently always already foreclosed counterfactual horizon—it could have been thus but at some level had to be thus—recurs, as if by repetition he can explain why a political opportunity that "had to fail" continues to enthrall his imagination (241).

What Weinbaum calls the book's "recursive historical rhythm"—which moves "from antagonism, to revolt, to crisis, to re-entrenchment, and then again to antagonism"—is condensed in these self-unraveling speculations.[38] In turn, they rehearse Du Bois's early account of the speculative importance of the Freedmen's Bureau as the embodiment of Reconstruction's foreclosed promise in *The Souls of Black Folk*. There he celebrates an organization that "established a beginning of peasant proprietorship" in the South during Reconstruction, maintaining that "had political exigencies been less pressing, the opposition to government guardianship of Negroes less bitter, and the attachment to the slave system less strong, the social seer can well imagine a far better policy,—a permanent Freedmen's Bureau," which may have "solved in a way we have not yet solved the most perplexing and persistent of the

Negro problems."[39] Immediately, though, he adds that "such an institution was unthinkable in 1870." Crucially, Du Bois is unclear about whether this unthinkability is a legacy of slavery or whether such a politics *became* unthinkable "because of certain actions of the Freedmen's Bureau itself," notably its failure to redistribute land. He frames this counterfactual ambiguity as the legacy of Reconstruction. "The passing of a great human institution before its work is done," he points out, "like the untimely passing of a single soul, but leaves a legacy of striving for other men. The legacy of the Freedmen's Bureau is the heavy heritage of this generation" (*SBF* 390).

The "heavy heritage" is not only the failure of Reconstruction but the "untimely" condition the contemporary observer is forced into when considering its counterfactual possibility. The divided logic of Du Bois's counterfactual speculations is underpinned by a broader question of perspective relating to the political subject they address, a question he highlights in *Black Reconstruction* when he asks whether his readers can "imagine this spectacular revolution." Rather than asserting that in the context of the Civil War the fugitive slave was a striking worker, Du Bois questions whether readers can imagine such a subject at all. When he claims there is "no point in thinking of this central figure in emancipation" unless "we think of these people as human beings like ourselves," he invokes a form of recognition that moves beyond the bounds of racial empathy. "Assuming this common humanity" involves "conceiv[ing] ourselves in a position where we are chattels and real estate, and then suddenly in a night become 'thenceforward and forever free'" (*BR* 121). Du Bois's challenging humanism makes a seemingly impossible act into a quotidian imperative; it requires a necessarily counterfactual confrontation with the limits of historical imagination. Picturing a political subject by conceiving them as "like ourselves" becomes an expression of inconceivable difference, which culminates in Du Bois's contention that understanding emancipation as revolution is an imaginative act equivalent to witnessing the Second Coming: "Suppose on some gray day, as you plod down Wall Street, you should see God sitting on the Treasury steps, in His Glory, with the Thunders curved about him? . . . Foolish talk, all of this, you say, of course; and that is because no American now believes in his religion . . . But to most of the four million black folk emancipated by civil war, God was real. They knew Him . . . and so on January 1, 1863, He made them free" (123–24).

Du Bois's counterfactual address establishes an epistemic contradiction. He neither allows readers to accept their difference from the enslaved, who experienced an apocalypse of sorts, nor to rest easily in "common humanity." The act of imagining the plantation's revolutionary subject thereby establishes the limit against which Du Bois's explicit counterfactuals inevitably come up. Singh has something like this speculative impulse in mind when he argues that Du Bois's seemingly tendentious materialism transcends the racialized empiricism of the New Deal Left. Singh convincingly locates *Black Reconstruction*'s speculative materialism in the racial politics of its era, but his gesture toward a literary capacity to "make the unthinkable thinkable" shares with other accounts of counterfactual writing (and of Du Bois's literary work) a tendency to conflate the negative function of critique with a utopian supplement located in aesthetics. Du Bois's peculiarly negative speculative impulse challenges this conflation.

Like Singh, Catherine Gallagher and Stephen Greenblatt identify counterfactual thought with a peculiarly literary, anecdotal approach to the past that enigmatically counters a sense of historical inevitability by making legible "the reality of unrealized possibilities" and recovering unrecognized subjects.[40] As Gallagher argues elsewhere, however, such contingency has a normative narrative function, insofar as counterfactual narratives isolate a point of historical contingency (usually an event or character) to assign deeper patterns of historical causation more absolutely and recognizably. She argues that this tendency paradoxically naturalizes history's so-called shaping forces by identifying what can, and what cannot, be removed them from the flux of events.[41] This "search for underlying processes" constitutes a counterfactual reality effect, reminiscent of the historical novelist's penchant for "giving plot to history."[42] Such an account tends to associate narrative per se (especially the kind associated with the historical novel) with conservatism, while displacing counterfactual thought's critical function onto a positive account of the utopian work of literary aesthetics. What is deemed radical here is contingency, celebrated as alterity and the negation of causation.[43] As Gallagher and Greenblatt parse it, the "counterhistorian's utopia" is an anti-narrative space in which all possible worlds become visible.[44]

My account of the historical novel of Reconstruction has been of a form in which narrative and contingency cannot be so categorically and normatively opposed, a form that gives plot to a history that does not proceed in line with a unidirectional account of historical transition. Certainly, Du Bois's counterfactual approach to Reconstruction seems as much concerned with specifying structural limits as transcending grand narratives. The hesitancy of his counterfactual scenarios reorients the search for underlying processes. By returning reflexively and recursively to the question of whether one can access the perspective of the plantation's political subject, he encourages readers to see a relationship between necessity and freedom conditioned specifically by the possible futures opened and foreclosed by revolution in a slave society.

Du Bois integrates his epistemic contradiction into the very political and economic concepts he uses to make his class subject and its political agency thinkable: "the black worker" and the general strike. He establishes his two major historical revisions—slavery's importance to modern capitalism and the slave as revolutionary subject—on the basis of a metonymic link between the enslaved "black worker" and the modern-day, colonial "dark proletariat," from whose exploitation "comes the surplus value filched from human beasts which in cultured lands the machine and harnessed power veil and conceal" (*BR* 15-16). However, having established this link between two proletarian subjects, whose centrality to capitalism has been obscured by racism, Du Bois resists his own metonym. While he argues that slavery was a modern iteration of industrial capitalism, he insists that the chattel slave was "the ultimate exploited," asserting that "there was in 1863 a real meaning to slavery different from that we may apply to the laborer today" (15, 9). Like his injunction to imagine slaves according to a "common humanity" and his self-unraveling counterfactual speculations, Du Bois's account of the slave as proletarian subject pulls in two directions. If slaves and colonial workers share an identity as "founding stone[s]" of a total industrial system, it is, he implies, one that is "veil[ed] and conceal[ed]" by that system's historical development. As in his earlier use of the metaphor, in *The Souls of Black Folk,* the veil is, on the one hand, a barrier between white and Black worlds, which in this case prevents white Euro-Americans from recognizing that the modern industrial system relies on coerced colonial labor. On the other hand, as in his earlier book, the veil is internal to the Black world. His use of the trope in *Black Reconstruction*—to conjoin past and present, slave and proletarian—suggests that Du Bois's revolutionary subject is itself veiled.[45] That this duality underpins his opening summary of the plantation economy indicates that the barrier to imagining a coherent revolutionary subject proceeds from the class character of plantation labor and its subsumption by capital.

If Du Bois's idea of a revolutionary agent forces readers to mediate between subject and structure in assigning narrative perspective, a similar split characterizes his account of that agent's political action. Rather than a decisive event, Du Bois describes the general strike as a form immanent to the capitalist logic of slave production, and he uses it to conceptualize the worldview of the planter. He argues that as a member of a class engaged in production entirely for the world market, the slave owner was forced, "unless he was willing to take lower profits, continually to beat down the cost of his slave labor" (*BR* 41). When unable to escape or to meet the planter in open rebellion, slaves were forced to cling to as much control of their life and labor as possible. Therefore, the planter, because of his economic position in relation to his slaves, "always faced the negative attitude of the general strike" (40).

Using Marxist analytical categories, Du Bois extends the concept of the strike from a single moment, characterized by the withdrawal of site-specific labor. Instead, he uses the term to designate a total social dynamic that reflects the everyday power relations and reproductive tensions of the plantation. He locates revolutionary agency in a socioeconomic relationship that cannot be fully subsumed under capital's laws of value production and in a subject that does not find its metonymic double in the industrial working class.[46] Nevertheless, he continues to maintain a tension that George Ciccariello-Maher argues is central to radical anticolonial dialectics; he approaches the "philosophy of life and action" of the enslaved through its uneven imbrication with the productive dynamics of the capitalist world-system, rather than "by [a] properly analectical separation and autonomy" from Marxist analysis.[47] Rather than representing the general strike as a decisive culmination of traditions of slave fugitivity and marronage, Du Bois frames it, at first, as an economic law given the character of a political act.[48] This "negative attitude" assumes the form not of an axial event—its generality is mundane, based on the frequency of individual acts rather than a collective occurrence—but of a central contradiction in slave production and plantation social life. Perpetual and cumulative, it is the tendency toward crisis that is "always" there in this system of production.[49] Always negative and general, this "strike" is raised conceptually by a moment of military conflict from a structural contradiction to a collective political consciousness.

I offer this close reading of two instances of a recurrent tension in Du Bois's political economy of the plantation to highlight how, time and again, he approaches the perspective of the emancipated slave only to establish an unresolved contradiction between structure and subject. He roots this contradiction in the specifics of the plantation's complex conjunction with the capitalist world-system. In this way, Du Bois requires readers to attend to a question that Chris Taylor argues should be at the forefront of any discussion of slavery and capitalism: "What gets left out when we assimilate the history of the plantation to the history of capitalism?" The answer, for Taylor, is "projections of plantation futures [by the formerly enslaved] that cannot be fully subsumed into the history of capitalism."[50] For Du Bois, articulating such a future from the perspective of a formerly enslaved peasantry involves facing an unresolved problem of the plantation's historical articulation with capital.[51]

This is a matter not just of historical categories but also of the kind of story Du Bois is trying to tell and the narrative perspective required to tell it. The problem of recognition staged by his imperative to imagine history from the point of view of the enslaved resembles a trope Fredric Jameson refers to as "historical anagnorisis." Confronting the late-capitalist global desegmentation of production, which forecloses simple class identity, Jameson suggests that the "coming into view of those multitudinous others suppressed from the official story and field of vision" can still precipitate a moment of recognition.[52] He distinguishes the narrative character of anagnorisis from both simple recognition and the identification of a multitude whose abjection by capital negates any unifying narrative structure.[53] Instead, anagnorisis precipitates a "changing of the valences" on connections between modes of exploitation and social collectivities, instigating "an act of theoretical production in which new characters are produced for our collective political discovery and recognition."[54]

Du Bois's injunction to imagine revolution from two unresolved narrative perspectives—and to see in their conjunction the key to a new political viewpoint—leads readers to question how the plantation shapes a revolutionary subject, rather than speculating from that subject's presumed perspective. At the center of this problem is a question of how to narrate what Du Bois called a new world peasantry in *Scorn*. To fully understand *Black Reconstruction*'s speculative form as part of a generative narrative process—an "act of theoretical production" characteristic of historical novels of Reconstruction—we should acknowledge that thirty years prior to asking readers to imagine Reconstruction as revolution, Du Bois had already drafted an answer in the form of a novel.

New World Counterfactuals

Like *Black Reconstruction, Scorn* returns to and forecloses Reconstruction's revolutionary horizon. The novel builds on and historicizes Du Bois's conception of Reconstruction as the moment of an ambivalent birth of a new people in *The Souls of Black Folk.* In *Souls,* Du Bois narrates this axial moment as the story of the Freedmen's Bureau's experiment in progressive government and uplift, attempted quixotically "as all the land was awakening from some wild dream to poverty and social revolution" (382). The grandeur and pathos of this experiment embody the emergent consciousness of a folk. By contrast, in *Scorn,* Du Bois approaches this moment of revolutionary birth as (and through) the decimated "wild dream" of the defeated slaveholders.

Du Bois narrates the same historical period three times, dividing *Scorn's* elusive central thought between its three main families. Each book reveals incrementally more information about the events of Reconstruction, turning the emergence of a new political subject into a prophetic moment. Before this moment arrives, however, readers witness emancipation through the eyes of white characters. Perhaps surprisingly, given Du Bois's desire to correct reactionary accounts of Reconstruction, he first frames emancipation's revolutionary nature by imagining it as an apocalyptic crisis for the slaveholding ideologue Irma Lloyd in a chapter entitled, "The End":

> And this was the end—the end of all her dreams and wide ambitions, a land sweating with blood and lawlessness, ruled by foreigners and looted by Negroes; a land of mobs and midnight murder: where gentlemen sneaked about masked at midnight and ladies cowered in poverty and terror. Where a Negro, a great black Negro had dared to enter her house and suffer her husband a chance in the world—an opportunity in his own state, a seat in the Legislature beside his own slaves . . . And yet the heavens did not open—the sun shone the rains fell and the flowers blushed in the spring-time; harvests ripened on her father's acres and were reaped by negroes whom once her husband in his burning young manhood had whipped in the very furrows. Oh it was pityful, infamous, monstrous. (*S* 97)

Du Bois seemingly decides that the best way to imagine revolution is in a passage that could almost be lifted from Dixon's racist screed *The Leopard's Spots.* While the caveat that "the heavens did not open" suggests disdain for Irma's racist hyperbole, this is more than satire. Du Bois's decision to approach revolutionary possibility by ventriloquizing a crisis of the proslavery future ("the end of all her dreams and wide ambitions") characterizes a novel whose structure draws readers repeatedly toward an ending in which the dreams of empire and accumulation harbored by white characters have been destroyed. He foreshadows the perspective of a new Black political subject by rendering it an impasse, or moment of crisis, in the mind of the master class.

This anachronistic narrative form—which, like *Black Reconstruction,* returns self-reflexively to Reconstruction's unfulfilled possibilities—holds the utopian potential that Du Bois locates in the new world peasantry alongside the novel's other counterfactual concern: the possible future created by an expanding slave economy. By holding these alternative visions of "the end" together and tracing how they recur and persist ("this was the end . . . and yet the heavens did not open"), Du Bois investigates how the structures of the plantation both enable and limit imagined futures. I will trace this simultaneously prophetic and recursive narrative through the novel's repetition of the qualifier *new world* to describe both the utopian horizon of the peasantry and the utopia outlined by proslavery political economy.

Only in book 3, which begins with rumors of the Emancipation Proclamation filtering across the plantations of the South Carolina coast, does Du Bois offer a direct account of how enslaved people experienced emancipation. Proceeding from a description of Tom Calhoun "as he looked across his forty acres" (*S* 205), Du Bois finally names this new class "a new world peasantry." Over the next two chapters, Du Bois uses *new world* on five occasions to describe how the enslaved experienced the dawn of freedom. However, the phrase quickly shifts from describing a new class subjectivity to suggesting a process of subjection. Tom Calhoun's son, Robert, experiencing freedom as an epiphany, attempts to explain the aspirations of his class to a disbelieving white aristocrat. Rebutting the suggestion that formerly enslaved people "expect to be like white people," he asserts that they "expect to be people in their own way just as you are in yours" (236). However, his epiphany degenerates into an argument about whether legislation will be required to prevent interracial marriage. "So it was," the narrator explains, "that Robert Calhoun entered the portals of a new world" (237).

Readers are prepared for this shift. Before Du Bois uses the phrase to name the new world peasantry, he repeatedly employs it to describe the imagined future in pursuit of which the novel's proslavery ideologues half-knowingly steer the South toward crisis. The phrase originates in John Calhoun's fantasy of a slaveholding empire, built on the annexation of Texas. Henry and Irma's imperial fantasies spring from a chance encounter with the senator on the eve of the Mexican-American War. Calhoun imagines a world in which "New Orleans and not New York would gather the shining wealth of the new cotton fields, and Charleston rather than Boston would speak the new world culture and show the wonderful social system built on the black corner stone of Africa." Du Bois reimagines Calhoun plagued by a theatrical Jeffersonian ambivalence because he realizes his proslavery utopia—in which slavery offers the South self-sufficiency and leaves slaveholding and non-slaveholding sections "forever safely balanced"—will inspire a generation set, as Henry puts it, on "the march of southern principles to the equator" (*S* 14, 12).

The novel roots this ambivalence, which haunts its white characters, in the economic imperatives of cotton monoculture. The commodity, which in John Calhoun's fantasy "binds the world to the South" (*S* 9), also binds the South to cotton's disastrous conditions of expanded reproduction. After signing the annexation order, Calhoun is struck by a "paroxysm of coughing"; bleeding from the mouth, "his weary head seized the refrain Blood! Blood the Beginning of the End." He imagines himself trapped in a net of cotton. Initially "white and silky," it becomes "black with dirt," before morphing into "a great dark formless mass of blackness with mighty arms and thick heavy countenance that seemed pressing, pressing on his sore chest" (16). Calhoun's "new world" produces an insurrectionary image of Blackness. He imagines a white colored commodity transformed, by a process of soiling, into a Black body, before further combining the sexual and economic aspects of this nightmare future by turning to "blood" as a figure for crisis. Du Bois fuses the novel's first image of a Black political subject (equal parts individual figure and "mass") with his first account of the new world promised by plantation slavery. Calhoun's metamorphic fantasy thereby locates a limit to speculative thought in the economic and reproductive crises that plagued a social form dependent on exponentially increasing its cotton production and supply of cheap slave labor in the buildup to the Civil War.[55]

The difference between Du Bois's representation of John Calhoun in his 1896 history, *The Suppression of the African Slave Trade,* and in *Scorn* clarifies how the novel stages a tension between counterfactual possibility and historical necessity specific to the plantation. Calhoun's fantasies in *Scorn* suggest a disparity between slaveholding as a vision of temporal and economic equilibrium and the reality that the plantation's economic imperatives fed what, in his earlier history, Du Bois calls an expansionist "theory of land and slave consumption."[56] In that book, he argues that the real John Calhoun was a keen advocate of this political response to slavery's imbrication in the capitalist world market, committing the slaveholding states to the pursuit of an ever-expanding territorial empire and hence to crisis. Read against Du Bois's historical Calhoun, his fictional avatar's ambivalence (repeated by the novel's white characters) locates the limit of speculative thought in the contradictions that haunt the plantation's conjunction with capitalism. Tellingly, in *Black Reconstruction,* Du Bois argues that from the 1830s onward, this conjunction constituted an "economic revolution" that "meant a new world" for American slavery (4–5).[57]

Du Bois's new world visions, then, locate counterfactual potential in historical desires and anxieties produced by the plantation and its staple commodity. He repeatedly leads readers to imagine the future from this perspective, in the process foregrounding political and economic crisis and contradiction as the conceptual limit of speculative thought. By using the same words to imagine the new world peasantry, Du Bois makes this tension central to his account of Reconstruction's political subject. Preempting *Black Reconstruction,* Du Bois's new world poetics, and the narrative form they shadow, orient his account of Reconstruction in two directions at once. There are two subjects of history in this speculative novel: the emancipated slave and the plantation itself. This duality conditions *Scorn's* simultaneously apocalyptic and recursive treatment of time. Calhoun's "new world culture" nods explicitly to the novel's anachronistic form by posing the emergent political subject as a crisis of narrative. His nightmare of insurrection foretells the collapse of slavery as a moment of narrative closure, "the beginning of the end," but also defers this moment. His prophecy reverts to a "refrain" before a nurse interjects, declaring that "Mr. Calhoun has fainted again" (*S* 16). Like the form of the novel, which twice promises to tell how the "end" of slavery becomes a new beginning, only to move backward in time to confront the crisis from another class perspective, Calhoun's is the first of several apocalyptic premonitions whose promised end never comes.

The pattern is repeated in Irma's apocalyptic account of Reconstruction in "The End." The following chapter, the last of book 1, is called "The Beginning" and recounts what is chronologically the novel's last event. In a scene that Du Bois repeats from Robert Calhoun's perspective in the novel's finale, Irma witnesses Robert preach from Isaiah's premonition of mankind saved by a despised messiah. Like John Calhoun, she seizes on a refrain: "the words, the words, how they burned, old yet new!" (*S* 102). Fleetingly, Irma recognizes the emergence of a new people (the scene in which Du Bois eventually names them as a class takes place outside the same church) after she is struck by Robert's "strange old new words" (103). The conflation of an emergent new world with "old new words" literally sounds like Du Bois reflecting on the problem of recognition that his novel stages. Irma cannot sustain her epiphany; a potential moment of anagnorisis breaks down, deferring the perspective of a new subject for a further hundred pages (when Du Bois takes it up again in book 3). The novel's apocalyptic promise to recover a coherent political subject from the history of Reconstruction instead reverts to an account of the contradictions that underpin the historical expansion of the plantation economy. Whenever this happens, as it so often does in *Scorn,* readers glimpse the concrete historical problematic that underpins Du Bois's speculative problem of imagining new worlds with old words.

Revising the Possible

Du Bois's tendency to voice a Black political subject through the language of the master class is reminiscent of what Nancy Bentley identifies as a form of counterfactual speculation developed by late-nineteenth-century African American novelists, under "the figure of catachresis." Focusing on racialized conceptions of family, Bentley argues that cultural and legal blindness to African American kinship relations developed in slavery created a form of literary "expression wherein strained or illogical language is necessary to name that which has no name." The positive value Bentley places on naming, however, risks negating the negation she rightly identifies in counterfactual form. Highlighting the dominant culture's absence of a language for what were, presumably, socially legible forms of experience for African Americans, she makes a counterfactual critique of the erasure enacted by dominant structures into a positive "epistemology of the outside."[58] Rather than recovering unpresentable social experience, I read *Scorn*'s catachrestic new world poetics as evidence of the productive tension between Du Bois's political and historical accounts of the plantation.

I do not wish to underplay the significance of his literary innovation here but only to highlight the specific historical determinants of the relationship between his creative and political thought. By engaging with the historical problematic I have outlined, Du Bois produced an ambitious experiment in novel writing. His almost metafictional treatment of historical time, which incorporates a modernist focus on psychological interiority, resembles what

Paul Gilroy identifies as "an intense and ambivalent negotiation of the novel form" by later Black writers who experimented with the historical novel to foreground slavery's centrality to the experience of modernity.[59] Elaborating, in particular, on Toni Morrison's ideas and fiction, Gilroy describes a "minority modernism," defined by a creative tension between ventriloquizing the recognizably modern perspective of enslaved subjects and locating this modernity in slavery's ultimately un-narratable trauma. Gilroy argues that this tension fractures the novel's humanist techniques of recovery. While *Scorn* in some ways predicts the representational fracture associated with novelizing slavery's history, Du Bois's aporetic narrative roots it in a particular moment, to capture what Gilroy refers to as the more elusive "specific dynamics of this [condition of] severance."[60] Du Bois's fascination with the intangible central thought of the plantation's revolutionary subject suggests that he located these "specific dynamics" in the relationship between the plantation and revolution. The nature of the tension motivating Du Bois's treatment of a forgotten historical subject reveals itself more fully in the revisions he made to *Scorn,* in particular in the stresses evident in his attempt to expand the novel's temporal and geographic focus.

In an early draft, Du Bois accompanies the emergence and collapse of the new world peasantry with a long account of Reconstruction politics from Tom Calhoun's perspective. He treats the period as a conflict over land, juxtaposing Robert's realization of the racialized "portals of a new world" with his father's attempt to redistribute plantation land to former slaves. The narrator recounts that "this same world it was that sorely puzzled [Robert's] father," but

> his world was simpler and solider was set with great metes and bounds, hemmed in with bog and mountain and mud . . . With his strong unlettered sense he strove persistently toward the gates called Peace and he thought they lay—he was sure they lay, in the silent flat soil round about. The Negroes must have land, little homes of their own, bits of soil to cultivate, havens of refuge against aggression and interference and a new slavery whose coming he foresaw. Day and night he worked toward this end. He wanted the state to buy up land and sell it cheap to Negroes or even give it to them.[61]

Tom's pursuit of a resolutely material freedom anchors a longer account of the political aspirations of his class. Imagining, through Tom's "unlettered sense," a politics both vernacular and previously unwritten, Du Bois frames the forgotten worldview of an emergent peasantry.

The excised passages treat with greater detail the hopes that the first generation of freed people invest in land, turning on General O. O. Howard's 1865 visit to the Sea Islands to order former slaves off lands they had settled during the war. The narrator describes how this anticipated "coming of the day of the Lord" turns into a messianic betrayal.[62] Through this betrayal, Du Bois attempts to narrate a politics beyond state pleading. Tom, who like Howard loses an arm fighting the Confederacy, turns to politics in support of the "maimed and stricken black peasant" who is abandoned by the government.[63] He is motivated by a combination of Howard's betrayal and his own experience of being sentenced to a chain gang when white dignitaries repossess his forty-acre plot. Closely approaching the perspective of a Black peasantry, Du Bois frames Tom's political struggle as a fleeting alternative to the community's reliance on the state.

Yet in the revised draft, the "unlettered sense" of this new class is prominent for its elision, an elision that the novel's recursive counterfactual form carries as a trace. In addition to significantly reducing his account of Tom's Reconstruction experience, Du Bois more than doubled the length of the first book, in the process giving Irma the first account of emancipation, treating more closely the new world of proslavery empire and bolstering his projection of a mechanics of historical determination created by slavery. Du Bois's revisions further suggest his unwillingness to separate his two subjects of history (the emancipated slave and the plantation). Tellingly, in the second draft, Du Bois also added the impossible birth of Robert Calhoun. In the first draft, Juno has one phenotypically white child after being raped by Henry. The novel suggests that the child is taken north and unwittingly adopted by John Reynolds. However, in the second version, Du Bois makes Robert the "black" twin of an impossible pairing and bizarrely attributes the twins' patronage simultaneously to Tom and Henry. He executes this strange plot twist deliberately: Juno tells Tom, "a child to you and to him both were born that red night. How the awful thing happened God only knows but it is true" (S 222–23). The narrative never gives the reader cause to question Juno's account. Whereas his contemporaries—Twain in *Pudd'nhead Wilson* and Pauline Hopkins in *Of One Blood* (1902–3)—use baby-swap narratives to emphasize the dependence of seemingly essential racial determinations on fictions of custom and fantasies of maternal descent, Du Bois literalizes the biopolitical fantasy of a segregated body politic played out in the reproductive body of a Black mother.[64] Not only are the Calhouns figuratively destroyers of, and heirs to, the contradictory future created by proslavery political economy (typified by the man whose name they share), but also Robert is literally reproduced by the fantasies (and fantasists) behind the crisis of John Calhoun's new world culture. In Du Bois's narrative of a new political subject, then, individual characters do not so much represent a class—as might be expected of characters in the classic nineteenth-century form of the historical novel—as collapse into a burlesque of the plantation class structure in crisis.

Du Bois rewrote the speculative core of his novel to lessen the sense of the new world peasantry as a personified subject, a move whose counterpart and condition was a plot structure that, in his publisher's words, failed to "advance and unfold itself in a logical sequence."[65] The link between subject and loss of temporal sequence is crucial to understanding the novel, its relationship to *Black Reconstruction,* and its link to the other novels examined in this book. Rather than rewriting to ventriloquize a class whose perspective he sought to write into history's gaps, Du Bois further suspended *Scorn* between the two political and historical perspectives whose tension would animate *Black Reconstruction* thirty years later. This tension characterizes Du Bois's specific engagement with the more general suspension between the historical and political that the other writers in this book employ to narrate Reconstruction as revolution. What's more, Du Bois clung to the conjunction of divergent perspectives that was his key aspiration for the novel, even at the cost of ruining his chances of publication. Responding to his publisher's complaint that *Scorn*'s anachronistic temporality and disregard for characterological verisimilitude spoiled the book's political "teaching" (and marketability), Du Bois insisted that the "tripartite scheme" that caused these problems was "an experiment and a rather bold one"; he added, "I may have to give it up but I do not want to."[66] The direction of travel between the two manuscripts, and the publisher's criticism that a later revision contained "just about the same" problems, suggests that Du Bois persisted in mining the history of Reconstruction for its counterfactual premonitions of a political subject whose central thought remained frustratingly elusive.[67]

Engaging with some of *Scorn*'s possible futures emphasizes how Du Bois's abortive narrative continued to frame his thinking about Reconstruction. While he laid *Scorn* aside, he refused to "give it up." At some point after World War I, from the horizon of his increasing interest in Black internationalism and connections between empire and slavery, Du Bois returned to the novel, amplifying the Golden Circle into a global force. In an undated plot summary for a revision of book 3, he has Irma's daughter adopt Robert's baby son after Robert's death. Unaware of his background, Robert Jr. travels to Europe, meets the "inner circle," and discovers "the great imperial conspiracy," which leads (in an elliptical insertion whose brevity suggests Du Bois was at the limits of the historical and imaginative connections his narrative could contain) to "World War."[68] Again, he conflates imperial capitalist conspiracy with a new political subject, only now on a global scale. In two key insertions to his notes, Du Bois has the great imperial conspiracy manifest itself at the 1911 Universal Races Congress in London, where Robert Jr. decides to acknowledge his Black heritage after meeting colonial delegates.

It is perhaps unsurprising that Du Bois returned to *Scorn* after 1914. The way that the novel locates a psychology of imperialism in slaveholding foreshadows connections he began to expand globally in his essay "The African Roots of War" (1915) and in the version of "The Souls of White Folk" that appears in *Darkwater* (1920). In *Scorn,* he began to dramatize and humanize the structural connections that are analogical and fleeting in those essays. These fragments reveal that Du Bois is at his most generative politically when at the limits of what he can process into narrative. Renaming the project "The Seat of the Scornful" (originally the title of book 3, which charts the experience of the Calhoun family), Du Bois begins one attempted rewrite in the first person, from the perspective of an enslaved woman. In a brief opening paragraph, entitled "The Story of Mary Calhoun" (he appears to have renamed Juno "Mary" or to have conflated the two characters), he has Mary recount her family history and experience of slavery.[69] In another fragment, Du Bois tries unsuccessfully to connect this ventriloquized perspective to his expanded plot outline, writing notes for himself in Mary Calhoun's voice. His outline contains such instructions as "my third baby is born and freedom comes." After two impressionistic pages, he begins the outline again in a detached third-person voice, carrying the plot forward in time and away from the South, to encompass the emergence of Black internationalism after World War I, before ending with a journey to Africa and a "postlude . . . on Mount Everest."[70]

Again, Du Bois suspends this novel between a moment of political possibility, through which he imagines the consciousness of a neglected subject, and a more impersonal historical architecture that puts the plantation at the center of a world historical narrative. The very features that led McClurg to reject *Scorn* offered Du Bois a means to reimagine the plantation's relationship to the capitalist world-system. It is a sign of the ambition and acuity of his political and literary imagination that the task of putting a subject at the heart of the historical development of the plantation was one that he refused to imagine in terms other than those suggested by a recursive counterfactual novel already deemed beyond the (very limited) pale of publishable political fiction.

An Untimely Subject

It remains for me to more fully historicize Du Bois's decision to revive *Scorn*'s recursive counterfactual impulse in *Black Reconstruction*. Du Bois's literary and historical treatments of the counterfactual possibility attaching to the peasantry are linked across thirty years by a historical problem, unresolved in the texts because it was unresolved in the world: namely, the plantation economy's structural reproduction of a potentially surplus peasant class. This historical problematic reveals itself in the complex temporality that Du Bois brought to the narrative framework he finally chose for Reconstruction: tragedy. His self-unraveling counterfactual speculations underpin *Black Reconstruction*'s account of the period as "a tragedy that beggared the Greek" (*BR* 727). The tragedy, as I have suggested, is not only that Reconstruction's "experiment in democracy" failed but also that, because of the plantation's centrality to capitalism, it "had to fail" (715). However, rather than an archetype for historical inevitability—tragedy emplotting history as "the eternal return of the same in the different"—Du Bois's tragic narrative adopts the anachronistic temporality he developed in *Scorn*.[71] In the process, he questions the temporal location of his political subject.

As Jeremy Matthew Glick argues in his study of the dramatic performance history of the Haitian revolution, Black radical writers have used tragedy's focus on temporal contingency to open up narratives of revolutionary history, "allow[ing] for different subjects—the peasantry, the ex-enslaved—to take center stage in the revolutionary drama."[72] Glick focuses on how plays stage the tragic contradiction between revolutionary masses and leadership. In *Black Reconstruction,* Du Bois mostly dispenses with leadership as his central problem. Accordingly, his tragic narrative plots the revolutionary potential of a formerly enslaved peasantry, but "the generative dance of contingency and necessity" serves less to introduce a new subject than to question its constitution.[73]

When Du Bois's counterfactual scenarios unravel in *Black Reconstruction,* so, too, does their utopian agrarian horizon. To the extent that Du Bois occasionally associates this horizon with "a chance . . . to keep the economic balance between farm and factory" (*BR* 368), such moments seem to suggest what Arnold Rampersad calls the "Jeffersonian affinities" of his political thought or a narrative Michael Denning dubs the "decline and fall of the Lincoln Republic," employed to Americanize socialism in the Popular Front era.[74] However, by confronting each moment of agrarian possibility with the language of economic necessity—and by consistently highlighting that the dream of a free labor republic depended on chattel slavery—Du Bois militates against such tendencies (not to mention the reactionary nostalgia of the Southern Agrarians in *I'll Take My Stand* [1930]). For these reasons, Du Bois's fascination with a moment and a class that "had to fail" requires explanation. His recursive counterfactual impulse produces a complex temporal framework in which he defines the modernity of the plantation by the backward look it continually motivates. As in *Scorn,* this narrative framework takes shape around the new world peasantry, and as with Du Bois's conception of the "black worker," its tragic sense requires readers to question whether the tragedy is limited to a moment in the past or whether it has a relationship to the present.

Du Bois's seeming inability to fix the peasantry, either in time or as a class subject, applies not only to Reconstruction but also to his sociological studies of sharecropping at the turn of the twentieth century. In *The Souls of Black Folk,* his attempt to locate a redemptive race consciousness in the everyday life and labor of "the massed millions of the black peasantry" is repeatedly mediated by his inability to identify a unified subject in a class who "are not all firmly fixed, but grow and shrink in number with the wavering of the cotton market" (*SBF* 359, 474). This sense of "class lines" that "vary, one might almost say, with the price of cotton" constitutes a peasantry whose defining feature is its precarity, its status as a single class being constantly in question (461). *Souls'* Black Belt chapters contain in miniature the book's larger ambivalence about the coherence of the concept of the "folk" by accounting for the Black peasantry as at once archetypically modern—"one of the chief figures in a great world-industry" (457)—and mired in a seemingly backward provincialism. This latter position is encapsulated by Du Bois's attack on Georgia's determination "to bind her own to sloth and misfortune as ruthlessly as ever England did" (451).

This tension structures *Souls'* prophetic narrative form. Shifting between history, sociology, philosophy, ethnography, economics, biography, and fiction (all in lyrical prose), Du Bois experiments with different forms through which to locate a redemptive historical consciousness in the rural folk, a consciousness hidden from the "car-window sociologist" blind to "life within the veil" (*SBF* 469). To do this, Du Bois frames the Black peasant as a "co-worker in the kingdom of culture," using his hybrid form to "sketch, in vague, uncertain outline, the spiritual world in which ten thousand Americans live and strive" (365, 359). Drawing out the valences of the word culture, Du Bois connects his own writing with a conception of the Black peasantry by figuring culture as unalienated labor: both culture and labor are forms of "striving." To be a "co-worker in the kingdom of culture," the Black subject must "husband and use his best powers and his latent genius" (365). Striving promises a fulfilling, unspecialized experience of work (intellectual and agricultural) as culture and culture as work. However, Du Bois's attempt to locate "the rights of all in the whirl of work," identifies a redemptive political consciousness in a concept of work that seems absolutely precarious, forcing his various scholarly and narrative voices up against the more literal experience of labor in the Black Belt, which seems always and inevitably to recall "a memory of forced human toil,—now, then, and before the war" (425, 451).

These conjunctions frame the Black southern worker as suspended between a peasantry and a proletariat. Du Bois's suspended account of the character of Black labor in the South accompanies broader shifts in perspective relevant to his conception of the tragic. What Gilroy refers to as Du Bois's utopian "polyphonic montage technique" fractures when faced with the precarity of the folk.[75] For all that *Souls* seeks to articulate intimate contact with those living "within the veil," confronting the scene of rural labor forces Du Bois repeatedly and explicitly back into the detached position he critiques. His central chapter, "Of the Black Belt," begins, "Out of the North the train thundered, and we woke to see the crimson soil of Georgia stretching away bare and monotonous right and left" (*SBF* 439). Swapping the more detached (and paternalistic) political program expressed in earlier chapters for an immersive account of Black life in the cotton belt, he informs the reader that "if you wish to ride with me you must come into the 'Jim Crow Car'" (440). The same perspective that articulates racial intimacy and connection places Du Bois in the position of the "car-window sociologist," "out of the North," struggling to fit this "perfect flood of black peasantry" into his prophetic political narrative (442).

Such narrative fracture reflects the precarity of the class whose perspective Du Bois articulates as the basis of the folk. As in *Black Reconstruction,* both perspectival and narrative precarity result from the counterfactual promise that Reconstruction could have created an independent peasantry. In *Souls,* that promise is the "heavy heritage" of the Freedmen's Bureau, a heritage that Du Bois roots in an ambivalent relationship to the land: "Those men of marvelous hindsight who are to-day seeking to preach the Negro back to the present peonage of the soil know well, or ought to know, that the opportunity of binding the Negro peasant willingly to the soil was lost on that day when the Commissioner of the Freedmen's Bureau had to go to South Carolina and tell the weeping freedmen, after their years of toil, that their land was not theirs, that there was a mistake—somewhere" (*SBF* 385).

Imagining a historical event that he returned to in *Scorn* and *Black Reconstruction,* Du Bois's syntax makes the Reconstruction-era dream of a Black peasantry inseparable from "the present peonage of the soil." The dream can only retrospectively be envisioned in a warped mirror image of a present and necessarily incomplete, because unwilling, bondage to the land. In turn, this new bondage is a movement "back to the present." As a subject, the "Negro peasant" shares this strange temporality. The term refers both to a subject never created by Reconstruction—and thereby "lost" to history, except in the burlesque of contemporary peonage—and to the modern Black laborers whose once "willing" attachment to the soil remains residual despite its co-option by capital. Du Bois clings ambivalently to a view of peasant life as the epistemological and experiential core of striving and of his elusive folk consciousness. However, in doing so, he suggests that to think the narrative of historical development since slavery through the peasantry is to describe how social relations that seem always to be a return to something—either a utopian aspiration located in the past or a retrenchment of slavery—are constitutive of new political and economic realities, new forms of immiseration, and new possibilities defined by the precariousness of a class.

In *Scorn,* Du Bois draws out the perspectival and temporal tensions contained in *Souls'* vision of work as the basis of a utopian folk consciousness. At the end of the novel, Robert Calhoun is reunited with his lost love, Hilda (who has become the leader of an Italian mill community), when they organize local sharecroppers in solidarity with a mill strike and overcome the mill owners' attempt to use croppers as strikebreakers. In the process, they save Robert's school from the control of these same capitalists. The novel closes with an image of the couple as they "walked down the world . . . thrilled [by] the chords of endless Love and Work," while a mad John Reynolds "reeled onward to his death," and Irma sits "staring white faced at the white faced sea" (*S* 303). Du Bois resolves the narrative of labor struggle that occupies the final section of the novel with an image of unalienated labor familiar from *Souls.* However, in line with *Scorn's* complex temporal structure and weaving of class perspectives, before the utopian desires lodged in the idea of work can signify the universalization of *Souls'* folk consciousness, they express that other new world fantasy. Repeatedly, Du Bois uses the language that he made famous for encapsulating the phenomenology of a Black folk consciousness to describe the historical desires created by slavery, as a system for the imperial domination of racialized labor. Some prominent examples prove illuminating.

Describing an audience of slaveholders transfigured by a John Calhoun speech advocating the annexation of Texas, *Scorn's* narrator applies the Hegelian overtones of Du Bois's description of double-consciousness to a crowd responding "as though a single-souled body had suddenly dissolved into its elemental individuals and they threatened all to drift in different ways. Still there was evident a certain striving, a silent breathless travail toward synthesis" (*S* 34). Similarly, escaping the "listlessness and languor and effeminacy" of the parochial South, Irma marries Henry to pursue a dream of slaveholding empire that is also a vision of "love and work" (44). "Real love," she tells Henry, "is a slow and awful growth—the knitting of human souls—the pain of life and development. The gradual coalescing of two wills and dreams and purposes into one great passion of love and striving" (50). Du Bois repurposes another of *Souls'* key expressive phrases when he describes the mysterious leader of the Golden Circle—who resurfaces in different guises throughout the novel as a deus ex machina, or figuration of the mechanics of historical causation created by slavery—announcing his plan for "a great slave empire stretching from Hudson Bay to the south Pacific and from Sea to Sea" (167). Enraptured by the figure, John Reynolds recalls the "unasked question" to which *Souls* is a response ("How does it feel to be a problem?") (*SBF* 363): "That vast mysterious power that lay in these men's hands, that power before which a continent was bowing, and the Five Seas resounding, seemed here suddenly incarnate flesh and blood and yet that flesh spiritualized and the blood, bloodless and thin. Over all his face and form hovered an appearance of extreme age, endless years, long, long, acquaintance with the infinite Past and Reynolds thought involuntarily perhaps, with—the Infinite Future . . . *ever the unasked question* slipped to Reynolds' lips—'Who is he?'" (*S* 166; emphasis added). In *Scorn,* the vocabulary that Du Bois previously used to describe Black experience becomes a language for summoning the contradictory fantasies generated by work in a plantation society. The novel's cyclical structure means that the vision of "love and work" with which it closes is also the inheritance of these fantasies. The new world peasantry is a class shaped by living in the ruins of a slave empire.

Perhaps unsurprisingly, it is Irma who articulates Du Bois's own sense of the anachronism involved in novelizing this conjuncture. After discovering Henry's involvement in the international slave trade by reading the "cabalistic figures" (another *Souls* reference) of the deeds for his recently acquired plantation, she writes him a tortured letter distinguishing dominance over slave laborers from the slave trade:

> I know they are and should be slaves and servants—they are a lower order of being fit for nothing else and never will be. But I have a horror of making money out of them just as I would shrink from selling worms and cats. Negroes may cringe at my feet—that is their place—but for me to use money made in their barter—I could never stoop to it, never—it would seem like a reversal of nature, of cringing to them. To make them work is right and the owner's share of their crops is less than is really due him for supervision. O dear, I am writing an essay on slavery and an incoherent one. (*S* 64)

Expressing a slave labor theory of millennial world making (which underpins the whole novel), Irma's reasoning fractures when an anachronistic vision of contemporary sharecropping impinges on her description of the master-slave relationship as the permanent core of racial dominance. It is hard not to hear Irma's anxiety about her incoherent "essay on slavery" as Du Bois's own wry commentary on the temporal experiment of his "tripartite" structure, an experiment driven by his desire to give novelistic form to the emergence (and political potential) of a class that his sociological analysis in *Souls* suggests would not sit still.

Scorn's anachronous form dramatizes the precarity of the subject at the center of *Souls*. *Precarity* might seem a strange word for rural workers often understood as being subject to a second slavery, in the shape of a labor system dominated by sharecropping and tenancy arrangements that tied Black workers to the land and ossified the class structure. I use the term not as a substitute for poverty (which dominated Black and white tenants in the Cotton South) but to capture Du Bois's tragic figuration of lives whose conditions are not fixed but in flux: a class whose experience seems suspended between rootedness and rootlessness; whose worldview seems poised between that of the peasant and the proletarian; and the nature of whose experience veers between an exploitation based on uncompensated toil and, to quote Marx's conception of a surplus population, a "misery . . . in inverse ratio to the amount of torture it has to undergo in the form of labor."[76]

Du Bois's nascent and shifting understandings of the Black folk document a precarity structural to what George L. Beckford calls the plantation's "social diseconomies." Beckford argues that as a "total social institution," which secures large supplies of cheap land and labor required for only part of the year, the plantation reproduces conditions for peasant life in accompaniment to its brutal dispossession of labor.[77] To keep labor cheap, and reserve against shifts in commodity price, to which they cannot respond at the point of production, owners must maintain a labor surplus tied to the land. Knowing work will be hard and unstable, laborers exploit their access to the land to reduce time spent working the planter's crop. This struggle to maintain independence is always partial and precarious because planters use debt and violence to secure land against alternative uses. As such, plantations are characterized simultaneously by overwork and underemployment, by proletarian labor and the conditions for peasant life.[78]

In the postbellum United States, this struggle produced what Gavin Wright identifies as a paradox of the Cotton South's circumscribed but real (and seasonal) labor mobility: namely, panic over Black vagrancy and labor shortages alongside the brutal limitation of tenant farmers' movement.[79] Highlighting how a "cycle of debt and dispossession" paradoxically reproduced affective attachment to the land, Pete Daniel characterizes the period between the 1890s and World War II as the South's long enclosure, whose "commodity cultures" shaped the life cycles of rural labor in ways typical of a peasantry, despite removing the fundamental conditions for independence.[80] The dispossession of the laborer and the precarious independence of the peasant are not disassociated in the postbellum South; they constitute a historical dialectic: the re-creation of a peasantry as a precarious labor surplus shapes what Beckford calls the "laws of motion governing [plantation] social change."[81]

These "laws of motion" bear similarities to Marx's "general law of capitalist accumulation," in which, to reproduce itself, capital must continually shed a relatively increasing proportion of workers from the labor process. What distinguishes work under capital from previous systems, for Marx, is that it provides the conditions for its own expansion by reproducing what Denning calls "wageless life" as a necessary accompaniment to waged work.[82] Capital "constantly 'sets free' a part of the working class," creating a mass of unemployed workers that "belongs to capital just as absolutely as if the latter had bred it at its own cost."[83] On the plantation—where a surplus population really does live in the interstices between Marx's twin image of emancipated slaves and the slave market—peasant production is both the means by which labor is subsumed by capital and the real and affective space for alternative existence. This structural contradiction of plantation development is glimpsed in *Souls*. The full temporal and generic implications of Du Bois's later tragic register remain nascent in that book's focus on a redemptive and unifying race consciousness. While such a consciousness is still present in *Scorn*, the novel's experimental historical form foregrounds the anachronistic problem of situating the revolutionary promise of the peasantry—and so, of Reconstruction—in relation to the changing class dynamics of the plantation. *Black Reconstruction*'s tragic counterfactuals develop this anachronism into an explicit theorization of Reconstruction's revolutionary temporality.

This trajectory can be seen in the way that Du Bois recycles his earlier counterfactual proposition from *Souls*, in a more self-consciously anachronistic fashion, to summarize *Black Reconstruction*'s tragic account of revolution. For all that *Black Reconstruction*'s counterfactual speculations foreclose Reconstruction's possible agrarian future, Du Bois refuses to situate his tragic moment squarely in the past. Instead, tragedy inheres in the fact that "for a moment, for the few years of an eternal second in a cycle of a thousand years, the orbits of two widely and utterly dissimilar economic systems coincided and the result was a revolution so vast and portentous that few minds ever fully conceived it" (*BR* 346). The two systems are not southern agrarianism and northern industrialism; he inverts the trope of "utterly dissimilar economic systems," drawn from Charles and Mary Beard's argument, in *The Rise of American Civilization* (1927), that the Civil War was a bourgeois revolution proceeding mechanistically from the clash between divergent economies.[84] Instead, Du Bois imagines Reconstruction as a clash of actual and possible systems. The moment in question, the possible creation of a revolutionary peasantry, is conceived both as a historical scene—the lost opportunity of agrarian democracy—and as the scene of counterfactual speculation itself, the latent and persistent possibility of the peasantry as revolutionary subject. The "few years" of Reconstruction form an "eternal second," inseparable from the future they produce. The "revolution" is indicative of the crisis of slavery, manifested by the emergence of a new class subject (the peasantry's single moment) and of crises to come (the peasantry's structural persistence).

The uncertain conditional tense Du Bois adopts for his counterfactual moment orients readers toward a political subject who seems to exist partly in a lost past, as the unrecoverable subject of Reconstruction's tragic failure, and partly in an unfulfilled present, as a continuing political problem.[85] The tragedy of Reconstruction is less the inevitability of failure than the experience of being out of time. This was a condition that was structural to the historical development of the plantation and its subsumption of labor between Du Bois's attempt to fictionalize the plantation's political subject in *Scorn* and to place it within a political economy of slavery and capital in *Black Reconstruction*. As Raymond Williams argues, tragedy suggests itself as a means of giving plot to revolution because it tests the historical limits of what constitutes inevitability. Tragedy dramatizes the strain placed on the "identification between a permanent order and a [particular] social system" at a given historical moment. As opposed to the epic, tragedy plots an experience of historical change perceived and lived but not yet fully comprehended, except as "the inevitable working through of a deep and tragic disorder."[86] Conceived in these terms, the untimely peasantry is both the tragic subject and historical precondition of the genealogy I have traced in Du Bois's writing. His persistent return to counterfactual speculations about the peasantry in *Black Reconstruction* mirrors that book's return to *Scorn*'s narrative form. Between them stretches thirty years in which the possibility of a peasant political subject was neither fully foreclosed nor rendered completely legible by "the laws of motion" that constituted the plantation's historical dynamic. In working through the question of how "the philosophy of life and action which slavery bred in the souls of black folk" was simultaneously preserved and negated, Du Bois's literary and historical accounts of Reconstruction imagine the peasantry as a revolutionary and a narrative problematic.

Through the false starts, revisions, and temporal uncertainties of Du Bois's long narrative process, I have tried to demonstrate that his speculative pursuit of a Black radical tradition placed a strain on his ability to unify the visionary and the historical. To that end, it is important that Du Bois could never finish *Scorn,* even if he did not precisely abandon it. The gaps remaining between his historical blind spots and literary speculations highlight the sustained work of historical and political inquiry in which he was engaged: this is the theoretical work of the historical novel of Reconstruction. Du Bois never allowed his historical thought to escape the political injunction, articulated in *Black Reconstruction*'s ambiguous rhetorical question about revolution, to imagine history from the perspective of the plantation's collective subject. At the same time, in his fiction, he refused to reduce that subject to a transhistorical identity. In the interests of summarizing this relationship between fictional and historical narrative (and between politics and history), I will end with my own hesitant counterfactual: Du Bois's necessarily unfinished (perhaps unfinishable) novel—premised on the reflexive what-if moment of Reconstruction's agrarian peasantry—was the necessary predicate to his theory of revolution in *Black Reconstruction.*

Conclusion
Narrative, Revolution, (Dis)Appearance

Du Bois's long attempt to narrate Reconstruction as revolution clarifies what I pointed out in my introduction was the full force of his observation that "the unending tragedy of Reconstruction is the utter inability of the American mind to grasp its real significance." Throughout this book, I have attempted to locate the "real significance" of Reconstruction in its revolutionary character. More importantly, though, I have been arguing that the inability to conceive this significance is not just a product of the fact that Reconstruction was ideologically written out of American (literary) history, though no doubt it has been in many ways. The elusive significance to which Du Bois refers is not a content that can simply be returned to a historical or literary record from which it has been erased. To grapple with the historical and literary liminality of Reconstruction is to tarry with real difficulties involved in narrating revolution in a slave society. These difficulties—which were shaped in the period this book has covered and which, in later years, hardened into the solid epistemic, political, and narrative categories through which we continue to measure the dynamics of change and continuity in the South—make revolution into Reconstruction's problematic. They also make the Reconstruction South a terrain for theorizing revolution.

Considered as a problematic, revolution is something that spurs narrative, as opposed to a category into which Reconstruction can be said to fit or not fit and which novels either endorse or contest ideologically. The novels I have discussed are linked by more than a theme (Reconstruction), by more even than a political category for understanding that theme (revolution). Avowedly political fictions, they also chart the intellectually and politically fraught process through which, despite Reconstruction's incompletion as a political project, past and present seemed to come apart in the act of representing it. Considering the emergence—both in the past and to our contemporary critical imagination—of a fragile historical sense defined by this problematic helps us to rethink the models of historical change that have brought the plantation South into the horizon of revolution while at the same time keeping slavery and revolution apart as awkward bedfellows. I have been arguing that the production and interpretation of novelistic narrative allows us to undertake such rethinking. And in treating fictional form as a kind of theoretical production in this way, I have inevitably written a book that is as much about reading, about reading historically, as about Reconstruction or revolution. Accordingly, I want to close with some observations on the kind of reading in which I have been engaged, a method that I think it is better to call historiographical than historicist.

Treating revolution as a narrative problematic has necessarily involved dealing with something of a negative presence. I have interpreted this presence by placing literary texts in relationship to the historical contexts and political discourses that have come to frame Reconstruction as an unfinished revolution. The development of a liberal public sphere, changing theories of republicanism and the state, understandings of racial embodiment, the emergence of a peasant class subject: these are frameworks for historicist reading. But the point in reconstructing them through fictional narrative has not been to return something absent or repressed to the texts, whether an unspoken ideological position on revolution or an unfinished utopian kernel present in Reconstruction. Rather than treat tension, aporia, and ellipsis as textual gaps to be filled in with historical material (or as literary apertures onto alternative political possibilities), I have read them as modes of historical argument in and of themselves. These forms of negativity are indeed symptomatic of the political discourses within which I have situated the texts, but the productive theoretical and historical work that the novels do comes from the way that writers make such tensions central to the acts of reading and interpretation that their novels elicit (and in varying degrees thematize).

I have, then, described a novelistic form engaged in a kind of historical critique, a critique that we as readers—reading from a present shaped by the historical development of the discourses these novels employ—can use to reframe our relationship to the past. This process requires an understanding of critique that does not see the practice as a suspicious exhumation of familiar historical and ideological contexts, to which writers are blind. In the case of these novels, such a conception of "the mentality of critique" fails to recognize the way that they structure, plot, and engage with aporia as a thematic concern.[1] Returning briefly to Sutton Griggs's *Imperium in Imperio,* addressed at the start of this book, helps to encapsulate this imaginative work. In that novel, the Black state, whose revelation the narrative's retrospective framing foreshadows, ultimately turns out to be "a compact government exercising all the functions of a nation" that is strikingly similar to the U.S. state (*II* 194). Griggs offers a scrupulously legalistic description of this political body. Formed in response to the catastrophic abandonment of Black citizens by the federal government, the new republic acts in almost exact parallel with the U.S. nation-state; its constitution, Belton explains, "except in a few, but important particulars, . . . was modeled after that of the United States" (194–95). Tinkering with "a defect in the Constitution," relating to the relationship between state and national power, is not the limit of Griggs's re-imagination of the postbellum political horizon, as confirmed by the brevity with which he treats the institutional body that might otherwise cap his narrative (194). A "form of government unexcelled by that of any nation" collapses almost immediately under the strain of a debate about whether political violence will be necessary to bring a Black state into being (199). Griggs's is only briefly a utopian novel. His precarious, almost satirical, move into utopian world-building trains the reader's focus onto a speculative impulse that is primarily historical, one that reimagines revolution contrapuntally by depicting the recent past as a revolutionary process unfolding in the absence of a transition toward the bourgeois-democratic nation-state.

The historical sense I have been charting comes from the struggle to see, to name, and to narrate the character of a situation that seems quite plainly to be revolutionary without culminating in the kind of telos that the nineteenth century has handed down to the present as the benchmark of categorizable political change. The historical perspective that we can glean from this form lies not in the excavation of an absent politics but in following writers as they plot the estrangement, and question the readability, of the frameworks through which we (as readers) necessarily encounter revolution in the past. To borrow a phrase from Timothy Bewes, reading this way involves "reading *with an eye to the reading that the text itself makes possible.*"[2] Without abandoning the insights of symptomatic interpretation, I have tried to remain sensitive to the greater and lesser degrees of authorial consciousness and intention involved in plotting the contours of a history that had not yet been fully theorized or narrated as revolution and that writers approached through political lenses whose subsequent development in the wake of Reconstruction made the social terrain of the plantation South seem an archetype of historical stasis. A central contention of this book has been that this kind of reading helps us to reconceive revolution as more like a convulsion than a transition, a crisis to which the postbellum racial terror was a long and unstable settlement, but not in any simple sense a recursion. By approaching historical convulsion through specific political frameworks, these writers give narrative to the dynamics of a period in which, to paraphrase an observer of revolution in another society shaped by combined and uneven development, "all changed, changed utterly," without a definite new birth of liberation becoming nameable.[3]

Together, Cable's "No South[s]," Tourgée's models of state citizenship, Chesnutt's and Harper's fragile deployment of sentimental poetics, and Du Bois's counterfactual revolutionary subject depict the difficulty of containing Reconstruction's legacy in the constitutional and political forms inaugurated in the postbellum period. Reading them through the tension between their political and historical perspectives, as I have done, helps us to understand revolution as a process that does not proceed in a straight line, with a single pattern of events and subjects. In focusing on the strained and straining legibility of political categories when they are used to plot the historical development of Reconstruction, I have charted a precariously historical form. But again, precarity need not be seen as something that the critic seeks to return to wholeness. One of my claims has been precisely that these novels do not constitute something that can be recovered as a singular political tradition or a genre neglected by critics. Walter Benjamin's famous claim that a revolution is an event that "make[s] the continuum of history explode" necessarily implies the difficulty (and, I have argued, the anachronism) of finding a narrative form in which to comprehend it.[4] This difficulty is useful to think with, and these novels provide a way of thinking with that difficulty as a problem of periodization and narrative temporality because they illuminate historical contradictions and conditions that did not produce the translatable and hegemonic terms of a full-blown genre.

From the perspective outlined in this book, Reconstruction's literary significance lies less in correcting than explaining its marginal presence in literary history, a marginality that is effectively emblematized in Chesnutt's most famous novel, *The Marrow of Tradition*. There Chesnutt moved away from the historical settings that dominate his earlier fiction, basing his most explicitly political novel on the real-world pogrom that overthrew an interra-

cial fusion government in Wilmington, North Carolina, in 1898.[5] Chesnutt's
shift from allusively to unabashedly political fiction is also an elaboration
on the impossibility of holding together the history of Reconstruction with
the emergent racial crisis of his present (so delicately balanced in *The House
behind the Cedars*). This novel turns on the power of print to control political
and historical perceptions. The riot that culminates the plot is engineered by a
cabal of white dignitaries who utilize the aristocratic Major Carteret's position
as editor of a newspaper, the *Morning Chronicle,* to sound "the tocsin of a new
crusade."[6] By publishing a series of race-baiting editorials, which almost trig-
ger a lynching before stoking the riot, Carteret and his coconspirators seize
control of political narrative to instrumentalize white supremacist violence:
by starting a pogrom, they disguise a "vulgar theft of power" as "a solemn act
of revolution" (*MT* 392). The link between print and political violence also
has a temporal function: it creates narrative simultaneity. Drawing together
plotlines linked by the different temporality of an inheritance plot, Chesnutt
uses the newspaper's political influence in creating the conditions for an impending riot as a backdrop that generates a catastrophic shared present for
the novel's characters. In a different way than Carteret, Chesnutt instrumen-
talizes print's relationship to this temporality, ending with a warning against
the political defeatism that his critique of white supremacy might engender:
"there's time enough but none to spare" (448).

Set against the ability of print to bring a political present into being is an
alternative history that Chesnutt implies is unable to enter print (and so the
present): the history of Reconstruction. This narrative turns on Olivia Carteret's attempt to conceal her father's lawful marriage to a Black woman during
Reconstruction and so mask the legitimate claim of the Black Miller family on
the Carterets' inheritance and social position. In a crucial scene, Olivia burns
evidence of a discovery that threatens her racialized sense of family legitimacy
all the more because it a legal rather than an illicit relationship.[7] What is striking about the way this novel treats Reconstruction is that Chesnutt does not
so much recover a forgotten history as dispense with it. Olivia's burning of her
father's will, his marriage contract, and a letter of testimony to the marriage
is more than the repression of "a chapter of family history" that anyway is
already known in "a general way" (*MT* 214). The written evidence indicates
an alternative history of Black rights during Reconstruction. Therefore, Olivia
burns the possibility of resolving Reconstruction's wrongs in the terms offered
by contract and an inheritance plot. As her father's will burns, she glimpses

a clause that makes provision for privately compensating Janet Miller while also rendering Olivia the main heir. Visible only fleetingly on "the carbon residue of one sheet" and set "out in ghostly black" as the will burns, the text is a way of making Reconstruction commensurate with the present order (396). With the will burned, the only way Olivia can reckon the past is total and public: it "would mean bankruptcy and ruin" (406). The ashes are evidence of a social history that cannot be contained by the mechanism of law and one that escapes the metaphorical (and printed) resolutions of the inheritance plot. Chesnutt stages the family dilemma that structures his political novel of the present as a burning of the thematic matter of his previous historical novel of Reconstruction. In a sense, what we see on the carbon residue is the disappearance from view of a historical tension that *The House behind the Cedars* held together: to borrow terms from Du Bois's *Scorn,* we witness the beginning of the end of a literary form.

Reconstruction is no more reclaimable as a political legacy for the novel's Black characters. Its other presence in the novel comes in the figure of Josh Green, who "ain' fergot" Reconstruction because he "wuz right in it" (*MT* 290–91). Having witnessed his mother being brutally beaten by the Klan as a child, the plebeian radical is a participant in what the reformist, Dr. Miller, calls a "page of history which most people are glad to forget" (289). His violent commitment to revenge seems to enable him to unite historical and political experience in a way that other characters cannot, by "shap[ing] his life to a definite purpose" (290). But when the novel shifts focus onto the impending catastrophe of the pogrom, Josh is murdered by a white mob. As both written record and experience, then, Chesnutt visibly erases Reconstruction from his most explicitly political novel. Insofar as *The Marrow of Tradition* questions what form the struggle for African American rights can take in the wake of a violent campaign of disfranchisement, it treats Reconstruction as a hiatus between past and present. If, as the sympathetic white physician Dr. Burns tells Dr. Miller, "the future of your race . . . is a serial story which we are all reading," Reconstruction interrupts the print run (246). Its history is difficult to incorporate into a political program because it looks toward a different horizon than the one suggested by rights to property and marriage, which are the focus of Chesnutt's novel, and even the franchise, the root of the real political crisis that the novel fictionalizes.

If *The Marrow of Tradition* depicts the end of a form, the image of Reconstruction as a ghostly residue might also be said to inaugurate the era's more familiarly gothic presence in twentieth-century American literature. As I have argued, an important aspect of the precariously historical form I have charted in this book is that it does not provide the readily adaptable aesthetic structure of a full-blown genre, one that is repeated across time. This is because its reading of the past as a revolutionary problematic emerges from the particular tension between political and historical narrative conditioned by the moment in which it was produced. In a sense, then, mine has been a historicist reading after all, because the precarious historicity that makes revolution appear as Reconstruction's historical problematic also disappeared as the Jim Crow order entrenched and became the political object through and against which writers approached the past. From the horizon of segregated America, the alternative to the Lost Cause parody of Reconstruction as an abject moment of disorder was to present the era in more or less mythic and spectral terms: either as a moment of foreclosed radical possibility or a traumatic recursion.

This is perhaps best demonstrated through the closest twentieth-century equivalent of the novels I have discussed. In his 1944 novel, *Freedom Road*, the popular socialist historical novelist Howard Fast resurrects Reconstruction as an interracial labor struggle and revolutionary forerunner of the Popular Front, dedicating his novel "to the men and women, black and white, yellow and brown, who have laid down their lives in the struggle against fascism."[8] Fast depicts Reconstruction as "an eight-year period of negro and white freedom and co-operation in the south," an "experiment [that] had worked" but whose "very memory was expunged" (*FR* 255–56).[9] The book has many features that would relate it to the novels I have discussed: it takes an avowedly activist stance to Reconstruction's significance, and it employs didactic set-piece political dialogues (some of which could almost be lifted from Tourgée) alongside a broader historical narrative that comes about as close to a fictionalization of *Black Reconstruction* as one can imagine. But in turning Reconstruction into an analogue for his hopes for post–World War II socialist politics—a moment of racial cooperation in the wake of what "at the time . . . [was] the greatest people's war the world had ever seen" (7)—and in trying to incorporate Reconstruction into a Popular Front–style national radical tradition, Fast enshrines its historicity as a mythic absence.

Stepping back from a fictional depiction of South Carolina's 1868 Constitutional Convention, depicted through the eyes of his protagonist, the former slave and Reconstruction leader Gideon Jackson, Fast's narrator takes on the role of historian: "The whole incident of the Convention was in the way of being a pause, a gap, a hole scooped in the developing stream of America by Union bayonets ... The plantation kings ... saw the impossible happen. The slaves emancipated, millions and millions and millions of dollars of capital they once owned taken from them and overnight dissolved into thin air. ... Perhaps never before in human history had a whole class, a ruling class of a nation, been so stunningly and quickly deprived of its property" (*FR* 69–70).

Leaning heavily on Du Bois, Fast recognizes that the best way to narrate Reconstruction's epochal dimension is to approach revolution as a crisis of the slaveholders' worldview. He goes on:

> When the first paralyzing shock passed, the planters bestirred themselves ... [They] saw a future, the same future they had always seen, propped up on the back of four million black slaves ... And then their house of cards fell down. A bitter, wrathful, revolutionary Congress that had fought one of the most terrible wars known to mankind, decided the blood spilt should not be in vain ... [They formed] Conventions which would frame new state constitutions and create a new democracy in the south, one in which the black man and the white man stood side by side, building together ... There was no future and no past in this moment. In the deep strange hole that had been violently scooped in the stream of history, something was happening ... And the planters waited. (*FR* 71–72)

Fast's elegiac tone incorporates Reconstruction into a broad historical sweep, only to close with the sign of coming failure. The conversion of Reconstruction into an unfulfilled political analogue for the present understandably leads Fast to turn a historical narrative of revolutionary crisis into a political myth. Twice named as a "hole" in history, Reconstruction's revolutionary character is defined overwhelmingly by its foreclosure and the fact that it has been forgotten; a moment with no past and no future is defined as much by its mythic detachment from history as its novelty: it is un-narratable as revolutionary process on its own terms. Like the gap in history that Fast conceives Reconstruction as, this passage is notable for its disconnection from the rest of the novel. Fast's narrator steps back only momentarily to speak as a historian, before returning to a plot that depicts Reconstruction as a proletarian romance in period dress: an analogue for Communist Party hopes for interracial organizing in the Jim Crow South.[10]

Gideon's comrade, the poor white tenant farmer Abner Lait, articulates the novel's historical sense when, facing the destruction of his and Gideon's plantation community of Carwell by the Klan, he says: "How in hell is anyone going to know that we're here? How in hell is anyone in this whole damned earth going to know what's happening here? Do we know what's happening anywhere else? They've sealed off this place; they've sealed it tighter than hell itself. Maybe everything in the South is sealed off that way. Maybe no one knows" (*FR* 251). Tellingly, in writing Reconstruction's historical elision and mythic foreclosure back onto the moment, Fast employs, for activist ends, a generalized sense of the South's gothic detachment from the streams of history and national life that could equally be voiced by Shreve in Faulkner's *Absalom, Absalom!*—"Tell about the South. What's it like there. What do they do there. Why do they live there. Why do they live at all."[11] Fast writes the Faulknerian South backward onto Reconstruction.

Of course, Faulkner's historical novel is *about* the complex and contemporary work of mythmaking (as well as the historical violence) involved in so sealing off from history "the deep South dead since 1865" (*AA* 6). But it is important which concealed history this gothic critique of New South mythmaking makes available. Faulkner's symptomology of the New South requires readers to unravel a history sublated into the retold tales of Rosa Coldfield. Insulted by Thomas Sutpen in 1866, Rosa retreats into a melancholic devotion to recounting the traumatic origin story of Sutpen's Hundred, as if—like the "nothusband" from whom she flees (5)—fighting "against the ponderable weight of the changed new time itself" (133). Rosa's refusal to continue the Sutpen line and her attempt to effectively freeze time into a recursive act of distended storytelling stop history at Reconstruction. Speaking through Quentin Compson's tortured reiteration of this history in 1909, Faulkner critiques a romantic nostalgia that renders his characters into "back-looking ghosts . . . still recovering, even forty-three years afterward from the fever which had cured the disease, waking from the fever without even knowing that it had been the fever itself which they fought against and not the sickness, looking with stubborn recalcitrance backward beyond the fever and into the disease with actual regret" (9). This critique, though, requires that Reconstruction's revolutionary creation of the "changed new time" (Quentin's "forty-three years" dates us to 1866, not the Civil War) be folded into the more general sense of belatedness and inertia conditioned by slavery's legacies:

that is to say, the confusion of disease and symptom that is the novel's critical object. To put it slightly differently, Faulkner can tell about the violence of slavery, can even tell in a displaced way about Black insurrection (in the Haitian origins of Sutpen's fortune), *because* he does not tell about Reconstruction.

My point in tracing briefly how the historical sense that I have explored passed into a different—more spectral and more mythic—kind of negativity is to suggest that Reconstruction's revolutionary problematic was overtaken by different historical and political questions in the twentieth century. Specifically, it was obscured by the pressing need to find ways of articulating and accounting for slavery's afterlives. In my introduction, I tweaked Toni Morrison's account of the legacies of slavery to suggest that the Reconstruction historical novel's fragile historical sense meant that it was not a genre to pass on. Since *Beloved,* it has been a critical commonplace to conceive of slavery's afterlives as the archetypically unpassable story (both in the sense of being impossible to avoid and inexpressible). I want to suggest that the gothic temporal frameworks that writers and cultural critics developed to recover, figure, and foreground slavery's traumatic history also made the institution's specifically revolutionary afterlives more difficult to conceive. We can see this dilemma condensed in the fact that the narrative present from which Morrison's characters iterate and reinterpret slavery into "re-memory" is (without it being spoken) Reconstruction.[12] In the sense preempted by Chesnutt, Reconstruction loses its epochal character to the same degree that the history of slavery is figured as a haunting presence.

In this changed context, Reconstruction became America's mythic unfinished revolution. A central argument of this book has been that conceiving of Reconstruction as America's *imagined* revolution changes the way we read its unfinished status. I want to end by venturing one possible further implication of this work and of the status of the unfinished as an organizing concept. In thinking about Reconstruction as revolution, I have engaged with work in literary, cultural, and historical studies that puts slavery and the plantation at the center of narratives of modernity. Much of this work is concerned with timelines of persistence and recurrence that seem anathema to the temporality of revolution. For this reason, a key question posed by this book as a whole is what place does revolution have, as a political and cultural afterlife of slavery, in these revised narratives? The concept of revolution—in particular, the social revolution as a thoroughgoing transformation in the fabric of society—is an important marker, and defining principle, of modernity that emerged in the long nineteenth century. And as I have argued, the history of Reconstruction gave rise to cultural attempts to imagine revolution. In this case, can the important scholarly attempt to reconstruct the plantation South as a locus of modernity—to find in its history and culture the outlines of what Amy Clukey calls a "plantation modernity"—dispense with revolution as a central political experience and rubric for cultural imaginaries?[13]

The answer given here is no. While I have sought to complicate the account of Reconstruction as unfinished revolution, the work done in this book is unfinished in an important regard. My argument suggests that more needs to be done to investigate the cultural forms that make revolution appear as a vital experience in the afterlife of slavery, even when slavery's effects continue into the present.

NOTES

Introduction: Revolution and the Historical Novel of Reconstruction

1. W. E. B. Du Bois, *Black Reconstruction in America, 1860–1880* (1935; New York: Free Press, 1992), 727.

2. Claude Bowers, *The Tragic Era: The Revolution after Lincoln* (Cambridge, MA: Riverside Press, 1929).

3. Eric Foner, *Reconstruction: America's Unfinished Revolution, 1863–1877* (New York: Perennial Classics, 1989). The phrase *second Reconstruction* is C. Vann Woodward's. *The Strange Career of Jim Crow*, 3rd rev. ed. (Oxford: Oxford University Press, 1974), 8–9. By hinging his account of Reconstruction's radicalism on the way it presaged the activist state of the twentieth-century civil rights revolution, Foner used Woodward's framework somewhat against Woodward's attempt to defend Reconstruction from its detractors on the basis of its "essentially nonrevolutionary and conservative" character. C. Vann Woodward, quoted in Eric Foner, "Reconstruction Revisited," *Reviews in American History* 10, no. 4 (1982): 84.

4. Du Bois, *Black Reconstruction,* 30.

5. For the classic account, see Georg Lukács, *The Historical Novel,* trans. Hannah Mitchell and Stanley Mitchell (1955; London: Merlin, 1962).

6. Haiti and the United States present different emancipatory contexts. However, despite their differences and the qualifications attending to U.S. emancipation—including the delay and limited scope of the constitutional amendments enforcing it—Haiti and the United States were unique among New World slave societies for ending slavery wholesale by armed violence.

7. Eric Foner, *The Second Founding: How the Civil War and Reconstruction Remade the Constitution* (New York: Norton, 2019), 3, 198.

8. Gregory P. Downs, *Declarations of Dependence: The Long Reconstruction of Popular Politics in the South, 1861–1908* (Chapel Hill: University of North Carolina Press, 2011), 1–2, 7–12, 77–78.

9. I am guided by social historians who trace how freed people transformed debates over political and civil freedoms into a broader resistance against the everyday practices of life and labor under plantation slavery, including direct supervision of work, physical punishment, management of free time, and control over mobility and public assembly. An inexhaustive list of these works includes Barbara J. Fields, *Slavery and Freedom on the Middle Ground: Maryland during the Nineteenth Century* (New Haven: Yale University Press, 1985); Julie Saville, *The Work of Reconstruction: From Slave to Wage Laborer in South Carolina, 1860–1870* (Cambridge: Cam-

bridge University Press, 1994); Steven Hahn, *A Nation under Our Feet: Black Political Struggles in the Rural South from Slavery to the Great Migration* (Cambridge: Harvard University Press, 2005); Susan E. O'Donovan, *Becoming Free in the Cotton South* (Cambridge: Harvard University Press, 2007); Thavolia Glymph, *Out of the House of Bondage: The Transformation of the Plantation Household* (Cambridge: Cambridge University Press, 2008).

10. Barbara J. Fields, "Ideology and Race in American History," in *Region, Race, and Reconstruction: Essays in Honor of C. Vann Woodward*, ed. J. Morgan Kousser and James M. McPherson (Oxford: Oxford University Press, 1982), 154.

11. Sutton Griggs, *Imperium in Imperio: A Study of the Negro Race Problem* (Cincinnati: Editor Publishing Company, 1899), 188. Hereafter cited parenthetically in the text.

12. Tess Chakkalakal and Kenneth W. Warren, "Introduction," in *Jim Crow, Literature, and the Legacy of Sutton E. Griggs*, ed. Tess Chakkalakal and Kenneth W. Warren (Athens: University of Georgia Press, 2013), 5.

13. Brook Thomas notes that the term *Reconstruction* mediated between restoration and revolution as possible outcomes of the Civil War. "The Literature of Reconstruction and the Worlds the Civil War Might Have Made," in *The Cambridge Companion to the Literature of the Civil War and Reconstruction* ed. Kathleen Diffley and Coleman Hutchison (Cambridge: Cambridge University Press, 2022), 170–71.

14. Reinhart Kosselleck, *Futures Past: On the Semantics of Historical Time* (New York: Columbia University Press, 2004), 44.

15. Kosselleck, *Futures Past*, 11.

16. Kosselleck, *Futures Past*, 49–50; Raymond Williams, *Keywords: A Vocabulary of Culture and Society*, rev. ed. (New York: Oxford University Press, 1985), 192–93.

17. Neil Davidson, *How Revolutionary Were the Bourgeois Revolutions?* (Chicago: Haymarket, 2012), 103–4; Michel-Rolph Trouillot, *Silencing the Past: Power and the Production of History* (1995; Boston: Beacon Press, 2005), 73–88; C. L. R. James, *The Black Jacobins* (1938; London: Penguin, 2001).

18. Saidiya Hartman, *Scenes of Subjection: Terror, Slavery, and Self-Making in Nineteenth Century America* (Oxford: Oxford University Press, 1997), 168–69; Hannah Arendt, *On Revolution* (London: Penguin, 1963), 72.

19. Sacvan Bercovitch, *The American Jeremiad* (1978; Madison: University of Wisconsin Press, 2012), 173–80.

20. George Bancroft, *The Necessity, the Reality, and the Promise of the Progress of the Human Race* (New York: New York Historical Society, 1854), 10.

21. Bancroft, *Necessity*, 36.

22. William Dunning, *Reconstruction, Political and Economic, 1865–1877* (New York: Harper and Brothers, 1907), 88, xvi, xv.

23. Dunning, *Reconstruction*, 142.

24. Bowers, *Tragic Era*, vi.

25. Bowers, *Tragic Era*, 538.

26. William Wells Brown, *The Negro in the American Rebellion: His Heroism and His Fidelity* (Boston: Lee and Shephard, 1867), v.

27. Brown, *Negro in the American Rebellion*, 45.

28. Brown, *Negro in the American Rebellion,* 53–54. On Brown's fragmented historical method as a riposte to Romantic historicism's failure to contend with slavery, see John Ernest, *"The Negro in the American Rebellion:* William Wells Brown and the Design of African American History," in *Literary Cultures of the Civil War,* ed. Timothy Sweet (Athens: University of Georgia Press, 2016).

29. Carl Schurtz, *Report on the Condition of the South* (1865; Salt Lake City: Project Gutenberg, 2005), https://www.gutenberg.org/cache/epub/8872/pg8872.html.

30. Schurtz, *Report on the Condition of the South,* n.p.

31. Schurtz, *Report on the Condition of the South,* n.p.

32. Notably, Schurtz abandoned Radical Reconstruction to join the Liberal Republicans after the passage of the Reconstruction Amendments, when "the logic of the great revolution" pulled the nation-state too far into the South's insurrectionary flux.

33. Foner is in part using Reconstruction to answer the question of why the United States did not develop a social democratic welfare state. As Noel Ignatiev argues, his understanding of revolution bears traces of the Popular Front conception of bourgeois revolution, which demonstrates the same focus on transition toward a revolutionary terminus in the form of the liberal state. "'The American Blindspot': Reconstruction According to Eric Foner and W. E. B. Du Bois," *Labor / Le Travail* 31 (Spring 1993): 243–51. For the strained attempt to make a Popular Front conception of bourgeois revolution fit the Civil War, see Andrew Zimmerman, "From the Second American Revolution to the Third International and Back Again: Marxism, the Popular Front, and the American Civil War," in *The World the Civil War Made,* ed. Gregory P. Downs and Kate Masur (Chapel Hill: University of North Carolina Press, 2015), 324–29. The novels I analyze do something of the dialectical work Zimmerman calls for when he emphasizes the need to return "the history of revolution to the centre of the American Civil War and the American Civil War to the centre of the history of revolution" (305).

34. Alain Badiou, *Being and Event,* trans. Oliver Fetham (London: Continuum, 2005), 16–18, 175–78.

35. Fredric Jameson, *The Antinomies of Realism* (London: Verso, 2013), 271–72.

36. Jameson, *Antinomies of Realism,* 272.

37. Louis Althusser et al., *Reading Capital: The Complete Edition,* trans. Ben Brewster and David Fernbach (London: Verso, 2015), 29.

38. Leigh Anne Duck, *The Nation's Region: Southern Modernism, Segregation, and U.S. Nationalism* (Athens: University of Georgia Press, 2009).

39. Sharon Kennedy-Nolle, *Writing Reconstruction: Race, Gender, and Citizenship in the Postwar South* (Chapel Hill: University of North Carolina Press, 2015), 4. With relation to literature's role in shaping political legitimacy, Scott Romine argues that "as political violence was organized into narrative form, fiction made history." "Fables of the Bloody Shirt: Reconstruction and the Problem of National Violence," in *A History of the Literature of the U.S. South,* ed. Harilous Stecopoulos (Cambridge: Cambridge University Press, 2021), 187.

40. See Arlin Turner, *George W. Cable: A Biography* (Durham, NC: Duke University Press, 1956), 269–70.

41. Tourgée's first biographer focuses on his political role in Reconstruction. Otto H. Olsen, *Carpetbagger's Crusade: The Life of Albion Winegar Tourgée* (Baltimore: Johns Hopkins Press,

1956). Two subsequent biographies interpret his literary career as central to his activism: Mark Elliott, *Color-Blind Justice: Albion Tourgée and the Quest for Racial Equality from the Civil War to Plessy v. Ferguson* (Oxford: Oxford University Press, 2006); Carolyn Karcher, *A Refugee from His Race: Albion W. Tourgée and His Fight against White Supremacy* (Chapel Hill: University of North Carolina Press, 2016).

42. Tourgée, "The South as a Field for Fiction," *Forum* 6 (1888): 404–13; "The Claim of 'Realism,'" *North American Review* 188, no. 388 (1889): 386–88.

43. Charles Chesnutt, *The Journals of Charles W. Chesnutt,* ed. Richard Broadhead (Durham, NC: Duke University Press, 1993), 125.

44. Chesnutt, *Journals,* 139–40.

45. Eric Gardner, *Black Print Unbound: The Christian Recorder, African American Literature, and Periodical Culture* (Oxford: Oxford University Press, 2015), 150.

46. David Blight, *Race and Reunion: The Civil War in American Memory* (Cambridge: Harvard University Press, 2001), 211–54.

47. Brook Thomas, *The Literature of Reconstruction: Not in Plain Black and White* (Baltimore: Johns Hopkins University Press, 2016), 2–3; Nina Silber, *The Romance of Reunion: Northerners and the South, 1865–1900* (Chapel Hill: University of North Carolina Press, 1993). For a critique of the "reunion" model, see K. Stephen Prince, *Stories of the South: Race and the Reconstruction of Southern Identity, 1865–1915* (Chapel Hill: University of North Carolina Press, 2014), 9.

48. Thomas, *Literature of Reconstruction,* 33–76. In *Writing Reconstruction,* Kennedy-Nolle focuses on how Reconstruction writers worked within the limits of racial and sectional ideologies to create more diverse ideas of the national polity grounded in local experience. For a similar reading of the myth of southern hospitality, in relation to Reconstruction, see Anthony Szczesiul, *The Southern Hospitality Myth: Ethics, Politics, and Race in American Memory* (Athens: University of Georgia Press, 2017), 130–68. For the (incompletely) inclusive and pedagogical nationalism of "citizen-building" in Reconstruction literature, see Peter Schmidt, *Sitting in Darkness: New South Fiction, Education, and the Rise of Jim Crow Colonialism, 1865–1920* (Jackson: University Press of Mississippi, 2008), 42, 35–75.

49. Jennifer Rae Greeson argues that the Reconstruction South was imagined as a "domestic Africa" that provided an exceptionalist origin story for American imperialism. *Our South: Geographic Fantasy and the Rise of National Literature* (Cambridge: Harvard University Press, 2010), 251. Scott Romine argues that white southern writers reinvented Reconstruction and redemption as colonial and postcolonial encounters as "a means of recolonizing white America." "Things Falling Apart: The Postcolonial Condition of *Red Rock* and *The Leopard's Spots,*" in *Look Away: The South in New World Studies,* ed. Jon Smith and Deborah Cohn (Durham, NC: Duke University Press, 2004), 195, 183–84. Peter Schmidt argues that "Reconstruction-era modes of creating subjects rather than citizens" helped construct an ideology of "Jim Crow colonialism." *Sitting in Darkness,* 90. For cultural histories that root segregationist conceptions of whiteness in Reconstruction memory, see Bruce E. Baker, *What Reconstruction Meant: Historical Memory in the U.S. South* (Charlottesville: University of Virginia Press, 2007), 45–53; Grace Elizabeth Hale, *Making Whiteness: The Culture of Segregation in the U.S. South, 1890–1940* (1998; New York: Vintage, 1999), 75–85.

50. For a state of the field essay that takes this approach to Reconstruction's neglect and recovery, see Elizabeth Renker, "Reconstruction Literature," in *American Literature in Transition, 1851–1877,* ed. Cody Marrs (Cambridge: Cambridge University Press, 2022), 322–36. Renker makes similar arguments about poetry in "What Is 'Reconstruction Poetry'?" *American Literary History* 30, no. 3 (2018): 509–10.

51. Cody Marrs and Christopher Hager, "Against 1865: Reperiodizing the Nineteenth Century," *J19: The Journal of Nineteenth-Century Americanists* 1, no. 2 (Fall 2013): 266. They argue against "the Civil War's status as a terminus in American literary history" (260).

52. In the introduction to their state of the field collection, Kathleen Diffley and Coleman Hutchison argue that the combination of temporal and political approaches I have identified—a "sense of continuity" and a "capacious definition" of literature—encapsulates what Reconstruction literature is. In *Cambridge Companion to the Literature of the Civil War and Reconstruction,* 4.

53. Marrs, "Three Theses on Reconstruction," *American Literary History* 30, no. 3 (Fall 2018): 408, 409–10. On "the Long Civil War," see Cody Marrs, *Nineteenth-Century American Literature and the Long Civil War* (Oxford: Oxford University Press, 2015).

54. Thomas, *Literature of Reconstruction,* 26–27. Signaling the order for federal troops in South Carolina and Louisiana not to intervene to defend Republican state governments following the disputed Hayes-Tilden election, the date forms an important moment in the transition to a solidly Democratic South. Thomas argues that it is not in any simple way the end of a political or literary era, which he dates to 1909.

55. Edward Sugden, *Emergent Worlds: Alternative States in Nineteenth-Century American Culture* (New York: New York University Press, 2018), 7. See Dana Luciano, *Arranging Grief: Sacred Time and the Body in Nineteenth-Century America* (New York: New York University Press, 2008); Lloyd Pratt, *Archives of American Time: Literature and Modernity in the Nineteenth Century* (Philadelphia: University of Pennsylvania Press, 2010); Peter Coviello, *Tomorrow's Parties: Sex and the Untimely in Nineteenth-Century America* (New York: New York University Press, 2013); Cindy Weinstein, *Time, Tense, and American Literature: When Is Now?* (Cambridge: Cambridge University Press, 2015); Jeffrey Insko, *History, Abolition, and the Ever-Present Now in Antebellum American Writing* (Oxford: Oxford University Press, 2018).

56. Marrs, "Three Theses," 414.

57. I have in mind Barbara Fields's critique of discussions of race in America that repeat Ulrich Bonnell Phillips's assertion that the attempt to enforce white supremacy is the central theme of southern history. "Ideology and Race," 143–77. See Ulrich B. Phillips "The Central Theme of Southern History," *American Historical Review* 34, no. 1 (1928): 30–43.

58. David Scott, *Conscripts of Modernity: The Tragedy of Colonial Enlightenment* (Durham, NC: Duke University Press, 2004), 4.

59. George Dekker, *The American Historical Romance* (Cambridge: Cambridge University Press, 1987), 8.

60. Toni Morrison, *Beloved* (1987; London: Vintage, 2010), 323.

61. Hartman, *Scenes of Subjection,* 116, 169.

62. Jared Sexton articulates its central question: "how does one mark time and think historicity . . . or make sense of lived experience, the lived experience of the black no less, without

break or interval or punctuation in the fact of (anti)blackness?" "The Social Life of Social Death," *InTensions* 5 (2011): 6.

63. Ian Baucom argues that the Atlantic slave trade haunts the historicist imagination as an "uncanny, reiterative temporality" because Romantic historicism shares a logic of abstraction with the commodity relations of slavery. I complicate the binary this poses between historicism and continuity throughout this book, particularly in my account of the relationship between embodied value in slavery and racial embodiment after emancipation, in chapter 3. *Spectres of the Atlantic: Finance Capital, Slavery, and the Philosophy of History* (Durham, NC: Duke University Press, 2005), 120; on historicism, see 43–47; on exchange, 65–72.

64. Steven Hahn, *The Political Worlds of Slavery and Freedom* (Cambridge: Harvard University Press, 2009), 114.

65. Lukács, *Historical Novel*, 60.

66. Cable's novel was initially serialized in *Century Magazine* before being published as a book in 1880.

67. Georg Lukács, *Historical Novel*, 19–24.

68. This argument has been central to Jameson's conception of the form, leading him to question whether it is still possible, under the conditions of late capitalism, to generate the "perception of the present as history; that is, as a relationship to the present which somehow defamiliarizes it and allows us that distance from immediacy which is at length characterized as a historical perspective." *Postmodernism, or, The Cultural Logic of Late Capitalism* (Durham, NC: Duke University Press, 1991), 284.

69. As Jameson notes, Lukács uses Scott's romance as a prehistory for his arguments about realism's capacity to historicize the present. Jameson, *The Antinomies of Realism* (London: Verso, 2013), 264.

70. George Dekker, *American Historical Romance*, 24–25.

71. It is worth recalling Lukács's argument in *The Theory of the Novel* that the novel is already an anachronistic approximation of epic wholeness because "the historico-philosophical moment at which great novels become possible" is precisely when capital's abstract totality supplants the epic's integrated world. (1915; London: Merlin, 1971), 88.

72. Lukács, *Historical Novel*, 61–62.

73. James Chandler, *England in 1819: The Politics of Literary Culture and the Case of Romantic Historicism* (Chicago: University of Chicago Press, 1998), 150–51; Lukács, *Historical Novel*, 26, 38–45, 60–63.

74. For the focus on systems of manners, see Chandler, *England in 1819*, 140, 149.

75. I borrow the claim about reading from Timothy Bewes's account of Lukács's *The Theory of the Novel* in "Reading with the Grain: A New World in Literary Criticism," *differences* 21, no. 3 (2010): 1–33.

76. Woodrow Wilson, "The Reconstruction of the Southern States," *Atlantic Monthly* 87 (1901): 1.

77. Wilson, "Reconstruction of the Southern States," 14. See also Romine, "Fables of the Bloody Shirt," 201–2.

78. Wilson, "Reconstruction of the Southern States," 1.

79. Thomas Dixon, *The Leopard's Spots: A Romance of the White Man's Burden—1865–1900* (1902; Gretna, LA: Pelican, 2001), 435. Hereafter cited parenthetically in the text.

80. For the way that Dixon exploits postcolonial defeat as an invented tradition, see Romine, "Postcolonial Condition," 193–94.

81. Michael Rogin, "The Sword Became a Flashing Vision: D. W. Griffith's *The Birth of a Nation,*" *Representations* 9 (1985): 151; Du Bois, *Black Reconstruction,* 711.

82. Thomas Nelson Page, *Red Rock: A Chronicle of Reconstruction* (New York: Charles Scribner's Sons, 1904), x. "The southerner's problem" is the subtitle of Page's 1904 essay collection. For Page, because "the only thing that stands between the people of the North and the Negroes is the South," the nation should allow the South its apparently "feudal instinct" in exchange for acting as labor managers, capable of integrating a subject population into the modern state. *The Negro: The Southerner's Problem* (New York: Charles Scribner's Sons, 1904), 28, 214.

83. Raymond Williams, *Modern Tragedy* (London: Chatto and Windus, 1966), 65.

84. Karl Marx, *The Eighteenth Brumaire of Louis Bonaparte* (1869; Moscow: Progress Publishers, 1972), 33–34.

85. Marx, *Eighteenth Brumaire,* 10. Even his famous speculative dictum that "the social revolution of the nineteenth century cannot draw its poetry from the past but only from the future" comes from an analysis of the revolutionary present as anachronous experience (12–13).

86. Not for nothing did Du Bois and C. L. R. James both find in the *Brumaire*'s moving dynamics of revolutionary contradiction the outlines for their own historical narratives of slave revolution, in *Black Reconstruction* and *The Black Jacobins* (1938), respectively.

87. Ernst Bloch, "Nonsynchronism and the Obligation to Its Dialectics," trans. Mark Ritter, *New German Critique* 11 (1977): 32. Bloch's ideas mediate between a discussion of a "synchronous contradiction" between bourgeois capitalism and the proletariat (influenced by Lukács) and the uneven development of revolutionary dialectics in a moment of German capitalist development when monopoly capitalism coexisted with a semi-incorporated peasant economy.

88. Mark Twain, *Adventures of Huckleberry Finn* (1885; Oxford: Oxford University Press, 1999), 261.

89. Du Bois, *Black Reconstruction,* 708.

1. Liberalism and George Washington Cable's Impossible Allegories

1. For the way Cable negotiated the local color genre's geographical fantasies about the national subsumption of quasi-colonial difference, see Greeson, *Our South,* 259–68; on the expropriative imaginary of literary regionalism more generally, see Richard Broadhead, *Cultures of Letters: Scenes of Reading and Writing in Nineteenth-Century America* (Chicago: University of Chicago Press, 1993), 107–42.

2. George Washington Cable, "Literature in the Southern States," in *The Negro Question: A Selection of Writings on Civil Rights in the South,* ed. Arlin Turner (New York: Norton, 1968), 43.

3. George Washington Cable, "The Negro Question," in *The Negro Question* (1890; New York: Charles Scribner's Sons, 1898), 27–28.

4. Cable, "Literature in the Southern States," 45

5. Cable, "Literature in the Southern States," 43.

6. For work that cites the speech as evidence of Cable's progressivism, see Katharine A. Burnett, "Moving toward a 'No South': George Washington Cable's Global Vision in *The Grandissimes,*" *Southern Literary Journal* 45, no. 1 (Fall 2012): 21–25; Karsten H. Piep, "Liberal Visions of Reconstruction: Lydia Maria Child's *Romance of the Republic* and George Washington Cable's *The Grandissimes,*" *Studies in American Fiction* 31, no. 2 (Fall 2003): 183; Joel Williamson, *The Crucible of Race: Black-White Relations in the American South since Emancipation* (Oxford: Oxford University Press, 1984), 96; Greeson, *Our South,* 266–68. Greeson sees the address's progressivism as tied to the imperialist imperatives of post-Reconstruction regionalism.

7. Cable, "Literature in the Southern States," 44.

8. George Washington Cable, "The Silent South," *Century Magazine* 30 (August 1885): 675.

9. C. Vann Woodward included Cable in his early roster of forgotten southern liberals. *American Counterpoint: Slavery and Racism in the North-South Dialogue* (1964; Oxford: Oxford University Press, 1983), 189, 212–13. See also Williamson, *Crucible of Race,* 93–108; Paul M. Gaston, *The New South Creed: A Study in Southern Myth-Making* (New York: Alfred A. Knopf, 1970), 140–45. For literary historians, see Louis D. Rubin, *George Washington Cable: The Life and Times of a Southern Heretic* (New York: Pegasus, 1969); Fred Hobson, *Tell about the South: The Southern Rage to Explain* (Baton Rouge: Louisiana State University Press, 1983), 105–26. From different political perspectives, Rubin and Hobson respond to Edmund Wilson's contention that Cable's liberalism was an imported trait: the result of "New England blood which was mingled in him with that of the Virginian." Wilson, *Patriotic Gore: Studies in the Literature of the American Civil War* (London: André Deutsch, 1962), 559.

10. For Ladd, *The Grandissimes* provides "an anatomy of the official optimism of the postbellum United States as it is constructed upon the tragic history of slavery and colonialism," one that nevertheless disavows the "fundamental ethno-centrism" underpinning his liberal nationalism. *Nationalism and the Color Line in George W. Cable, Mark Twain, and William Faulkner* (Baton Rouge: Louisiana State University Press, 1996), 77, 41. Wagner argues that Cable's construction of folk culture makes racism a product of the southern patriarchal past, disavowing the anti-Black violence of the modern police power. "Disarmed and Dangerous: The Strange Career of Bras-Coupé," *Representations* 92, no. 1 (Fall 2005): 125–31. Best and Hartman contend that Cable's anti-segregationism disavows the role of the state in structuring apparently inevitable "private" racial judgments. Hartman, *Scenes of Subjection,* 166–70, 203–4; Stephen Best, *The Fugitive's Properties: Law and the Poetics of Possession* (Chicago: University of Chicago Press, 2004), 209–17.

11. Best, *Fugitive's Properties,* 209.

12. Cable, "Negro Question," 27–28.

13. Daniel Immerwahr, "Caste or Colony: Indianizing Race in the United States," *Modern Intellectual History* 4, no. 2 (2007): 275–301.

14. Oliver Cromwell Cox, *Caste, Class, and Race: A Study in Social Dynamics* (1948; New York: Monthly Review Press, 1959), 450–53, 489–508.

15. Cox, *Caste, Class, and Race,* 312–13, 485–88, 528–38. Much of the definitional ambiguity Cox critiqued in midcentury liberal approaches to caste characterizes the term's recent popular rejuvenation to describe contemporary American racism. See Isabel Wilkerson, *Caste: The Lies That Divide Us* (New York: Allen Lane, 2020), which sees race less as a changing system of domination than a timeless expression of insidious beliefs in caste hierarchy.

16. Cox, *Caste, Class, and Race,* 505–6.

17. Charles Sumner, "The Question of Caste," *The Works of Charles Sumner,* 20 vols. (Boston: Lee and Sheppard, 1870–83), 13:141, 161.

18. Charles Sumner, "Question of Caste," 168.

19. For the latter, see Greeson, *Our South,* 254–68; Schmidt, *Sitting in Darkness,* 3–31; Romine, "Things Falling Apart," 175–200.

20. Cable, "Negro Question," 27.

21. Cable, "Silent South," 674.

22. "Topics of the Time: Battles and Leaders of the Civil War," *Century Magazine* 28 (October 1884): 943.

23. *Civil Rights Cases,* 109 U.S. 3 (1883): 13, https://www.loc.gov/item/usrep109003.

24. George Washington Cable, "The Freedmen's Case in Equity," *Century Magazine* 29 (January 1885): 409, 417. Hereafter cited parenthetically in the text.

25. Sharon Monteith and Suzanne W. Jones, "Introduction: South to New Places," in *South to a New Place: Region, Literature, Culture,* ed. Suzanne W. Jones and Sharon Monteith (Baton Rouge: Louisiana State University Press, 2002), 2.

26. I have in mind Rubin's portrait of Cable as a "southern heretic," both in the sense that his ideas constituted heresy in the New South and that his heresy was somehow traditionally "southern." Rubin, *George W. Cable.*

27. Eric Foner, *Politics and Ideology in the Age of the Civil War* (Oxford: Oxford University Press, 1980), 98.

28. Foner, *Politics and Ideology,* 108, see also 101–11. On the formerly enslaved plantation household as the social and productive unit central to resisting the contractual demands of free labor (especially for women), see Thavolia Glymph, *Out of the House of Bondage: The Transformation of the Plantation Household* (Cambridge: Cambridge University Press, 2008), 122–24, 150–55, 209–18.

29. Scott Marler, "Fables of the Reconstruction, Reconstruction of the Fables," *Journal of the Historical Society* 4, no. 1 (Winter 2004): 128, 118–26. See also Foner, *Reconstruction,* 170–74, 210–13, 230–35. According to Stacy L. Smith, as both the site in which the federal government interceded to arbitrate against bonded labor and the terrain in which new coercive labor relations were established, the plantation South formed a key reference point for jurists and capitalists seeking to define and reconstruct the boundaries of bonded labor on a national scale, especially in the West. "Emancipating Peons, Excluding Coolies: Reconstructing Coercion in the American West," in Downs and Masur, *World the Civil War Made,* 46–74.

30. For C. Vann Woodward, this combination defines the South's "colonial economy." His schematic separation of northern and southern capital risks misrecognizing white southerners as the region's colonial subjects, but he captures how an influx of speculative capital for railroads, extractive industries, and manufacturing existed alongside systems of agrarian monoculture whose primary reproductive mechanism (bound labor) limited the "developmental" horizons of capital. This tension created the conditions for what Woodward argues was a periodically hysterical cultural investment in modernization alongside the ephemeral impact of economic investment. *Origins of the New South* (1951; Baton Rouge: Louisiana State University Press, 1971), 291–320.

31. Turner, *George W. Cable*, 72.

32. Turner, *George W. Cable*, 223. On the awkward coexistence between New Orleans merchant capital and the "country store," see Scott Marler, *The Merchant's Capital: New Orleans and the Political Economy of the Nineteenth-Century South* (Cambridge: Cambridge University Press, 2013), 210–24.

33. Edward L. Ayres, *The Promise of the New South: Life after Reconstruction* (Oxford: Oxford University Press, 1992), 159.

34. George Washington Cable, *Old Creole Days* (1879; New York: Charles Scribner's Sons, 1883), 142. Hereafter cited parenthetically in the text.

35. William Faulkner, *As I Lay Dying* (1930; London: Vintage, 2004), 40.

36. Antonio Gramsci, *Selections from the Prison Notebooks,* ed. Quintin Hoare and Geoffrey Nowell-Smith (London: Lawrence and Wishart, 1971), 276.

37. Nasser Mufti, *Civilizing War: Imperial Politics and the Poetics of National Rupture* (Evanston, IL: Northwestern University Press, 2017), 168.

38. Mufti, *Civilizing War,* 166, 168.

39. George Washington Cable, *The Grandissimes: A Story of Creole Life* (1880; London: Penguin, 1988), 269. Hereafter cited parenthetically in the text.

40. Gramsci, *Selections from the Prison Notebooks,* 276.

41. *Civil Rights Cases,* 17.

42. *Civil Rights Cases,* 25; Colin Dayan, *The Law Is a White Dog* (Princeton: Princeton University Press, 2011), 239.

43. Henry Grady, "In Plain Black and White: A Reply to Mr. Cable," *Century Magazine* 29 (April 1885): 912.

44. Grady, "In Plain Black and White," 910–11, 912.

45. Cable, "Silent South," 678.

46. For the class argument, see Hale, *Making Whiteness,* 44–51. On Cable's attachments to race, see Hartman, *Scenes of Subjection,* 203–4; Best, *Fugitives Properties,* 206–16.

47. Hartman, *Scenes of Subjection,* 203–4. Wagner makes a similar argument about *The Grandissimes* and the police power. "Disarmed and Dangerous," 125–31.

48. Scott Romine, "Southern Affects: Field and Feeling in a Skeptical Age," in *The Oxford Handbook of the Literature of the U.S. South,* ed. Fred Hobson and Barbara Ladd (Oxford: Oxford University Press, 2016), 165, 169.

49. Michael Kreyling notes the post–*Brown v. Board* reconstruction of Cable's literary reputation in these terms in his introduction to the Penguin Classics edition of *The Grandissimes* (xvii–xix). In an early attempt to return *The Grandissimes* to the American literary canon, Richard Chase notes its "truly Faulknerian strain of dark melodrama." *The American Novel and Its Tradition* (1957; Baltimore: Johns Hopkins University Press, 1980), 168. More recently, Ladd, in *Nationalism and the Color Line,* places *The Grandissimes* alongside *Absalom, Absalom!* as key texts in her analysis of U.S. nationalism and the color line. Romine identifies Cable as a progenitor of an affect, if not ideology, that underpins "multiple discourses of 'I [don't] hate it.'" "Southern Affects," 170.

50. For the relationship between these two periods as plotted by another version of the historical novel of Reconstruction, see chapter 3.

51. The disjunction of allegorical spaces itself is more important to my reading than the question of whether Cable embraces or disavows this hemispheric space. See Burnett, "Moving toward a 'No South,'" 21–38. On the Bras Coupé folktale and the Haitian revolution, see Ladd, *Nationalism and the Color Line*, 65–77; Wagner, "Disarmed and Dangerous." For two important collections that use transnational approaches to uncover literary histories of alternative Souths, see Jones and Monteith, *South to a New Place*; Smith and Cohen, *Look Away*.

52. Wagner, "Disarmed and Dangerous," 128; Ladd, *Nationalism and the Color Line*, 47–48.

53. The difficulty might be avoided by imagining that Cable intends the parallel to be 1876/7, in which case the compromise that settled the disputed Hayes-Tilden election might be read as a second secession, but this would ignore the extent to which Cable depicts the Creole elite in terminal crisis.

54. Jameson, *Antinomies of Realism*, 270–71.

55. Charles Swann, "*The Grandissimes*: A Story-Shaped World," *Literature and History* 13, no. 2 (1987): 257–77.

56. See Greeson, *Our South*, 241–51, 261.

57. Mrs. John S. Kendall, "Cable, George Washington (1844–)," in *Library of Southern Literature*, 17 vols., ed. Edwin Anderson Alderman and Joel Chandler Harris (Atlanta: Martin and Hoyte, 1909–13), 2:622.

58. Ladd, *Nationalism and the Color Line*, 47–51; Swann, "Story Shaped World," 270.

59. Michel Foucault, "Nietzsche, Genealogy, History," in *The Foucault Reader*, ed. Paul Rabinow (New York: Pantheon Books, 1984), 77. Werner Sollors details how in segregationist thought genealogy "usurp[s] the terms of blood and kinship," producing an illusory authority for the category of race by conflating it with descent. *Neither Black nor White, yet Both: Thematic Explorations of Interracial Literature* (Oxford: Oxford University Press, 1997), 43–44.

60. Ladd argues that Cable uses Creole anxieties about the displacement of French civil law by American common law—in which descent from the mother became the legal basis for proving one's race, and hence for justifying inheritance—to focus the reader's attention on mixed-race histories. *Nationalism and the Color Line*, 48–51.

61. Charles Gayarré, *The Creoles of History and the Creoles of Romance: A Lecture Delivered in the Hall of the Tulane University, New Orleans* (New Orleans: C. E. Hopkins, 1885), 28.

62. Alfred Tennyson, "Flower in the Crannied Wall," in *The Major Works* (Oxford: Oxford University Press, 2000), 379.

63. Foucault, "Nietzsche," 83, 86.

2. Albion Tourgée and the Ironies of the Reconstruction State

1. Karl Marx, "Address of the International Workingmen's Association to Abraham Lincoln," in Robin Blackburn, *An Unfinished Revolution: Karl Marx and Abraham Lincoln* (London: Verso, 2011), 211–12.

2. On Marx's "social republicanism," see William Clare Roberts, *Marx's Inferno: The Political Theory of Capital* (Princeton: Princeton University Press, 2017).

3. Albion Tourgée, *A Fool's Errand* (New York: Fords, Howard, and Hulbert, 1879), 337. Hereafter cited parenthetically in the text.

4. Duck, *Nation's Region*, 22.

5. *Plessy v. Ferguson,* 163 U.S. 537 (1896), 550, https://www.loc.gov/item/usrep163537.

6. Foner, *Reconstruction,* 233, On how this ideological tension shaped Radical Republican labor policy in the South and constitutional ideas, see 142–70, 228–80.

7. Du Bois, *Black Reconstruction,* 183.

8. Straining somewhat to capture this genealogy, Tourgée's biographer Mark Elliott frames it as an "ontological notion of the self" rather than an ideology, which avoids the laissez-faire determinism that overtook the Republican Party from the 1870s. *Color-Blind Justice,* 7.

9. Karcher, *Refugee from His Race,* xi. David Blight places Tourgée's work in a tradition forged by the conflict between activist memory and a culture of forgetting following the Civil War. *Race and Reunion,* 217–21. A similar periodization frames Brook Thomas's dating of the era of Reconstruction in his book *The Literature of Reconstruction,* in which Tourgée is a central figure.

10. Christopher Taylor, *Empire of Neglect: The West Indies in the Wake of British Liberalism* (Durham, NC: Duke University Press, 2018), 76.

11. Arendt, *On Revolution,* 33, 65, 88, 88–100.

12. Arendt, *On Revolution,* 72. See Seyla Benhabib, *The Reluctant Modernism of Hannah Arendt* (London: Sage Publications, 1996), 160; Richard H. King, *Arendt and America* (Chicago: University of Chicago Press, 2015), 8; Hartman, *Scenes of Subjection,* 168–69.

13. Albion Tourgée, *Bricks without Straw* (New York: Fords, Howard, and Hulbert, 1880), 512, 508. Hereafter cited parenthetically in the text.

14. Brook Thomas demonstrates that Tourgée fuses Thaddeus Stevens's theory of "territorial acquisition" with Sumner's of "state suicide." *Literature of Reconstruction,* 78–84; Mark Elliot also draws the link to Stevens. *Color-Blind Justice,* 165–66.

15. Sumner, "Are We a Nation," 12:191–92, 192–93, 232, 244.

16. Thaddeus Stevens, "Reconstruction: Hon. Thaddeus Stevens on the Great Topic of the Hour. An Address Delivered to the Citizens of Lancaster, Sept. 6, 1865," *New York Times,* September 10, 1865, 2.

17. Stevens, "Reconstruction," 2.

18. Du Bois, *Black Reconstruction,* 121.

19. Greeson, *Our South,* 255. Mark Elliott calls the novel "one of the first shots fired in the struggle over the historical meaning of Reconstruction." *Color-Blind Justice,* 165. While Elliot notes the "often overlooked . . . possibility of renewed intervention on behalf of Black civil rights by the Federal Government," he does not elaborate on the irony of Tourgée promoting this possibility by enshrining Reconstruction's tragically inevitable failure (166).

20. James McPherson, *The Abolitionist Legacy: From Reconstruction to the NAACP* (Princeton: Princeton University Press, 1975), 102, 100.

21. See Romine, "Fables of the Bloody Shirt."

22. James S. Pike, *The Prostrate State: South Carolina under Negro Government* (New York: D. Appleton and Company, 1874), 12, 4.

23. Edward King, *The Great South* (Hartford, CT: American Publishing Company, 1875), I, 572, 465.

24. Albion Tourgée, *The Invisible Empire* (New York: Fords, Howard, and Hulbert, 1880), 385. The description of *A Fool's Errand* is taken from the enlarged subtitle on the book's title page.

25. Anna Julia Cooper, *A Voice from the South* (1892; Oxford: Oxford University Press, 1988), 89.

26. Quoted in Turner, *George W. Cable*, 291.

27. Sandra M. Gustafson, "Reimagining the Republic: Tourgée on Citizenship," in *Reimagining the Republic: Race, Citizenship, and Nation in the Literary Work of Albion W. Tourgée*, ed. Sandra M. Gustafson and Robert S. Levine (New York: Fordham University Press, 2022), 97–109. Kathryn Hamilton Warren argues that Tourgée employs empathy as a rhetorical model for democracy. "Empathetic Persuasion in Albion Tourgée's *A Fool's Errand*," *American Literary Realism* 44, no. 1 (Fall 2011): 49, 51–56. On empathy as Tourgée's democratic literary mode, see Karcher, *Refugee from His Race*, 53. Ben Railton sees a democratic model for the Republic in Tourgée's "heteroglossic" form. *Contesting the Past, Reconstructing the Nation: American Literature and Culture in the Gilded Age, 1876–1893* (Tuscaloosa: University of Alabama Press, 2007), 194–97. While she argues that Tourgée "embraces coercion," Gretchen Short sees democracy as his literary ideal. "The Dilemmas of Reconstructing the Nation in Albion W. Tourgée's *A Fool's Errand* and Charles W. Chesnutt's *The Marrow of Tradition*," *REAL* 14 (1998): 258.

28. Lionel Trilling, *Sincerity and Authenticity* (Oxford: Oxford University Press, 1972), 7.

29. Trilling, *Sincerity and Authenticity*, 70, 7–9. His quibble, in particular, is with Sartre and Marcuse (144–72).

30. See Adam Kelly, "Dialectic of Sincerity: Lionel Trilling and David Foster Wallace," *Post45*, October 17, 2014. https://post45.org/2014/10/dialectic-of-sincerity-lionel-trilling-and-david-foster-wallace. On the relationship between Arendt's and Trilling's attempts to rethink postwar liberalism through republican political ideas, see Anthony Hutchison, *Writing the Republic: Liberalism and Morality in American Fiction* (New York: Columbia University Press, 2007), 92–95.

31. Michael Elliott, *The Culture Concept: Writing and Difference in the Age of Realism* (Minneapolis: University of Minnesota Press, 2002), 61.

32. Tourgée, "Claim of 'Realism,'" 386.

33. Henry James, *The Bostonians* (1886; London: Penguin, 2000), 139.

34. Despite thinking Verena's speeches reflect "the crazy character of an age where such a performance . . . was treated as an intellectual effort, a contribution to a question," Basil nonetheless "felt her presence, tasted her voice," and is led to feel "a joyous sincerity" in his and Verena's committed disagreement (209–10). For Verena's part, Basil's desire to possess her "just as you are"—to render commitment personal and erotic rather than political—leads her to abandon "the feminine revolution" for "the revolution which was taking place in her," one that makes "the idea of giving herself to a man more agreeable to her than that of giving herself to a movement" (64, 127, 299–300).

35. Whereas Tourgée argued that the realists "tell only the weakest and meanest part of the grand truth which makes up the continued story of every life," he contended that the experience of heroism and pathos would put southern writers (and notably Black southerners) in the "very front rank" of American literature: "The history of literature shows that it is those who were cradled amid the smoke of battle, the sons and daughters of heroes yet red with slaughter, the inheritors of national woe or racial degradation, who have given utterance to the loftiest strains of genius." "South as a Field for Fiction," 411, 413.

36. For a reading of Tourgee's account of literary realism that also places him in ironic proximity to James, see Kenneth W. Warren, "Tourgee, Democracy, Romance, and the Art of Fiction," in Gustafson and Levine, *Reimagining the Republic*, 110–23.

37. Du Bois, *Black Reconstruction*, 57.

38. For important critiques of agency in the historiography of slavery, see Walter Johnson, "Agency: A Ghost Story," in *Slavery's Ghost: The Problem of Freedom in the Age of Emancipation*, ed. Jarod Roll (Baltimore: Johns Hopkins University Press, 2011); Hartman, *Scenes of Subjection*.

39. Du Bois, *Black Reconstruction*, 121.

40. Du Bois, *Black Reconstruction*, 121. See also chapter 4 of this book.

41. That this is, properly speaking, a difficulty is emphasized by David Roediger's important argument that historians' sympathetic take-up of Du Bois tends to privilege the revolutionary agency of the Republican Party. Even in highlighting slave revolution as Du Bois's theme, Roediger forces the problem back into the heroic binary. *Seizing Freedom: Slave Emancipation and Liberty for All* (London: Verso, 2015), 6–9.

42. For the way that formerly enslaved people appropriated access to the means of violence by using institutions such as the Republican Party and the Union League for paramilitary ends, see Hahn, *Nation under Our Feet*, 266–76.

43. Gregory P. Downs and Kate Masur, "Echoes of War: Rethinking Post–Civil War Governance and Politics," in Downs and Masur, *World the Civil War Made*, 7.

44. Downs, *Declarations of Dependence*, 75–100. While this may not have represented "bayonet rule," the struggle over the new means of violence still demonstrates that "political power in the Reconstruction South grew out of the barrel of a gun." Hahn, *Nation under Our Feet*, 283.

45. Bensel, *Yankee Leviathan*, 14, 238–43, 413.

46. Barbara J. Fields, "The Advent of Capitalist Agriculture: The New South in a Bourgeois World," in *Essays on the Postbellum Southern Economy*, ed. Thavolia Glymph and John J. Kushma (College Station: Texas A&M University Press, 1985), 87.

47. Hahn, *Nation under Our Feet*, 312.

48. Bensel, *Yankee Leviathan*, 415. See also Steven Hahn, "Class and State in Postemancipation Societies: Southern Planters in Comparative Perspective," *American Historical Review* 95, no. 1 (February 1990): 83–85, 93–98; Sven Beckert, *Empire of Cotton: A Global History* (New York: Vintage, 2015), 272–75, 310.

49. My questioning of the Reconstruction state as "project" draws on Nicos Poulantzas, who argues that "the state is not a simple tool or instrument manipulated by the ruling class" but a "relatively autonomous" structure through which "the differences and relations between fractions of capital" are fought out, asserted, and challenged. "The Problem of the Capitalist State," in *Ideology in Social Science: Readings in Critical Social Theory*, ed. Robin Blackburn (London: Fontana Press, 1972), 247, 244.

50. He refers to redemption as revolution on three occasions and only once as a counterrevolution.

51. See Hahn, *Nation under Our Feet*, 283, 313.

52. Brook Thomas argues that Tourgée's exaggerations highlight the government's unfulfilled promises because by the letter of the 1870/71 Enforcement Acts, "intervention by the national government required proof of an organized conspiracy." *Literature of Reconstruction*, 160.

53. Wilson, *Patriotic Gore,* 537.

54. See Everett Carter, "Edmund Wilson Refights the Civil War: The Revision of Albion Tourgée's Novels," *American Literary Realism* 29, no. 2 (Winter 1997): 69–70, 72.

55. Albion Tourgée, *An Appeal to Caesar* (New York: Fords, Howard, and Hulbert, 1884), 142–43.

56. On Tourgée as neo-Lamarckian, see Brook Thomas, *American Literary Realism and the Failed Promise of Contract* (Berkeley: University of California Press, 1997), 203–4.

57. Nancy Bentley argues that by metaphorizing citizenship through the kinship practices of formerly enslaved people, Tourgée foregrounds the messy instrumentality of the state in tying political to intimate life, rather than endorsing an organic (and allegorical) relationship between marriage and the nation, as does the traditional marriage plot. "Queer Synecdoche: Tourgée's *Bricks without Straw* and Black Kinship," in Gustafson and Levine, *Reimagining the Republic,* 44–56.

58. Tess Chakkalakal argues that African American writers reworked marriage and inheritance plots to imagine "the terms of a public sphere that was predicated upon the non-legal nature of the [marriage] relation." *Novel Bondage: Slavery, Marriage, and Freedom in Nineteenth-Century America* (Urbana: University of Illinois Press, 2011), 13–14. For Peter Coviello, slave narratives use "civically certified" marriage (and the legitimized sanction it provides for inheritance) to imagine a freedom not wholly ascribable to "autonomous self-possession" and "contractual citizenship." *Tomorrow's Parties,* 109. In particular, Tourgée's account of Nimbus's relationship to naming and property borrows heavily from Frederick Douglass's *Narrative of the Life of Frederick Douglass* (1845).

59. Blackness being conceived, through matrilineage, as at once an absence of inheritance and an inheritance of racial abjection. Hortense Spillers, "Mama's Baby, Papa's Maybe: An American Grammar Book," *Diacritics* 17, no. 2 (Summer 1987): 69, 74–76.

60. Hartman, *Scenes of Subjection,* 117.

61. This is Sharon Kennedy-Nolle's phrase for Tourgée's republican worldview in his first novel, *Toinette* (1874). *Writing Reconstruction,* 78–79. On the educational dynamic of paternalism and agency in *Bricks without Straw,* see Schmidt, *Sitting in Darkness,* 34, 55–56.

62. Karcher locates the origin of Nimbus's name in Tourgée's Civil War diary, arguing that its inclusion in the novel "embodies the unforgettable image of black manhood that his real-life model imprinted on the future author's memory." Strangely, she does not question why he reattributes his act to a slaveholder. "Introduction," *Bricks without Straw,* by Albion Tourgée, ed. Carolyn Karcher (Durham, NC: Duke University Press, 2009), 7.

63. Aaron Carico, *Black Market: The Slave's Value in National Culture after 1865* (Chapel Hill: University of North Carolina Press, 2020), 13.

64. Hartman, *Scenes of Subjection,* 115, 123. Another key critical reference point is Cheryl I. Harris, "Whiteness as Property," *Harvard Law Review* 106, no. 8 (1993): 1707–91.

65. Hartman, *Scenes of Subjection,* 6.

66. For Wilderson, this "scandal" is the continuity of anti-Blackness, which is "not only in excess of any semiotics of exploitation, but a grammar of suffering beyond signification itself." Frank Wilderson III, "Gramsci's Black Marx: Whither the Slave in Civil Society?" *Social Identities* 9, no. 2 (2003): 230. Best, *Fugitives Properties,* 13. More recently, Best has offered a different model of slavery's afterlife. Critiquing "melancholy historicism" as the dominant epis-

temological approach to "recovering" the history of slavery, he asks: "Why must we predicate having an ethical relation to the past on the idea that there is a continuity between that past and our present?" While he seems to question his previous argument about slavery and rights discourse, the essay's treatment of historicity as a question of recovery and belonging renders discontinuity an ontological rather than historical problem. This makes incommunicable that decidedly noncontinuous link between past and present called revolution. Stephen Best, *None Like Us: Blackness, Belonging, Aesthetic Life* (Durham, NC: Duke University Press, 2018), 72.

67. Jennifer Rae Greeson, "The Pre-History of Possessive Individualism," *PMLA* 127, no. 4 (October 2012): 918–24.

68. Hartman and Best argue for a "focus on sovereignlessness and statelessness," as they are masked in notions of liberal personhood's relationship to slavery, a focus that they argue "heralds a new direction in studies of slavery, one that takes a keen interest in the state and its designation of dispensable subjects." "Fugitive Justice," *Representations* 91, no. 2. (2005): 12.

69. The logical demand also becomes a better *language* of justice rather than a more just world. Wai-Chee Dimock reads segregated conceptions of the human capacity for reason in the *Plessy* Court's majority decision as characteristic of the era's rights discourse, before calling for "an alternate language, a language that, responsive to the many shades and meanings of reason, will perhaps bring to our awareness not only the absolute claim of rights, not only the absolute claim of justice, but also what is not resolved by these concepts." *Residues of Justice: Law, Literature, Philosophy* (Berkeley: University of California Press, 1996), 223.

70. C. B. MacPherson, *The Political Theory of Possessive Individualism: Hobbes to Locke* (Oxford: Oxford University Press, 1964), 227, 231.

71. MacPherson, *Political Theory of Possessive Individualism*, 273–74.

72. Carico, *Black Market*, 42.

73. I have in mind Stuart Hall's account of race and the crisis of the British postwar state: "In one of its principal dimensions, the crisis is *thematized through race*. Race is the prism through which British people are called upon to 'live through,' to understand, and then to deal with crisis conditions." "Race and 'Moral Panics' in Postwar Britain," in *Selected Writings on Race and Difference*, ed. Paul Gilroy and Ruth Wilson Gilmore (Durham, NC: Duke University Press, 2021), 63.

74. Mark Elliot, *Color-Blind Justice*, 262–96; Mark Golub, "*Plessy* as Passing: Judicial Responses to Ambiguously Raced Bodies in *Plessy v. Ferguson*," *Law and Society Review* 39 (September 2005): 565–68; Thomas J. Davies, "Race, Identity, and the Law: *Plessy v. Ferguson* (1896)," in *Race on Trial: Law and Justice in American History*, ed. Annette Gordon-Reed (Oxford: Oxford University Press, 2002), 70; J. Allen Douglas, "The 'Most Valuable Sort of Property': Constructing White Identity in America Law, 1880–1940," *San Diego Law Review* 40, no. 3 (August–September 2003): 891–93, 902, 912–16; Hartman, *Scenes of Subjection*, 194–95. Eric Sundquist argues that Tourgée constructs such an argument but also reveals ideas about race symptomatic of the late-century solidification of the color line. *To Wake the Nations: Race in the Making of American Literature* (Cambridge: Harvard University Press, 1993), 246–49.

75. *Plessy v. Ferguson*, 163 U.S. 537 (1896), 544.

76. Albion Tourgée, "Brief of the Plaintiff in Error," in *Undaunted Radical: The Selected Writings and Speeches of Albion W. Tourgée*, ed. Mark Elliot and John David Smith (Baton

Rouge: Louisiana State University Press, 2010), 318. Hereafter cited parenthetically in the text. Sundquist points out that Tourgée's anachronistic citations highlight the Court's role in "transfiguring dual *constitutional* citizenship into dual *racial* citizenship after Reconstruction." *To Wake the Nations*, 240–41.

77. Elliot, *Color-Blind Justice*, 286; Otto H. Olsen, *The Thin Disguise: Plessy v. Ferguson* (New York: Humanities Press, 1967), 16.

78. Elliot, *Color-Blind Justice*, 286.

79. Woodward, *American Counterpoint*, 224.

80. Sundquist argues that the "ironic . . . import" of Tourgée's argument exposes the "hallucinatory character of the Jim Crow laws that were ushered in by *Plessy*," but realizing its "rank paradoxicalness," he could not sustain it. *To Wake the Nations*, 247, 249. Mark Golub claims the argument is "an ironic commentary on the arbitrary nature of racial classifications." *Plessy* as Passing," 571. Mark Elliot calls it "a passage that dripped with irony" and argues that Tourgée raises it to appeal to a conservatively minded Court interested in defending property rights. *Color-Blind Justice*, 288, 284.

81. Rebecca Scott convincingly argues that the Comité des Citoyens appealed to a Creole discourse of "public rights," drawn from the local experience of Reconstruction in Louisiana. She argues that this category rejected the "imagined taxonomy of civil, political, and social rights" that structured the racist demonization of "social equality." "Public Rights, Social Equality, and the Conceptual Roots of the *Plessy* Challenge," *Michigan Law Review* 106, no. 5 (2008): 781.

82. In J. Allen Douglas's words, Plessy holds a curiously alienated "property right in passing for white." "'Most Valuable Sort of Property,'" 891.

83. Otto H. Olsen notes that the planning of the *Plessy* case was "encouraged when the state legislature pigeonholed a bill prohibiting the not unfamiliar practice of racial intermarriage." *Thin Disguise*, 12.

3. Charles Chesnutt, Frances Harper, and Passing's Revolutionary Event

1. W. E. B. Du Bois, *The Souls of Black Folk*, in *Writings*, ed. Nathan Huggins (1903; New York: Library of America, 1986), 359.

2. Eva Saks, "Representing Miscegenation Law," in *Interracialism: Black-White Intermarriage in American History, Literature, and Law*, ed. Werner Sollors (Oxford: Oxford University Press, 2000), 79. For the link between Tourgée's novel and the legal case, see Thomas, *American Literary Realism*, 201–2.

3. Saks, "Representing Miscegenation Law," 63.

4. Elaine K. Ginsburg, "Introduction: The Politics of Passing," in *Passing and the Fictions of Identity*, ed. Elaine K. Ginsburg (Durham, NC: Duke University Press, 1996), 2. Eric Sundquist takes the phrase *second slavery* from Twain's *Pudd'nhead Wilson* to describe the uncanny repetitions of slavery in racial discourse of the 1890s. *To Wake the Nations*, 230.

5. I lean here on Anthony Hutchison's distinction between the "politics of representation" and the representation of politics. *Writing the Republic*, xvii.

6. Rayford Logan, *The Betrayal of the Negro: From Rutherford B. Hayes to Woodrow Wilson* (1954; New York: Collier Books, 1965), 62.

7. "The nadir was reached . . . not because of a lack of attention. On the contrary, the plight of the negro worsened precisely because of the efforts made to improve it." Logan, *Betrayal of the Negro,* 62.

8. Stein dates the hegemonic influence of this idea, which shaped twentieth-century understandings of Black politics, to the late 1880s. "'Of Mr. Booker T. Washington and Others': The Political Economy of Racism in the United States," in *Renewing Black Intellectual History: The Ideological and Material Foundations of African American Thought,* ed. Adolph Reed Jr. and Kenneth W. Warren (Boulder: Paradigm Publishers, 2010). The violent response to fusionism is the topic of Chesnutt's novelistic depiction of the 1898 Wilmington massacre in *The Marrow of Tradition* (1901).

9. C. Vann Woodward, *The Strange Career of Jim Crow,* 3rd rev. ed. (Oxford: Oxford University Press, 1974), 7–8, 102–9. I take this shift from uneven and locally determined practice into a logic (or imperative) implemented by bureaucratic and standardized means to be Woodward's lasting insight regarding the noncontinuity of segregation (34, 44, 68, 93–98). Barbara Fields calls this process the "nationalization of race." She does not mean that racism was ever unique to the South but that the destruction of the master-slave relation as a localized basis of sovereignty (and domination) led to a standardization of race as the explanatory framework for difference and inequality, such that it came to seem like a self-determining logic. "Slavery, Race and Ideology in the United States of America," *New Left Review* 181 (1990): 115.

10. Werner Sollors argues that as an offshoot of melodrama, passing fiction uses acts of discovery, mistaken identities, and coincidences to highlight the persistence of the past and the pull of (racial) origins in the present. *Neither Black nor White yet Both,* 232, 250. For Mikko Tuhkanen, postbellum representations of racial hybridity construct "a haunted history that cannot be put behind us because it is ceaselessly passing in the present, suspended and unacknowledged." "'Out of Joint': Passing, Haunting, and the Time of Slavery in *Hagar's Daughter,*" *American Literature* 79, no. 2 (June 2007): 337. A similarly recursive account of slavery's temporality underpins Stephen Knadler's account of nineteenth-century African American passing novels as "traumatized texts." "Traumatized Racial Performativity: Passing in Nineteenth-Century African-American Testimonies," *Cultural Critique* 55 (Fall 2003): 64. On this temporality as a "meta-critical and meta-fictional tool" for the resurfacing of racial imperatives in contemporary literature, see Sinéad Moynihan, *Passing into the Present: Contemporary American Fiction of Race and Gender Passing* (Manchester: Manchester University Press, 2010), 5.

11. The novel is set on the eve of the 1888 presidential election.

12. Albion Tourgée, *Pactolus Prime* (1890; Upper Saddle River, NJ: Gregg Press, 1968), 140. Hereafter cited parenthetically in the text.

13. William Dean Howells, *An Imperative Duty* (1891; New York: Harper and Brothers, 1892), 77. Hereafter cited parenthetically in the text.

14. See Melanie Dawson, *Emotional Reinventions: Realist-Era Representations beyond Sympathy* (Ann Arbor: University of Michigan Press, 2015), 178; Debra J. Rosenthal, "The White Blackbird: Miscegenation, Genre, and the Tragic Mulatta in Howells, Harper, and the Babes of Romance," *Nineteenth-Century Literature* 56, no. 4 (2002): 508–10.

15. Lukács, *Historical Novel,* 60.

16. Mikhail Bakhtin, *The Dialogic Imagination: Four Essays,* ed. and trans. Michael Holquist (Austin: University of Texas Press, 1981), 105, 247.

17. Charles Chesnutt, *The House behind the Cedars* (1900; New York: Modern Library, 2003), 108. Hereafter cited parenthetically in the text.

18. Broadhead, *Cultures of Letters,* 133.

19. Chesnutt's hometown of Fayetteville, North Carolina—for which Patesville is a literary stand-in—was effectively reoccupied throughout 1867, becoming an outpost of the "stockade state" after Congress passed the Reconstruction Act to overcome Presidential Reconstruction. Chesnutt's novel takes place in the wake of this occupation, which ended in Fayetteville in December 1867 but continued elsewhere in North Carolina until the state was returned to the Union in July 1868. *The House behind the Cedars* takes place across a period of around a year and a half that saw the enfranchisement of Black voters, the ratification of the state's new constitution, and North Carolina's return to the Union following the ratification of the Fourteenth Amendment. For a mapped timeline of these troop movements, see Gregory Downs and Scott Nesbit, *Mapping Occupation: Force, Freedom, and the Army in Reconstruction,* March 2015, https://www.mappingoccupation.org.

20. Discussing literary responses to the Haitian revolution, Jonathan Elmer conceives misprision as a symptomatic phenomenology of "the event," as described by Badiou. "Babo's Razor; or Discerning the Event in an Age of Differences," *Differences: A Journal of Feminist Cultural Studies* 19, no. 2 (2008): 54–81. For a discussion of passing as a Badiouian event that calls into being a new racial subject in Chesnutt's later fiction, see Erica Stevens, "Absolutely Novel: The Event and Charles Chesnutt's *Paul Marchand, F.M.C.,*" *Studies in the Novel* 50, no. 4 (Winter 2018): 523–42. I am less interested in the philosophical repercussions of Badiou's theory than in the shifting historical conditions for imagining revolution as such.

21. Frances Harper, *Iola Leroy, or Shadows Uplifted* (1892; Oxford: Oxford University Press, 1988), 122, 81. Hereafter cited parenthetically in the text.

22. Karen Sanchez-Eppler, *Touching Liberty: Abolition, Feminism, and the Politics of the Body* (Berkeley: University of California Press, 1993), 26. A key tenet of the nineteenth-century "culture of sentiment" was print culture's ability to construct "the sentimental subject who consumes the work" by depicting emotional responses to shared suffering as proof of universal humanity. Shirley Samuels, "Introduction," in *The Culture of Sentiment: Race, Gender, and Sentimentality in Nineteenth-Century America,* ed. Shirley Samuels (Oxford: Oxford University Press, 1993), 6. Jane Tompkins laid the basis for much subsequent work on sentimental fiction by arguing that sentimental texts were "agents of cultural formation," intended to be "heuristic and didactic rather than mimetic." *Sensational Designs: The Cultural Work of American Fiction, 1790–1860* (Oxford: Oxford University Press, 1985), xvii. On the way that this heuristic function of a "sentimental public" relies on an impulse to "love conventionality," reinforcing the social differences between women that it proposes to bridge, see Lauren Berlant, *The Female Complaint: The Unfinished Business of Sentiment in American Culture* (Durham, NC: Duke University Press, 2008), 3.

23. See Hazel Carby, *Reconstructing Womanhood: The Emergence of the Afro-American Woman Novelist* (Oxford: Oxford University Press, 1987), 71–77. Claudia Tate emphasizes how Black women's fiction of the period turned the tropes of sentimental domestic fiction into a

"symbolic" and speculative means to imagine the emergence of a politically engaged Black female readership. *Domestic Allegories of Political Desire: The Black Heroine's Text at the Turn of the Century* (Oxford: Oxford University Press, 1993), 107–8. Elizabeth Ammons argues that *Iola Leroy* narrates "the political enabling of women's art in the 1890s" through intertextual invocations of Ida B. Wells's anti-lynching journalism. *Conflicting Stories: American Women Writers at the Turn into the Twentieth Century* (Oxford: Oxford University Press, 1992), 29. On this point, see also P. Gabrielle Foreman, *Activist Sentiments: Reading Black Women in the Nineteenth Century* (Urbana: University of Illinois Press, 2009), 90–96.

24. Berlant argues that the avowal of fractured maternal kinship is a "utopian political imaginary activity" that rewrites sentimental suffering according to the experiences of Black women. "The Queen of America Goes to Washington City: Harriet Jacobs, Frances Harper, Anita Hill," *American Literary History* 65, no. 3 (September 1993): 561–62. See also Foreman, *Activist Sentiments*, 89.

25. *An Imperative Duty* and *Pactolus Prime* solve the problem of racial recognition by expelling their heroines, to Florence and a convent, respectively. On Harper's and Chesnutt's response to Howells and Tourgée, see Thomas, *Literature of Reconstruction* 295–301; Thomas, *American Literary Realism*, 156–63; Rosenthal, "White Blackbird," 510–17; Kenneth W. Warren, *Black and White Strangers: Race and American Literary Realism* (Chicago: University of Chicago Press, 1993), 66–67. Writing eight years later than Harper—after the resurgence of political support for renewing Reconstruction policies in the South had been quelled, in part by *Plessy*—Chesnutt depicts Rena's decision as one with tragic consequences, as opposed to Harper's optimistic portrayal of racial kinship. Nevertheless, these are consequences born of Rena's concrete experience, not of the sudden discovery of Blackness to which Howells and Tourgée subject their heroines.

26. Carby argues that "the overall structure of *Iola Leroy* progressed increasingly toward a complete separation of the black community from the white world and thus implicitly accepted the failure of Reconstruction . . . In this regard, *Iola Leroy* was a textbook for the educated black person in the crisis of disfranchisement, lynching, and the Jim Crow laws." *Reconstructing Womanhood*, 93.

27. Ammons, *Conflicting Stories*, 23. See also Stephen Knadler, "The Bright Side: African American Women and the Affective Archive of Southern Racial Uplift," in Hobson and Ladd, *Oxford Handbook of the Literature of the U.S. South*, 238–39, 242–46.

28. Carla L. Peterson, "Commemorative Ceremonies and Invented Traditions: History, Memory, and Modernity in the 'New Negro' Novel of the Nadir," in *Post-Bellum, Pre-Harlem: African American Literature and Culture, 1877–1919*, ed. Barbara McCaskill and Caroline Gebhard (New York: New York University Press, 2006), 35–39. In their introduction to this collection, which uses "Post-Bellum, Pre-Harlem" (a coinage of Chesnutt's) as a period marker, McCaskill and Gebhard argue that the conversion of a seemingly dire contemporary political history into an artistic resource characterizes the era culturally. They offer this cultural history as a corrective means of "renaming the Nadir" (2–6).

29. Russ Castronovo understands the history it discloses to be "the mulatta's cultural memory" of enslavement and sexual abuse, an embodied history of slavery repressed by legal definitions of emancipation that dominated the interpretation of citizenship by the end of the century.

Necro Citizenship: Death, Eroticism, and the Public Sphere (Durham, NC: Duke University Press, 2001), 225.

30. Broadhead, *Cultures of Letters,* 204–8; Sundquist, *To Wake the Nations,* 359–92.

31. Broadhead, *Cultures of Letters,* 207. See also Sundquist, *To Wake the Nations,* 397–406. Werner Sollors posits Chesnutt as the first self-consciously historical African American novelist to emerge before the 1930s. Focusing on his conjure tales and later fiction, he deems *The House behind the Cedars* to be an imaginative trial run. He understands Chesnutt's guiding historical question to be how "the historical trauma of slavery [could] be represented so that its continuing effect on the gilded age and fin-de-siècle would become apparent." "Charles W. Chesnutt's Historical Imagination," in *Passing in the Works of Charles W. Chesnutt,* ed. Susan Prothro Wright and Ernestine Pickens Glass (Jackson: University Press of Mississippi, 2010), 4.

32. Stacey Margolis, *The Public Life of Privacy in Nineteenth-Century America* (Durham, NC: Duke University Press, 2005), 108; emphasis added. For Cane, the novel recovers "a higher law version of republican virtue in the era of Jim Crow positivism." *Race, Citizenship, and Law in American Literature* (Cambridge: Cambridge University Press, 2002), 204. Relating the novel's representation of race to legal ideas of contract and equity, Thomas orients his discussion toward the "post-Reconstruction" era. *American Literary Realism,* 160–61. Strikingly, in rereading the novel as part of his canon of Reconstruction literature, Thomas focuses on the question of what can be inherited from slavery but acknowledges the book's Reconstruction setting only by noting that it is "set before redemption." *Literature of Reconstruction,* 305. Moddelmog stresses the continuity between Reconstruction legislation and "racialized conceptions of ownership" characteristic of slavery. *Reconstituting Authority: American Fiction in the Province of the Law* (Iowa City: University of Iowa Press, 2000), 142–43.

33. Woodward, *Strange Career of Jim Crow,* 7.

34. Woodward, *Strange Career of Jim Crow,* 102–9. Woodward updated the book three times (in 1957, 1966, and 1974). To avoid confusion, I have quoted from the 1974 edition, noting in the text when passages *did not* appear in the original.

35. Woodward, *Strange Career of Jim Crow,* 25. For his distinction between exploitation and ostracism (present in the original edition), see 43–44. On Woodward's amendments, see Harold Rabinowitz, "More than the Woodward Thesis: Assessing *The Strange Career of Jim Crow,*" *Journal of American History* 75, no. 3 (December 1988): 842–56.

36. Woodward, *Strange Career of Jim Crow,* 32.

37. Notably, the critics who most successfully disputed the absence of segregation in Reconstruction also credit Woodward for identifying the 1890s as the moment segregation's character changed. For Joel Williamson, the fundamental transition was in the increasingly violent and all-encompassing policing of the color line by "Radical racists." *Crucible of Race,* ix, 111–39. Harold Rabinowitz locates this backlash as a response to a changed terrain of struggle: where, after emancipation, a formerly enslaved (and socially excluded) population fought for access to social provision, the development of *new* systems of welfare and public accommodation (like transport) in the South at the end of the nineteenth century led Black movements to challenge the *terms* of access (a struggle over segregation rather than exclusion). *Race Relations in the Urban South: 1865–1890* (1978; Athens: University of Georgia Press, 1996), 333–39.

38. Woodward, *Strange Career of Jim Crow,* 8–9; Michael O'Brien, "C. Vann Woodward and the Burden of Southern Liberalism," *American Historical Review* 78, no. 3 (1973): 596. For the way in which the tension between Woodward's account of discontinuity in southern history and his faith in an archetypical, redemptive southern identity played out across his work, see Leigh Anne Duck, "Woodward's Southerner: History, Literature, and the Question of Identity," in *The Ongoing Burden of Southern History: Politics and Identity in the Twenty-First-Century South,* ed. Angie Maxwell, Todd Shields, and Jeannie Whayne (Baton Rouge: Louisiana State University Press, 2012), 31–61.

39. Woodward, *Strange Career of Jim Crow,* 10.

40. Mark Twain, *Pudd'nhead Wilson* (1893; London: Penguin, 1986), 225.

41. W. E. B. Du Bois, *Dusk of Dawn,* in Du Bois, *Writings,* 716. Hereafter cited parenthetically in the text.

42. Du Bois, *Dusk of Dawn,* 639, 555.

43. See Anthony Appiah, "The Uncompleted Argument: Du Bois and the Illusion of Race," *Critical Inquiry* 12, no. 1 (1985): 21–37. The problem is central to Kenneth Warren's historicization of the concept of African American literature, in *What Was African American Literature?* (Cambridge: Harvard University Press, 2011).

44. The judge's advice mirrors Chesnutt's journalistic account of the farcical nature of the regional differences between laws designating whiteness across the postbellum South. In his 1889 essay "What Is a White Man?" Chesnutt discusses the emergence in South Carolina of a mixed-race population whose members have "come in from the surrounding states" and "taken their social position as white people." "What Is a White Man?" in *Charles W. Chesnutt: Essays and Speeches,* eds. Joseph R. McElrath Jr., Robert C. Leitz III, and Jesse S. Crisler (Stanford: Stanford University Press, 1999), 71.

45. On the pairing of incest and interracial sex as sentimental responses to the chattel relationship in abolitionist fiction, see Shirley Samuels, "The Identity of Slavery," in Samuels, *Culture of Sentiment,* 167–68.

46. The link between coverture and chattel slavery was a key rhetorical tool for abolitionist feminists who drew on the sentimental tradition, one that Sanchez-Eppler argues was "so normative as to be unavoidable." *Touching Liberty,* 41. See also Caroline Karcher, "Rape, Murder, and Revenge in 'Slavery's Pleasant Homes': Lydia Maria Child's Antislavery Fiction and the Limits of Genre," in Samuels, *Culture of Sentiment,* 59–60. For the trope's afterlife in postbellum culture, see Amy Dru Stanley, *From Bondage to Contract: Wage Labor, Marriage, and the Market in the Age of Slave Emancipation* (Cambridge: Cambridge University Press, 1998), 179–86, 216–17.

47. Margolis, *Public Life of Privacy,* 108–9, 125; Thomas, *Literature of Reconstruction,* 322–23.

48. U.S. Constitution, amend. 14, sec. 4.

49. On the way in which the chattel status of slaves underpinned the liquidity required to expand cotton production between the 1830s and the Civil War, see Walter Johnson, *River of Dark Dreams: Slavery and Empire in the Cotton Kingdom* (Cambridge: Harvard University Press, 2013), 86–87. John J. Clegg argues that the laws (unique to new world colonies) that allowed the chattel and real property of estates (slaves and land) to be seized by creditors in foreclosure arrangements were fundamental to the "credit market discipline" that expanded productivity in U.S. cotton slavery. Slave sale allowed the plantation economy's dependence

on credit and foreclosure to function as a means of expansion. "Credit Market Discipline and Capitalist Slavery in Antebellum South Carolina," *Social Science History* 42, no. 4 (Summer 2018): 348, 353–55, 363–65. For credit as the site of a class struggle at least as important as land to the transformation of the plantation economy in the immediate wake of emancipation, see Eric Foner, *Nothing but Freedom: Emancipation and Its Legacy* (Baton Rouge: Louisiana State University Press, 1983), 35–44, 61.

50. Michael Germana, *Standards of Value: Money, Race, and Literature in America* (Des Moines: University of Iowa Press, 2010), 87.

51. Charles Chesnutt, *The Conjure Woman and Other Conjure Tales,* ed. Richard H. Broadhead (Durham, NC: Duke University Press, 1993), 61.

52. Germana, *Standards of Value,* 85, 87–89.

53. The theory behind this reading is drawn from Michael O'Malley's account of the racial language underpinning the money question. For O'Malley, race and money are analogous "shorthand way[s] of assigning value to difference." He sees the rhetoric of hard money and biological determinism as shared essentialist discourses about value that outlived slavery. In this account, value and race are purely discursive, a move that ignores the effect that a fundamental change in the nature of property (and the capacity for economic value to be embodied) has on the understanding of racial embodiment. *Face Value: The Entwined Histories of Money and Race in American History* (Chicago: University of Chicago Press, 2012), 5, 83–123.

54. Roland Barthes, "The Reality Effect," *The Rustle of Language,* trans. Richard Howard (Berkeley: University of California Press, 1989), 142.

55. Chesnutt's use of Confederate debt to thicken his historical scene is also on display in his earlier lynching story, "The Sheriff's Children," in which the crime that eventuates the lynching is the murder of a Confederate captain, rumored to have a store of greenbacks, but who actually has "two bairls of Confedrit money, which he 'spected 'ud be good some day 'er nuther." Chesnutt lifts elements of his opening description of Patesville in *The House behind the Cedars* almost verbatim from his opening account of the village of Troy in his short story, whose racial narrative also has a largely unremarked upon Reconstruction setting ("about ten years after the war"). *The Wife of His Youth: And Other Stories of the Color Line* (1898; Boston: Houghton, Mifflin, 1901), 65, 63.

56. Barthes, "Reality Effect," 146.

57. For the novel's negotiation of sentimental and realist approaches to the color line, see Dawson, *Emotional Reinventions,* 173–77; Thomas, *American Literary Realism,* 166–68.

58. Sanchez-Eppler, *Touching Liberty,* 5. Dawson identifies a similar transition in literary genre, arguing that American realists reinvented sentiment to contribute to "the work of social analysis" rather than political reform. She argues that rather than using emotion to make universal political claims, they created quasi-social scientific taxonomies of affect. *Emotional Reinventions,* 10.

59. Stanley, *From Bondage to Contract,* 262; see also 184, 254–58.

60. Tim Armstrong, *The Logic of Slavery: Debt, Technology, and Pain in American Literature* (Cambridge: Cambridge University Press, 2012), 3, 5.

61. Spillers, "Momma's Baby, Papa's Maybe," 68–69.

62. See Thomas, *Literature of Reconstruction,* 289–90.

63. Berlant, "Queen of America," 562.

64. Geoffrey Sanborn, "Mother's Milk: Frances Harper, and the Circulation of Blood," *ELH* 72, no. 3 (2005): 692.

65. Darlene Clark Hine, "Rape and the Inner Lives of Back Women: Thoughts on the Culture of Dissemblance," in *Hine Sight: Black Women and the Re-Construction of American History* (Bloomington: Indiana University Press, 1994), 41.

66. Sanborn notes the "the unparalleled strangeness" of "a body that disappears into the word-filled air in every way but one." For him, what constitutes this exception (and Iola's strangeness) is her tendency to flush, a sensation caused by rushing blood that Sanborn argues Harper uses to develop a distinctively Black, female language of vitalist energy that counters the abstraction of debates over Black rights. "Mother's Milk," 693.

67. Harriet Jacobs, *Incidents in the Life of a Slave Girl* (Boston: Published for the author, 1861), 46.

68. Jacobs, *Incidents in the Life of a Slave Girl,* 304, 300.

69. After the flashback, Iola describes the same events to Gresham; another flashback repeats her experience through her letter to Harry; she narrates her story to Robert after emancipation; on finding their mother, Harry and Iola separately retell their stories; Iola retraces events after reencountering Gresham in the North; finally, Iola gives her conditional account of her life to Dr. Latimer after he narrates her own story to her, so as to encourage her to see it as material for a book.

70. Tompkins, *Sensational Designs,* 62, 66–68.

71. See Carby, *Reconstructing Womanhood,* 88–94; Carla L. Peterson, "Frances Harper, Charlotte Forten, and African American Literary Reconstruction," in *Challenging Boundaries: Gender and Periodization,* ed. Joyce W. Warren and Margaret Dickie (Athens: University of Georgia Press, 2000), 42–46; Tate, *Domestic Allegories,* 144–47.

72. Peterson, "Frances Harper," 44–45.

73. Frances Harper, *Minnie's Sacrifice: A Rediscovered Novel,* ed. Frances Smith Foster (1868; Project Gutenberg, 2004), chap. 20, accessed May 21, 2019, http://www.gutenberg.org/cache /epub/11053/pg11053-images.html. (As this edition is unpaginated, I have referenced chapter numbers.)

74. Harper, *Minnie's Sacrifice,* chap. 20.

75. Harper, *Minnie's Sacrifice,* chap. 18.

76. I borrow the reference to history's active voice from Hayden White's account of *The Communist Manifesto* in *Metahistory: The Historical Imagination in Nineteenth-Century Europe* (Baltimore: Johns Hopkins Press, 1973), 329.

4. W. E. B. Du Bois's Counterfactual Peasantry

1. Brian Kelly argues that Du Bois depicts a revolutionary moment in which "agency and restraint rubbed up against one another more dramatically" than during perhaps any other revolution in history. "W. E. B. Du Bois, Black Agency and the Slaves' Civil War," *International Socialist Review* 100 (Spring 2016): 52.

2. Du Bois, *Black Reconstruction,* 64–67, 15. Hereafter cited parenthetically in the text.

3. Cedric Robinson credits Du Bois with introducing the problem of revolutionary sponta-
neity and agrarian radicalism to an American Left increasingly devoted to the vanguard party
in the 1930s. *Black Marxism: The Making of the Black Radical Tradition* (1983; Chapel Hill:
University of North Carolina Press, 2000), 200–232.

4. Robinson, *Black Marxism.*

5. Nikhil Pal Singh, *Black Is a Country: Race and the Unfinished Struggle for Democracy*
(Cambridge: Harvard University Press, 2004), 93–95, 78.

6. Robinson, *Black Marxism*, 241, 171, 169.

7. W. E. B. Du Bois, *Scorn: A Romance,* ca. 1905, mums312-b231-i120, W. E. B. Du Bois Papers
(MS 312), Special Collections and University Archives, University of Massachusetts Amherst
Libraries, http://credo.library.umass.edu/view/full/mums312-b231-i120. Hereafter cited paren-
thetically in the text.

8. For the connection between the study and *Quest,* see Maria Farland, "W. E. B. Du Bois,
Anthropometric Science, and the Limits of Racial Uplift," *American Quarterly* 58, no. 4 (2006):
1017–44.

9. W. E. B. Du Bois, ed., *Economic Co-operation among Negro Americans* (Atlanta: Atlanta
University Press, 1907), 10.

10. Du Bois, *Economic Co-operation among Negro Americans,* 26, 24–45.

11. For an account of the early development of Du Bois's socialism in relation to his fiction,
see Mark Van Wienen and Julie Kraft, "How the Socialism of W. E. B. Du Bois Still Matters: Black
Socialism in *The Quest of the Silver Fleece*," *African American Review* 31, no. 1 (2007): 67–85. For
a biographical account of his early socialism and its hesitant engagement with Marxism, see
Michael J. Saman, "Du Bois and Marx, Du Bois and Marxism," *Du Bois Review* 17, no. 1 (2020):
33–54. For a study that roots Du Bois's early socialism in technocratic ideologies of progressivist
collectivism, see Adolph Reed, *W. E. B. Du Bois and American Political Thought: Fabianism across
the Color Line* (Oxford: Oxford University Press, 1997), 18–32, 53–67, 85–87.

12. Brent Hayes Edwards, "The Autonomy of Black Radicalism," *Social Text* 67, vol. 19, no.
2 (2001): 6.

13. I take this phrase from George Ciccariello-Maher's account of anticolonial dialectics,
Decolonizing Dialectics (Durham, NC: Duke University Press, 2017), 7.

14. A. C. McClurg to W. E. B. Du Bois (fragment), ca. 1905, mums312-b003-i281, Du Bois
Papers, http://credo.library.umass.edu/view/full/mums312-b003-i281.

15. Adolph Reed argues that Du Bois's political thought consistently reflected a Fabianism
hostile to revolutionary mass action. Tellingly, he does not analyze *Black Reconstruction. W. E. B.
Du Bois and American Political Thought.*

16. W. E. B. Du Bois, *John Brown* (1909; New York: M. E. Sharpe, 1997), 201.

17. Du Bois, *John Brown,* 173. The founding document of the reformist Niagara Movement,
the activist group that Du Bois formed in 1905 while writing *Scorn,* opens up this contradiction
similarly without closure: "We do not believe in violence . . . but we do believe in John Brown."
Quoted in Du Bois, *Dusk of Dawn,* 621.

18. W. E. B. Du Bois, "The Negro and Communism," in *W. E. B. Du Bois: A Reader,* ed. David
Levering Lewis (New York: Henry Holt, 1995), 591.

19. W. E. B. Du Bois, "Marxism and the Negro Problem," in Lewis, *W. E. B. Du Bois,* 540.

20. Bill Mullen, *Un-American: W. E. B. Du Bois and the Century of World Revolution* (Philadelphia: Temple University Press, 2015), 60, 44, 78–85.

21. Paul Ricoeur. *Time and Narrative,* trans. Kathleen McLoughlin and David Pellauer (Chicago: University of Chicago Press, 1984), 1:179.

22. The only discussions I know of are Autumn Womack, "W. E. B. Du Bois's Apocalyptic Ambivalence," in *Apocalypse in American Literature and Culture,* ed. John Hay (Cambridge: Cambridge University Press, 2020), 239–51; James B. Stewart, "Psychic Duality of Afro-Americans in the Novels of W. E. B. Du Bois," *Phylon* 44, no. 2 (1983): 93–107.

23. David Levering Lewis, *W. E. B. Du Bois: Biography of a Race, 1868–1919* (New York: Henry Holt, 1993), 444. Manning Marable, *W. E. B. Du Bois: Black Radical Democrat* (Boston: Twayne, 1986), 66–67. Stewart's brief treatment of the novel in "Psychic Duality" also frames it as a precursor to Du Bois's later fiction.

24. Paul Gilroy, *The Black Atlantic: Modernity and Double Consciousness* (London: Verso, 1993), 89, 121–22; Susan Gillman, *Blood Talk: American Race Melodrama and the Culture of the Occult* (Chicago: University of Chicago Press, 2003), 148–50.

25. Jarvis C. McInnis, "'Behold the Land': W. E. B. Du Bois, Cotton Futures, and the Afterlife of the Plantation in the U.S. South," *Global South* 10, no. 2 (2016): 79, 89–92; Mullen, *Un-American,* 12–13, 67–71, 79; Alys Eve Weinbaum, *Wayward Reproductions: Genealogies of Race and Nation in Transatlantic Modern Thought* (Durham, NC: Duke University Press, 2004), 214–15; Lily Wiatrowski Phillips, "*The Black Flame* Revisited: Recursion and Return in the Reading of W. E. B. Du Bois's Trilogy," *CR: The New Centennial Review* 15, no. 2 (2015): 167–68.

26. Though most material on *Scorn* in the archive is dated 1905 (the date of the manuscripts), I will discuss fragments whose content clearly dates them after World War I. Blake Spitz, archivist for the Du Bois Papers, has confirmed to me that 1905 was assumed as a "circa" date for undated materials relating to *Scorn.* My citations retain the archive's dates, but I indicate in the text when material was written later. For all material, I have corrected any obvious transcription errors but otherwise retained Du Bois's text.

27. On this point, see also Womack "Apocalyptic Ambivalence," 243-44.

28. A. C. McClurg to W. E. B. Du Bois, July 20, 1904, mums312-b003-i269, Du Bois Papers, http://credo.library.umass.edu/view/full/mums312-b003-i269.

29. On the novel's apocalypticism, see Womack, "W. E. B. Du Bois's Apocalyptic Ambivalence."

30. A. C. McClurg to W. E. B. Du Bois (fragment).

31. His assertion that the novel was "none the less a work of art" damned Chesnutt with faint praise. William Dean Howells, "A Psychological Counter-Current in Recent Fiction," *North American Review* 173, no. 541 (1901): 882–83.

32. For the role of editors in making a depoliticized account of race relations central to genteel realist aesthetics (a tradition against which Du Bois was surely writing), see Warren, *Black and White Strangers,* 48–71.

33. Du Bois proposed that meetings of the Niagara Movement be held in joint commemoration of William Lloyd Garrison and Tourgée. "Niagara Movement membership letter No. 2, October 7, 1905," mums312-b004-i098, Du Bois Papers, https://credo.library.umass.edu/view

/full/mums312-b004-i098. In *Black Reconstruction,* he cites both Cable's *The Silent South* (1885) and Tourgée's novels in his suggestions for further reading as well as calling Tourgee "one of the ablest and most honest of the carpetbaggers" (536). On his reading of Tourgée in high school and college, see "Letter from W. E. B. Du Bois to Otto H. Olsen, June 4, 1956," mums312-b145-i336, Du Bois Papers, https://credo.library.umass.edu/view/full/mums312-b145-i336.

34. W. E. B. Du Bois, "Possibilities of the Negro: The Advanced Guard of the Race," *Book-lovers Magazine* 2 (July 1903): 13.

35. For this reading of turn-of-the-century African American writing, see Nancy Bentley, "The Fourth Dimension: Kinlessness and African American Narrative," *Critical Enquiry* 35, no. 2 (2009): 270–92; Stephen Knadler, "Narrating Slow Violence: Post-Reconstruction's Necropolitics and Speculating beyond Liberal Anti-Race Fiction," *J19: The Journal of Nineteenth-Century Americanists* 5, no. 1 (2017): 21–50.

36. Fanny Hale Gardiner, *The Golden Fleece,* ca. June 17, 1910, mums312-b003-i452, Du Bois Papers, http://credo.library.umass.edu/view/full/mums312-b003-i452.

37. Gardiner, Golden Fleece.

38. Alys Eve Weinbaum, "Gendering the General Strike: W. E. B. Du Bois's *Black Reconstruction* and Black Feminism's 'Propaganda of History,'" *South Atlantic Quarterly* 112, no. 3 (Summer 2013): 444.

39. Du Bois, *Souls of Black Folk,* 387, 389–90. Hereafter cited parenthetically in the text.

40. Catherine Gallagher and Stephen Greenblatt, *Practicing New Historicism* (Chicago: University of Chicago Press, 2000), 54.

41. Catherine Gallagher, *Telling It like It Wasn't: The Counterfactual Imagination in History and Fiction* (Chicago: University of Chicago Press, 2018), 11. Stephen Best identifies this normative function with the formalist ideology of the legally culpable individual, characteristic of nineteenth-century jurisprudence. *Fugitive's Properties,* 213–16.

42. Catherine Gallagher, "When Did the Confederate States of America Free the Slaves?" *Representations* 98, no. 1 (2007): 58, 60.

43. See Best, *Fugitive's Properties,* 213–16.

44. Gallagher and Greenblatt, *Practicing New Historicism,* 72.

45. I am paraphrasing Malcolm Bull's argument that in *The Souls of Black Folk,* "unveiling the truth about black people means not just revealing that something is veiled" (i.e., Black life within white America) "but revealing something veiled, something that continues to be partially hidden even as it is uncovered." *Seeing Things Hidden: Apocalypse, Vision and Totality* (London: Verso, 1999), 241.

46. My argument about the unevenness of Du Bois's metonymic link between slavery and capitalism is indebted to Nikhil Pal Singh's analysis of Marx's elliptical considerations of slave labor. Acknowledging Marx's blind spots, Singh emphasizes the moments in which "Marx evinces a refusal of the historicist separation between capitalism and slavery," to arrive at the following redefinition of capital's always partial universalizing tendencies: "Capital ceases to be capital without the ongoing differentiation of free labor and slavery, waged labor and unpaid labor." "On Race, Violence, and So-Called Primitive Accumulation," *Social Text* 128, vol. 34, no. 3 (2016): 39, 37.

47. Ciccariello-Maher, *Decolonizing Dialectics,* 162–63.

48. As Kelly argues, Du Bois refuses to generalize a fugitive political consciousness, focusing on the unevenness of the phenomenon and the restrictions facing slaves on isolated plantations. "W. E. B. Du Bois," 51–53.

49. For a discussion of slavery's relationship to capitalism in terms of its crisis tendency, see John J. Clegg, "Capitalism and Slavery," *Critical Historical Studies* 2, no. 2 (2015): 281–304.

50. Chris Taylor, "The Plantation Road to Socialism," *Amerikastudien / American Studies* 62, no. 4 (2017): 552, 554. Taylor characterizes the slavery-capitalism relationship as one of "immanent exteriority" (553).

51. On the way that socioeconomic articulation of modes and relations of production is (in the other sense of the word) articulated at the level of ideology (particularly race), see Stuart Hall, "Race, Articulation, and Societies Structured in Dominance," in Gilroy and Gilmore, *Selected Writings on Race and Difference*, 195–245.

52. Fredric Jameson, *Valences of the Dialectic* (London: Verso, 2009), 565.

53. Jameson, *Valences of the Dialectic*, 572.

54. Jameson, *Valences of the Dialectic*, 48, 579, 582.

55. For the crisis tendency in slavery's "conditions of expanded reproduction," see Charles Post, *The American Road to Capitalism* (Leiden: Brill, 2011), 221–26. I am also borrowing Weinbaum's sense of "reproduction," which refers to modernist thought's frequent conflation of socioeconomic and biological reproduction to link anxieties about historical reproduction with racialized accounts of the nation-state. She argues that Du Bois turned this "race/reproduction bind" toward a critical account of race. Weinbaum, *Wayward Reproductions*, 13–14, 188. The link is crucial to *Scorn*, which approaches the crises that plague its white characters' economic fantasies through their paranoiac recognition and displacement of their own mixed bloodlines.

56. W. E. B. Du Bois, *The Suppression of the African Slave Trade*, in *Writings*, ed. Nathan Huggins (1896; New York: Library of America, 1986), 155.

57. In *Scorn*, the phrase refers to the imagined futures conditioned by the plantation's economic imperatives on two other occasions, prior to naming the "new world peasantry": first in Henry Jones's observation that "if a new world like Texas opens up, new stock of slaves is needed" (131); and later to describe John Reynolds's "vision of a strange new world," glimpsed "among the dying and the dead" Black bodies of a Civil War battlefield. Realizing that "never before had he really looked upon black men as men," Reynolds experiences an epiphany (176). However, his recognition of a new people proves merely to be financial opportunism, expressed by his son's desire to "to stay here forever and make money" (179). The phrase is notably absent in *The Souls of Black Folk*, which is seemingly more focused on the perspective of the folk. There Du Bois uses it only once to refer broadly to U.S. culture, as a counterpoint to his argument that the Sorrow Songs are the first indigenously American music: "the human spirit in this new world has expressed itself in vigor and ingenuity rather than beauty" (*SBF* 536).

58. Bentley, "Fourth Dimension," 276, 278.

59. Gilroy, *Black Atlantic*, 218. Bentley makes this link with Gilroy. "Fourth Dimension," 277.

60. Gilroy, *Black Atlantic*, 222–23.

61. W. E. B. Du Bois, *Scorn: A Romance*, ca. 1905, 51–52, mums312-b231-i123, Du Bois Papers, (MS 312), Special Collections and University Archives, University of Massachusetts Amherst Libraries, http://credo.library.umass.edu/view/full/mums312-b231-i123. The page numbers vary

so much between drafts because in this earlier draft, Du Bois paginated each book of the novel separately. The references quoted here all relate to book 3 of this earlier draft.

62. Du Bois, *Scorn,* ca. 1905, 43. Du Bois later named the chapter of *Black Reconstruction* that questions the reader's ability to imagine revolution "The Coming of the Lord."

63. Du Bois, *Scorn,* ca. 1905, 42.

64. For the centrality of Black maternity to Du Bois's novelistic figuration of race and empire, see Weinbaum, *Wayward Reproductions,* 214–18.

65. A. C. McClurg to Du Bois (fragment).

66. W. E. B. Du Bois to Francis G. Brown, October 28, 1905, mums312-b003-i282, Du Bois Papers, http://credo.library.umass.edu/view/full/mums312-b003-i282.

67. A. C. McClurg to W. E. B. Du Bois, May 11, 1906, mums312-b003-i285, Du Bois Papers, http://credo.library.umass.edu/view/full/mums312-b003-i285. There is no copy of this revised manuscript in either Du Bois's or A. C. McClurg's archive. The revisions are unlikely to have been substantial, given that Du Bois informed Walter Hines Page that he considered the novel "virtually finished" less than a month after responding to McClurg's initial criticisms. In this same letter, Du Bois poured cold water on Page's open advance for him to send Doubleday and Page future work; despite McClurg's coolness about his novel, Du Bois rebuffed Page, asserting that he was reluctant to send his work to "the exploiters of Thomas Dixon." Walter H. Page to W. E. B. Du Bois, November 22, 1905, mums312-b002-i140, Du Bois Papers, http://credo.library .umass.edu/view/full/mums312-b002-i140.

68. W. E. B. Du Bois, *Scorn: A Romance* (fragment), ca. 1905, mums312-b232 i010, Du Bois Papers, http://credo.library.umass.edu/view/full/mums312-b232-i010.

69. W. E. B. Du Bois, "The Seat of the Scornful: The Story of Mary Calhoun" (fragment), ca. 1905, mums312-b232-i004, Du Bois Papers, http://credo.library.umass.edu/view/full/mums312 -b232-i004.

70. W. E. B. Du Bois, *Scorn: A Romance* (fragment), ca. 1905, 2, mums312-b232-i009 Du Bois Papers, http://credo.library.umass.edu/view/full/mums312-b232-i009. Although it has the same title as a previously cited fragment, this is a separate draft, with a different archival identifier.

71. White, *Metahistory,* 11.

72. Jeremy Matthew Glick, *The Black Radical Tragic: Performance, Aesthetics, and the Unfinished Haitian Revolution* (New York: New York University Press, 2016), 88.

73. Glick, *Black Radical Tragic,* 124. This does not mean, as David Scott argues, that tragedy plots the loss of revolutionary possibility previously narrated as romance (along with its time-bound utopian future imagined by the anticolonial struggle). The similarities between Du Bois's historical romance and his tragic history are precisely what I am drawing attention to. *Conscripts of Modernity: The Tragedy of Colonial Enlightenment* (Durham, NC: Duke University Press, 2004), 11–14, 65.

74. Arnold Rampersad, *The Art and Imagination of W. E. B. Du Bois* (1976; New York: Schocken, 1990), 217; Michael Denning, *The Cultural Front: The Laboring of American Culture in the Twentieth Century* (London: Verso, 1997), 163–68.

75. Gilroy, *Black Atlantic,* 89. For readings that highlight the utopian aspects of Du Bois's mixed form, see Gilman, *Blood Talk,* 148–50; Peter Coviello, "Intimacy and Affliction: Du Bois, Race, and Psychoanalysis," *Modern Language Quarterly* 64, no. 1 (March 2003): 8, 20; Russ Cas-

tronovo, "Within the Veil of Interdisciplinary Knowledge? Jefferson, Du Bois, and the Negation of Politics," *New Literary History* 31, no. 4 (Fall 2000): 793–96, 798–99. Castronovo focuses on Du Bois's opposition of history and counterfactual speculation.

76. Karl Marx, *Capital*, trans. Ben Fawkes (London: Penguin, 1990), 1:798.

77. George L. Beckford, *Persistent Poverty: Underdevelopment in Plantation Economies of the Third World* (Oxford: Oxford University Press, 1972), 55, 177.

78. Beckford, *Persistent Poverty*, 177, 50, 86, 170–80.

79. Gavin Wright, *Old South, New South: Revolutions in the Southern Economy since the Civil War* (New York: Basic Books, 1986), 90–98.

80. Pete Daniel, *Breaking the Land: The Transformation of Cotton, Tobacco, and Rice Cultures since 1880* (Urbana: University of Illinois Press, 1985), xii, 155, 163.

81. Beckford, *Persistent Poverty*, 55.

82. Michael Denning, "Wageless Life," *New Left Review* 66 (November 2010): 80–81.

83. Marx, *Capital*, 786, 784. Beckford does not draw the comparison, but Marx's recourse to metaphors of slavery to describe the link between production and reproduction—in particular, his discussion of capital's reproduction of a surplus population as a false emancipation or afterlife of the slave market—indicates that he probably had. Marx wrote the first edition of *Capital* between 1866 and 1867, in the wake of Presidential Reconstruction, as southern legislatures pushed through Black Codes to secure their disappearing labor reserves. Andrew Zimmerman points out that Marx and Engels corresponded keenly about American slave emancipation. Following their mutual disappointment at Johnson's failure to break up the plantation estates, Engels predicted a drawn-out crisis in which the emancipated slaves "will turn into small squatters as in Jamaica" and "the oligarchy will go to pot after all." While the prediction did not materialize, the planters' struggle to maintain a labor force suggests a historical precedent for Marx's understanding of capitalist crisis as simultaneously one of production and population. "Engels to Marx, 15th July 1865," *Marx and Engels Collected Works*, trans. Christopher Upward and John Peet, 50 vols. (London: Lawrence and Wishart, 1975–2004), 42:168; Andrew Zimmerman, "Introduction," in *The Civil War in the United States*, by Karl Marx and Friedrich Engels, ed. Andrew Zimmerman (New York: International Publishers, 2017), xi–xxx; Singh, "On Race," 32–35.

84. See Zimmerman, "From the Second American Revolution," 324.

85. For an account of how C. L. R. James's ethnography of sharecropping employs similar temporal anachronisms to make solidarity between croppers and wage laborers central to a critique of developmentalist socialism, see Christopher Taylor, "Sharing Time: C. L. R. James and Southern Agrarian Movements," *Social Text* 111, vol. 30, no. 2 (2012): 75–98.

86. Williams, *Modern Tragedy*, 67, 64, 75.

Conclusion: Narrative, Revolution, (Dis)Appearance

1. Rita Felski, *The Limits of Critique* (Chicago: University of Chicago Press, 2015), 15–16.

2. Bewes, "Reading with the Grain," 21.

3. W. B. Yeats, "Easter, 1916," in *The Poems*, ed. Daniel Albright (London: Everyman's Library, 1992), 228.

4. Walter Benjamin, "Theses on the Philosophy of History," in *Illuminations*, ed. Hannah

Arendt; trans. Harry Zorn (London: Pimlico, 1999), 253.

5. Chesnutt's 1898 collection, *The Wife of His Youth and Other Stories of the Color Line*, might seem to be an exception, but in keeping with the argument in chapter 3, the majority of these "stories of the color line" have historical settings, even when they are only referred to allusively. Of the nine stories, three are set during Reconstruction ("A Matter of Principle," "The Sheriff's Children," and "Uncle Wellington's Wives") and two during slavery ("Cicely's Dream" and "The Passing of Grandison").

6. Charles Chesnutt, *The Marrow of Tradition*, in *The Portable Charles W. Chesnutt*, ed. William L. Andrews (1901; London: Penguin, 2008), 237. Hereafter cited parenthetically in the text.

7. For an account of Chesnutt's treatment of legitimate interracial marriage as an inexpressible history, see Nancy Bentley, "The Strange Career of Love and Slavery: Chesnutt, Engels, Masoch," *American Literary History* 17, no. 3 (2005): 469–73.

8. Howard Fast, *Freedom Road* (1944; London: Bodley Head, 1949), n.p. Hereafter cited parenthetically in the text.

9. Fast seems to be directly borrowing Du Bois's account of Reconstruction as an "experiment in democracy" (*BR* 715). Du Bois uses these words to criticize the "sweeping mechanistic interpretation" of the Civil War as a revolution, advanced by Charles and Mary Beard and later adopted by Popular Front historians, between the publication of Du Bois's book and Fast's, to describe the Civil War as a bourgeois revolution. See Zimmerman, "From the Second American Revolution," 324–28.

10. The novel was published in the year that the Congress of Industrial Organizations launched Operation Dixie.

11. William Faulkner, *Absalom, Absalom!* (1936; London: Penguin, 1971), 143. Hereafter cited parenthetically in the text.

12. Morrison, *Beloved*, 43.

13. Amy Clukey, "Plantation Modernity: *Gone with the Wind* and Irish-Southern Culture," *American Literature* 85, no. 3 (September 2013): 505–11.

BIBLIOGRAPHY

Archival Material and Legal Documents

Civil Rights Cases, 109 U.S. 3 (1883). https://www.loc.gov/item/usrep109003.

W. E. B. Du Bois Papers. MS 312. Special Collections and University Archives, University of Massachusetts Amherst Libraries. http://credo.library.umass.edu/view/collection/mums312.

Plessy v. Ferguson, 163 U.S. 537 (1896). https://www.loc.gov/item/usrep163537.

U.S. Constitution, amend. 14, sec. 4. General Records of the United States Government. Record Group 11. National Archives. https://www.archives.gov/milestone-documents/14th-amendment.

Books

Ammons, Elizabeth. *Conflicting Stories: American Women Writers at the Turn into the Twentieth Century.* Oxford: Oxford University Press, 1992.

Arendt, Hannah. *On Revolution.* London: Penguin, 1963.

Armstrong, Tim. *The Logic of Slavery: Debt, Technology, and Pain in American Literature.* Cambridge: Cambridge University Press, 2012.

Ayres, Edward L. *The Promise of the New South: Life after Reconstruction.* Oxford: Oxford University Press, 1992.

Badiou, Alain. *Being and Event.* Translated by Oliver Fetham. London: Continuum, 2005.

Baker, Bruce E. *What Reconstruction Meant: Historical Memory in the U.S. South.* Charlottesville: University of Virginia Press, 2007.

Bancroft, George. *The Necessity, the Reality, and the Promise of the Progress of the Human Race.* New York: New York Historical Society, 1854.

Baucom, Ian. *Specters of the Atlantic: Finance Capital, Slavery, and the Philosophy of History.* Durham, NC: Duke University Press, 2005.

Beckert, Sven. *Empire of Cotton: A Global History.* New York: Vintage, 2015.

Beckford, George L. *Persistent Poverty: Underdevelopment in Plantation Economies of the Third World.* Oxford: Oxford University Press, 1972.

Benhabib, Seyla. *The Reluctant Modernism of Hannah Arendt*. London: Sage Publications, 1996.

Bensel, Richard Franklin. *Yankee Leviathan: The Origins of Central State Authority in America, 1859–1877.* Cambridge: Cambridge University Press, 1990.

Bercovitch, Sacvan. *The American Jeremiad*. 1978; Madison: University of Wisconsin Press, 2012.

Berlant, Lauren. *The Female Complaint: The Unfinished Business of Sentiment in American Culture*. Durham, NC: Duke University Press, 2008.

Best, Stephen. *The Fugitive's Properties: Law and the Poetics of Possession*. Chicago: University of Chicago Press, 2004.

———. *None Like Us: Blackness, Belonging, Aesthetic Life*. Durham, NC: Duke University Press, 2018.

Blight, David. *Race and Reunion: The Civil War in American Memory*. Cambridge: Harvard University Press, 2001.

Bowers, Claude. *The Tragic Era: The Revolution after Lincoln*. Cambridge, MA: Riverside Press, 1929.

Broadhead, Richard. *Cultures of Letters: Scenes of Reading and Writing in Nineteenth-Century Literature*. Chicago: University of Chicago Press, 1993.

Brown, William Wells. *The Negro in the American Rebellion: His Heroism and His Fidelity*. Boston: Lee and Shephard, 1867.

Bull, Malcolm. *Seeing Things Hidden: Apocalypse, Vision, and Totality*. London: Verso, 1999.

Cable, George Washington. *The Grandissimes: A Story of Creole Life*. 1880; London: Penguin, 1988.

———. *John March, Southerner*. New York: Charles Scribner's Sons, 1894.

———. *Old Creole Days*. 1879; New York: Charles Scribner's Sons, 1893.

Carby, Hazel. *Reconstructing Womanhood: The Emergence of the Afro-American Woman Novelist*. Oxford: Oxford University Press, 1987.

Carico, Aaron. *Black Market: The Slave's Value in National Culture after 1865*. Chapel Hill: University of North Carolina Press, 2020.

Castronovo, Russ. *Necro Citizenship: Death, Eroticism, and the Public Sphere in the Nineteenth-Century United States*. Durham, NC: Duke University Press, 2001.

Chakkalakal, Tess. *Novel Bondage: Slavery, Marriage, and Freedom in Nineteenth-Century America*. Urbana: University of Illinois Press, 2011.

Chandler, James. *England in 1819: The Politics of Literary Culture and the Case of Romantic Historicism*. Chicago: University of Chicago Press, 1998.

Chase, Richard. *The American Novel and Its Tradition*. 1957, Baltimore: Johns Hopkins University Press, 1980.

Chesnutt, Charles. *The Conjure Woman and Other Conjure Tales*. Edited by Richard H. Broadhead. Durham, NC: Duke University Press, 1993.

———. *The House behind the Cedars*. New York: Modern Library, 2003.

———. *The Journals of Charles W. Chesnutt*. Edited by Richard Broadhead. Durham, NC: Duke University Press, 1993.

———. *The Marrow of Tradition*. In *The Portable Charles W. Chesnutt*, edited by William L. Andrews. 1901; London: Penguin, 2000.

———. *The Wife of His Youth and Other Stories of the Color Line*. 1898; Boston: Houghton, Mifflin, 1901.

Childs, Lydia Maria. *A Romance of the Republic*. Boston: Ticknor and Fields, 1867.

Ciccariello-Maher, George. *Decolonizing Dialectics*. Durham, NC: Duke University Press, 2017.

Cooper, Anna Julia. *A Voice from the South*. 1892; Oxford: Oxford University Press, 1988.

Coviello, Peter. *Tomorrow's Parties: Sex and the Untimely in Nineteenth-Century America*. New York: New York University Press, 2013.

Cox, Oliver Cromwell. *Caste, Class, and Race: A Study in Social Dynamics*. 1948; New York: Monthly Review Press, 1959.

Crane, Gregg D. *Race, Citizenship, and Law in American Literature*. Cambridge: Cambridge University Press, 2002.

Daniel, Pete. *Breaking the Land: The Transformation of Cotton, Tobacco, and Rice Cultures since 1880*. Urbana: University of Illinois Press, 1985.

Davidson, Neil. *How Revolutionary Were the Bourgeois Revolutions?* Chicago: Haymarket, 2012.

Davis, Rebecca Harding. *Waiting for the Verdict*. New York: Sheldon and Company, 1868.

Dawson, Melanie. *Emotional Reinventions: Realist-Era Representations beyond Sympathy*. Ann Arbor: University of Michigan Press, 2015.

Dayan, Colin. *The Law Is a White Dog*. Princeton: Princeton University Press, 2011.

Dekker, George. *The American Historical Romance*. Cambridge: Cambridge University Press, 1987.

Denning, Michael. *The Cultural Front: The Laboring of American Culture in the Twentieth Century*. London: Verso, 1997.

Dimock, Wai-Chee. *Residues of Justice: Law, Literature, Philosophy*. Berkeley: University of California Press, 1996.

Dixon, Thomas. *The Clansman: An Historical Romance of the Ku Klux Klan*. 1905; Gretna, LA: Pelican.

———. *The Leopard's Spots: A Romance of the White Man's Burden—1865–1900*. 1902; Gretna, LA: Pelican, 2001.

Downs, Gregory P. *Declarations of Dependence: The Long Reconstruction of Popular Politics in the South, 1861–1908*. Chapel Hill: University of North Carolina Press, 2011.

Du Bois, W. E. B. *Black Reconstruction in America, 1860–1880.* 1935; New York: Free Press, 1992.

———. *Darkwater: Voices from within the Veil.* 1920; London: Verso, 2016.

———. *Dusk of Dawn.* In *Writings,* by W. E. B. Du Bois. Edited by Nathan Huggins, 549–802. 1940; New York: Library of America, 1986.

———. *Economic Co-operation among Negro Americans.* Atlanta: Atlanta University Press, 1907.

———. *John Brown.* 1909; New York: M. E. Sharpe, 1997.

———. *The Quest of the Silver Fleece.* 1911; Mineola, NY: Dover, 2008.

———. *The Souls of Black Folk.* In Du Bois, *Writings.*

———. *The Suppression of the African Slave Trade.* In Du Bois, *Writings.*

Duck, Leigh Anne. *The Nation's Region: Southern Modernism, Segregation, and U.S. Nationalism.* Athens: University of Georgia Press, 2009.

Dunning, William. *Reconstruction Political and Economic, 1865–1877.* New York: Harper and Brothers, 1907.

Elliott, Mark. *Color-Blind Justice: Albion Tourgée and the Quest for Racial Equality from the Civil War to* Plessy v. Ferguson. Oxford: Oxford University Press, 2006.

Elliott, Michael. *The Culture Concept: Writing and Difference in the Age of Realism.* Minneapolis: University of Minnesota Press, 2002.

Fast, Howard. *Freedom Road.* 1946; London: Bodley Head, 1949.

Faulkner, William. *Absalom, Absalom!* 1936; London: Penguin, 1971.

———. *As I Lay Dying.* 1930; London: Vintage, 2004.

Felski, Rita. *The Limits of Critique.* Chicago: University of Chicago Press, 2015.

Fields, Barbara J. *Slavery and Freedom on the Middle Ground: Maryland during the Nineteenth Century.* New Haven: Yale University Press, 1985.

Foner, Eric. *Nothing but Freedom: Emancipation and Its Legacy.* Baton Rouge: Louisiana State University Press, 1983.

———. *Politics and Ideology in the Age of the Civil War.* Oxford: Oxford University Press, 1980.

———. *Reconstruction: America's Unfinished Revolution, 1863–1877.* New York: Perennial Classics, 1989.

———. *The Second Founding: How the Civil War and Reconstruction Remade the Constitution.* New York: Norton, 2019.

Foreman, P. Gabrielle. *Activist Sentiments: Reading Black Women in the Nineteenth Century.* Urbana: University of Illinois Press, 2009.

Gallagher, Catherine. *Telling It Like It Wasn't: The Counterfactual Imagination in History and Fiction.* Chicago: University of Chicago Press, 2018.

Gallagher, Catherine, and Stephen Greenblatt. *Practicing New Historicism.* Chicago: University of Chicago Press, 2000.

Gardner, Eric. *Black Print Unbound: The Christian Recorder, African American Literature, and Periodical Culture.* Oxford: Oxford University Press, 2015.

Gaston, Paul M. *The New South Creed: A Study in Southern Myth-Making.* New York: Alfred A. Knopf, 1970.

Gayarré, Charles. *The Creoles of History and the Creoles of Romance: A Lecture Delivered in the Hall of the Tulane University, New Orleans.* New Orleans: C. E. Hopkins, 1885.

Germana, Michael. *Standards of Value: Money, Race, and Literature in America.* Des Moines: University of Iowa Press, 2010.

Gillman, Susan. *Blood Talk: American Race Melodrama and the Culture of the Occult.* Chicago: University of Chicago Press, 2003.

Gilroy, Paul. *The Black Atlantic: Modernity and Double Consciousness.* London: Verso, 1993.

Glick, Jeremy Matthew. *The Black Radical Tragic: Performance, Aesthetics, and the Unfinished Haitian Revolution.* New York: New York University Press, 2016.

Glymph, Thavolia. *Out of the House of Bondage: The Transformation of the Plantation Household.* Cambridge: Cambridge University Press, 2008.

Gramsci, Antonio. *Selections from the Prison Notebooks.* Edited by Quintin Hoare and Geoffrey Nowell-Smith. London: Lawrence and Wishart, 1971.

Greeson, Jennifer Rae. *Our South: Geographic Fantasy and the Rise of National Literature.* Cambridge: Harvard University Press, 2010.

Griggs, Sutton. *Imperium in Imperio: A Study of the Negro Race Problem.* Cincinnati: Editor Publishing Company, 1899.

Gustafson, Sandra M., and Robert S. Levine, eds. *Reimagining the Republic: Race, Citizenship, and Nation in the Literary Work of Albion W. Tourgée.* New York: Fordham University Press, 2022.

Hahn, Steven. *A Nation under Our Feet: Black Political Struggles in the Rural South from Slavery to the Great Migration.* Cambridge: Harvard University Press, 2003.

———. *The Political Worlds of Slavery and Freedom.* Cambridge: Harvard University Press, 2009.

Hale, Grace Elizabeth. *Making Whiteness: The Culture of Segregation in the U.S. South, 1890–1940.* 1998; New York: Vintage, 1999.

Harper, Frances. *Iola Leroy, or Shadows Uplifted.* 1892; Oxford: Oxford University Press, 1988.

———. *Minnie's Sacrifice: A Rediscovered Novel.* Edited by Frances Smith Foster. 1868; Project Gutenberg, 2004. http://www.gutenberg.org/cache/epub/11053/pg11053 -images.html.

Hartman, Saidiya V. *Scenes of Subjection: Terror, Slavery, and Self-Making in Nineteenth-Century America.* Oxford: Oxford University Press, 1993.

Hobson, Fred. *Tell about the South: The Southern Rage to Explain.* Baton Rouge: Louisiana State University Press, 1983.

Hopkins, Pauline E. *Contending Forces: A Romance Illustrative of Negro Life North and South.* 1900; Oxford: Oxford University Press, 1988.

———. *Of One Blood.* 1902–3; New York: Washington Square Press, 2004.

Howells, William Dean. *An Imperative Duty.* 1891; New York: Harper and Brothers, 1892.

Hutchison, Anthony. *Writing the Republic: Liberalism and Morality in American Fiction.* New York: Columbia University Press, 2007.

Insko, Jeffrey. *History, Abolition, and the Ever-Present Now in Antebellum American Writing.* Oxford: Oxford University Press, 2018.

Jacobs, Harriet. *Incidents in the Life of a Slave Girl.* Boston: Published for the author, 1861.

James, C. L. R. *The Black Jacobins.* 1938; London: Penguin, 2001.

James, Henry. *The Bostonians.* 1886; London: Penguin, 2000.

Jameson, Fredric. *The Antinomies of Realism.* London: Verso, 2013.

———. *Postmodernism, or, The Cultural Logic of Late Capitalism.* Durham, NC: Duke University Press, 1991.

———. *Valences of the Dialectic.* London: Verso, 2009.

Johnson, Walter. *River of Dark Dreams: Slavery and Empire in the Cotton Kingdom.* Cambridge: Harvard University Press, 2013.

Karcher, Carolyn. *A Refugee from His Race: Albion W. Tourgée and His Fight against White Supremacy.* Chapel Hill: University of North Carolina Press, 2016.

Kennedy-Nolle, Sharon D. *Writing Reconstruction: Race, Gender, and Citizenship in the Postwar South.* Chapel Hill: University of North Carolina Press, 2015.

King, Edward. *The Great South.* Hartford, CT: American Publishing Company, 1875.

King, Richard H. *Arendt and America.* Chicago: University of Chicago Press, 2015.

Kosselleck, Reinhart. *Futures Past: On the Semantics of Historical Time.* New York: Columbia University Press, 2004.

Ladd, Barbara. *Nationalism and the Color Line in George W. Cable, Mark Twain, and William Faulkner.* Baton Rouge: Louisiana State University Press, 1996.

Lewis, David Levering. *W. E. B. Du Bois: Biography of a Race, 1868–1919.* New York: Henry Holt, 1993.

Logan, Rayford. *The Betrayal of the Negro: From Rutherford B. Hayes to Woodrow Wilson.* New York: Collier Books, 1965.

Luciano, Dana. *Arranging Grief: Sacred Time and the Body in Nineteenth-Century America.* New York: New York University Press, 2008.

Lukács, Georg. *The Historical Novel.* Translated by Hannah Mitchell and Stanley Mitchell. 1955; London: Merlin, 1962.

———. *The Theory of the Novel.* 1915; London: Merlin, 1971.

MacPherson, C. B. *The Political Theory of Possessive Individualism: Hobbes to Locke.* Oxford: Oxford University Press, 1964.

McPherson, James. *The Abolitionist Legacy: From Reconstruction to the NAACP.* Princeton: Princeton University Press, 1975.

Marable, Manning. *W. E. B. Du Bois: Black Radical Democrat.* Boston: Twayne, 1986.

Margolis, Stacey. *The Public Life of Privacy in Nineteenth-Century America.* Durham, NC: Duke University Press, 2005.

Marler, Scott. *The Merchant's Capital: New Orleans and the Political Economy of the Nineteenth-Century South.* Cambridge: Cambridge University Press, 2013.

Marrs, Cody. *Nineteenth-Century American Literature and the Long Civil War.* Oxford: Oxford University Press, 2015.

Marx, Karl. *Capital.* Vol. 1. Translated by Ben Fawkes. 1867; London: Penguin, 1990.

———. *The Eighteenth Brumaire of Louis Bonaparte.* 1852; Moscow: Progress Publishers, 1972.

Moddelmog, William E. *Reconstituting Authority: American Fiction in the Province of the Law.* Iowa City: University of Iowa Press, 2000.

Morrison, Toni. *Beloved.* 1987; London: Vintage, 2010.

Moynihan, Sinéad. *Passing into the Present: Contemporary American Fiction of Race and Gender Passing.* Manchester: Manchester University Press, 2010.

Mufti, Nasser. *Civilizing War: Imperial Politics and the Poetics of National Rupture.* Evanston, IL: Northwestern University Press, 2017.

Mullen, Bill. *Un-American: W. E. B. Du Bois and the Century of World Revolution.* Philadelphia: Temple University Press, 2015.

O'Donovan, Susan E. *Becoming Free in the Cotton South.* Cambridge: Harvard University Press, 2007.

O'Malley, Michael. *Face Value: The Entwined Histories of Money and Race in American History.* Chicago: University of Chicago Press, 2012.

Olsen, Otto H. *Carpetbagger's Crusade: The Life of Albion Winegar Tourgée.* Baltimore: Johns Hopkins Press, 1965.

———. *The Thin Disguise:* Plessy v. Ferguson. New York: Humanities Press, 1967.

Page, Thomas Nelson. *The Negro: The Southerner's Problem.* New York: Charles Scribner's Sons, 1904.

———. *Red Rock: A Chronicle of Reconstruction.* New York: Charles Scribner's Sons, 1898.

Pike, James S. *The Prostrate State: South Carolina under Negro Government.* New York: D. Appleton and Company, 1874.

Post, Charles. *The American Road to Capitalism.* Leiden: Brill, 2011.

Pratt, Lloyd. *Archives of American Time: Literature and Modernity in the Nineteenth Century.* Philadelphia: University of Pennsylvania Press, 2010.

Prince, K. Stephen. *Stories of the South: Race and the Reconstruction of Southern Identity, 1865–1915.* Chapel Hill: University of North Carolina Press, 2014.

Rabinowitz, Harold. *Race Relations in the Urban South: 1865–1890.* 1978; Athens: University of Georgia Press, 1996.

Railton, Ben. *Contesting the Past, Reconstructing the Nation: American Literature and Culture in the Gilded Age, 1876–1893.* Tuscaloosa: University of Alabama Press, 2007.

Rampersad, Arnold. *The Art and Imagination of W. E. B. Du Bois.* 1976; New York: Schocken, 1990.

Reed, Adolph. *W. E. B. Du Bois and American Political Thought: Fabianism across the Color Line.* Oxford: Oxford University Press, 1997.

Ricoeur, Paul. *Time and Narrative.* Vol. 1. Translated by Kathleen McLoughlin and David Pellauer. Chicago: University of Chicago Press, 1984.

Roberts, William Clare. *Marx's Inferno: The Political Theory of Capital.* Princeton: Princeton University Press, 2017.

Robinson, Cedric. *Black Marxism: The Making of the Black Radical Tradition.* 1983; Chapel Hill: University of North Carolina Press, 2000.

Roediger, David. *Seizing Freedom: Slave Emancipation and Liberty for All.* London: Verso, 2014.

Rubin, Louis D. *George Washington Cable: The Life and Times of a Southern Heretic.* New York: Pegasus, 1969.

Sánchez-Eppler, Karen. *Touching Liberty: Abolition, Feminism, and the Politics of the Body.* Berkeley: University of California Press, 1993.

Saville, Julie. *The Work of Reconstruction: From Slave to Wage Laborer in South Carolina, 1860–1870.* Cambridge: Cambridge University Press, 1994.

Scott, David. *Conscripts of Modernity: The Tragedy of Colonial Enlightenment.* Durham, NC: Duke University Press, 2004.

Schmidt, Peter. *Sitting in Darkness: New South Fiction, Education, and the Rise of Jim Crow Colonialism, 1865–1920.* Jackson: University Press of Mississippi, 2008.

Silber, Nina. *The Romance of Reunion: Northerners and the South, 1865–1900.* Chapel Hill: University of North Carolina Press, 1993.

Singh, Nikhil Pal. *Black Is a Country: Race and the Unfinished Struggle for Democracy.* Cambridge: Harvard University Press, 2004.

Sollors, Werner. *Neither Black nor White yet Both: Thematic Explorations of Interracial Literature.* Oxford: Oxford University Press, 1997.

Stanley, Amy Dru. *From Bondage to Contract: Wage Labor, Marriage, and the Market in the Age of Slave Emancipation.* Cambridge: Cambridge University Press, 1998.

Sugden, Edward. *Emergent Worlds: Alternative States in Nineteenth-Century American Culture.* New York: New York University Press, 2018.

Sundquist, Eric. *To Wake the Nations: Race in the Making of American Literature.* Cambridge: Harvard University Press, 1993.

Szczesiul, Anthony. *The Southern Hospitality Myth: Ethics, Politics, and Race in American Memory.* Athens: University of Georgia Press, 2017.

Tate, Claudia. *Domestic Allegories of Political Desire: The Black Heroine's Text at the Turn of the Century.* Oxford: Oxford University Press, 1993.

Taylor, Christopher. *Empire of Neglect: The West Indies in the Wake of British Liberalism.* Durham, NC: Duke University Press, 2018.

Thomas, Brook. *American Literary Realism and the Failed Promise of Contract.* Berkeley: University of California Press, 1997.

———. *The Literature of Reconstruction: Not in Plain Black and White.* Baltimore: Johns Hopkins University Press, 2016.

Tompkins, Jane. *Sensational Designs: The Cultural Work of American Fiction, 1790–1860.* Oxford: Oxford University Press, 1985.

Tourgée, Albion. *An Appeal to Caesar.* New York: Fords, Howard, and Hulbert, 1884.

———. *Bricks without Straw.* New York: Fords, Howard, and Hulbert, 1880.

———. *A Fool's Errand.* New York: Fords, Howard, and Hulbert, 1879.

———. *The Invisible Empire.* New York: Fords, Howard, and Hulbert, 1880.

———. *Pactolus Prime.* 1890; Upper Saddle River, NJ: Gregg Press, 1968.

Trilling, Lionel. *Sincerity and Authenticity.* Oxford: Oxford University Press, 1972.

Trouillot, Michel-Rolph. *Silencing the Past: Power and the Production of History.* 1995; Boston: Beacon Press, 2005.

Turner, Arlin. *George W. Cable: A Biography.* Durham, NC: Duke University Press, 1956.

Twain, Mark. *Adventures of Huckleberry Finn.* 1885; Oxford: Oxford University Press, 1999.

———. *Pudd'nhead Wilson.* 1893; London: Penguin, 1986.

Warren, Kenneth W. *Black and White Strangers: Race and American Literary Realism.* Chicago: University of Chicago Press, 1993.

———. *What Was African American Literature?* Cambridge: Harvard University Press, 2011.

Weinbaum, Alys Eve. *Wayward Reproductions: Genealogies of Race and Nation in Transatlantic Modern Thought.* Durham, NC: Duke University Press, 2004.

Weinstein, Cindy. *Time, Tense, and American Literature: When Is Now?* Cambridge: Cambridge University Press, 2015.

White, Hayden. *Metahistory: The Historical Imagination in Nineteenth-Century Europe.* Baltimore: Johns Hopkins University Press, 1973.

Wilkerson, Isabel. *Caste: The Lies That Divide Us.* New York: Allen Lane, 2020.

Williams, Raymond. *Keywords: A Vocabulary of Culture and Society.* Rev. ed. New York: Oxford University Press, 1985.

———. *Modern Tragedy.* London: Chatto and Windus, 1966.

Williamson, Joel. *The Crucible of Race: Black-White Relations in the American South since Emancipation.* Oxford: Oxford University Press, 1984.

Wilson, Edmund. *Patriotic Gore: Studies in the Literature of the American Civil War.* London: André Deutsch, 1962.

Woodward, C. Van. *American Counterpoint: Slavery and Racism in the North-South Dialogue.* 1964; Oxford: Oxford University Press, 1983.

——. *The Origins of the New South.* Baton Rouge: Louisiana State University Press, 1951.

——. *The Strange Career of Jim Crow.* 3rd rev. ed. Oxford: Oxford University Press, 1974.

Wright, Gavin. *Old South, New South: Revolutions in the Southern Economy since the Civil War.* New York: Basic Books, 1986.

Articles and Book Chapters

Althusser, Louis. "From *Capital* to Marx's Philosophy." In *Reading Capital: The Complete Edition,* edited by Louis Althusser, Etienne Balibar, Roger Establet, Pierre Machery, and Jacques Rancière; translated by Ben Brewster and David Fernbach. London: Verso, 2015.

Appiah, Anthony. "The Uncompleted Argument: Du Bois and the Illusion of Race." *Critical Inquiry* 12, no. 1 (1985): 21–37.

Bakhtin, Mikhail. "Forms of Time and of the Chronotope in the Novel." In *The Dialogic Imagination: Four Essays,* edited and translated by Michael Holquist, 84–258. Austin: University of Texas Press, 1981.

Barthes, Roland. "The Reality Effect." In *The Rustle of Language,* 141–48. Translated by Richard Howard. Berkeley: University of California Press, 1989.

Benjamin, Walter. "Theses on the Philosophy of History." In *Illuminations,* edited by Hannah Arendt; translated by Harry Zorn, 245–55. London: Pimlico, 1999.

Bentley, Nancy. "The Fourth Dimension: Kinlessness and African American Narrative." *Critical Inquiry* 35, no. 2 (2009): 270–92.

——. "Queer Synecdoche: Tourgée's *Bricks without Straw* and Black Kinship." In *Reimagining the Republic: Race, Citizenship and Nation in the Literary Work of Albion W. Tourgée,* edited by Sandra M. Gustafson, and Robert Levine, 44–56. New York: Fordham University Press, 2022.

——. "The Strange Career of Love and Slavery: Chesnutt, Engels, Masoch." *American Literary History* 17, no. 3 (2005): 460–85.

Berlant, Lauren. "The Queen of America Goes to Washington City: Harriet Jacobs, Frances Harper, Anita Hill." *American Literary History* 65, no. 3 (1993): 549–74.

Best, Stephen, and Saidiya Hartman. "Fugitive Justice." *Representations* 91, no. 2. (2005): 1–15.

Bewes, Timothy. "Reading with the Grain: A New World in Literary Criticism." *Differences: A Journal of Feminist Cultural Studies* 21, no. 3 (2010): 1–33.

Bloch, Ernst. "Nonsynchronism and the Obligation to Its Dialectics." Translated by Mark Ritter. *New German Critique* 11 (1977): 22–38.

Burnett, Katharine A. "Moving toward a 'No South': George Washington Cable's Global Vision in *The Grandissimes.*" *Southern Literary Journal* 45, no. 1 (2012): 21–38.

Cable, George Washington. "The Freedman's Case in Equity." *Century Magazine* 29 (January 1885): 409–18.

———. "Literature in the Southern States." In *The Negro Question: A Selection of Writings on Civil Rights in the South,* edited by Arlin Turner, 37–46. New York: Norton, 1968.

———. "The Negro Question." *The Negro Question,* 1–58. 1890; New York: Charles Scribner's Sons, 1898.

———. "The Silent South." *Century Magazine* 30 (August 1885): 674–91.

Carter, Everett. "Edmund Wilson Refights the Civil War: The Revision of Albion Tourgée's Novels." *American Literary Realism* 29, no. 2 (1997): 68–75.

Castronovo, Russ. "Within the Veil of Interdisciplinary Knowledge? Jefferson, Du Bois, and the Negation of Politics." *New Literary History* 31, no. 4 (2000): 781–804.

Chakkalakal, Tess, and Kenneth W. Warren. "Introduction." In *Jim Crow, Literature, and the Legacy of Sutton E. Griggs,* edited by Tess Chakkalakal and Kenneth W. Warren, 1–20. Athens: University of Georgia Press, 2013.

Chesnutt, Charles. "What Is a White Man?" In *Charles W. Chesnutt: Essays and Speeches,* edited by Joseph R. McElrath Jr., Robert C. Leitz III, and Jesse S. Crisler, 68–73. Stanford: Stanford University Press, 1999.

Clegg, John J. "Capitalism and Slavery." *Critical Historical Studies* 2, no. 2 (2015): 281–304.

———. "Credit Market Discipline and Capitalist Slavery in Antebellum South Carolina." *Social Science History* 42, no. 4 (Summer 2018): 1–34.

Clukey, Amy. "Plantation Modernity: *Gone with the Wind* and Irish-Southern Culture." *American Literature* 85, no. 3 (September 2013): 505–30.

Coviello, Peter. "Intimacy and Affliction: Du Bois, Race, and Psychoanalysis." *Modern Language Quarterly* 64, no. 1 (March 2003): 1–32.

Davies, Thomas J. "Race, Identity and the Law: *Plessy v. Ferguson* (1896)." In *Race on Trial: Law and Justice in American History,* edited by Annette Gordon-Reed, 61–76. Oxford: Oxford University Press, 2002.

Denning, Michael. "Wageless Life." *New Left Review* 66 (November 2010): 79–97.

Diffley, Kathleen, and Coleman Hutchison. "Introduction." In *The Cambridge Companion to the Literature of the Civil War and Reconstruction,* edited by Kathleen Diffley and Coleman Hutchison, 1–12. Cambridge: Cambridge University Press, 2022.

Douglas, J. Allen. "The 'Most Valuable Sort of Property': Constructing White Identity in America Law, 1880–1940." *San Diego Law Review* 40, no. 3 (August–September 2003): 881–946.

Downs, Gregory P., and Kate Masur. "Echoes of War: Rethinking Post–Civil War Governance and Politics." In *The World the Civil War Made,* edited by Gregory P. Downs and Kate Masur, 1–21. Chapel Hill: University of North Carolina Press, 2015.

Du Bois, W. E. B. "The African Roots of War." *Atlantic Monthly* 115 (May 1915): 707–14.

———. "Marxism and the Negro Problem." In *W. E. B. Du Bois: A Reader,* edited by David Levering Lewis, 538–44. New York: Henry Holt, 1995.

———. "The Negro and Communism." In Lewis, *W. E. B. Du Bois,* 583–93.

———. "Possibilities of the Negro: The Advanced Guard of the Race." *Booklovers Magazine* 2 (July 1903): 3–15.

Duck, Leigh Anne. "Woodward's Southerner: History, Literature, and the Question of Identity." In *The Ongoing Burden of Southern History: Politics and Identity in the Twenty-First Century South,* edited by Angie Maxwell, Todd Shields, and Jeannie Whayne, 31–61. Baton Rouge: Louisiana State University Press, 2012.

Edwards, Brent Hayes. "The Autonomy of Black Radicalism." *Social Text* 67, vol. 19, no. 2 (2001): 1–13.

Elmer, Jonathan. "Babo's Razor; or Discerning the Event in an Age of Differences." *Differences: A Journal of Feminist Cultural Studies* 19, no. 2 (2008): 54–81.

Engels Friedrich. "Engels to Marx, 15th July 1865." *Marx and Engels Collected Works.* Translated by Christopher Upward and John Peet, 42:167–68. 50 vols. London: Lawrence and Wishart, 1975–2004.

Ernest, John. "*The Negro in the American Rebellion:* William Wells Brown and the Design of African American History." In *Literary Cultures of the Civil War,* edited by Timothy Sweet, 57–75. Athens: University of Georgia Press, 2016.

Farland, Maria. "W. E. B. Du Bois, Anthropometric Science and the Limits of Racial Uplift." *American Quarterly* 58, no. 4 (2006): 1017–44.

Fields, Barbara Jeanne. "The Advent of Capitalist Agriculture: The New South in a Bourgeois World." In *Essays on the Postbellum Southern Economy,* edited by Thavolia Glymph and John J. Kushma, 73–94. College Station: Texas A&M University Press, 1985.

———. "Ideology and Race in American History." In *Region, Race, and Reconstruction: Essays in Honor of C. Vann Woodward,* edited by J. Morgan Kousser and James M. McPherson, 143–77. Oxford: Oxford University Press, 1982.

———. "Slavery, Race and Ideology in the United States of America." *New Left Review* 181 (May–June 1990): 143–77.

Foner, Eric. "Reconstruction Revisited." *Reviews in American History* 10, no. 4 (1982): 82–100.

Foucault, Michel. "Nietzsche, Genealogy, History." In *The Foucault Reader,* edited by Paul Rabinow, 76–100. New York: Pantheon Books, 1984.

Gallagher, Catherine. "When Did the Confederate States of America Free the Slaves?" *Representations* 98, no. 1 (2007): 53–61.

Gardner, Eric. "African American Literary Reconstructions and the 'Propaganda of History.'" *American Literary History* 30, no. 3 (Fall 2018): 429–49.

Gebhard, Caroline, and Barbara McCaskill. "Introduction." In *Post-Bellum, Pre-Harlem,* edited by Barbara McCaskill and Caroline Gebhard, 1–16. New York: New York University Press, 2006.

Ginsburg, Elaine K. "Introduction: The Politics of Passing." In *Passing and the Fictions of Identity,* edited by Elaine K. Ginsburg, 1–18. Durham, NC: Duke University Press, 1996.

Golub, Mark. "*Plessy* as Passing: Judicial Responses to Ambiguously Raced Bodies in *Plessy v. Ferguson.*" *Law and Society Review* 39 (September 2005): 563–600.

Grady, Henry. "In Plain Black and White: A Reply to Mr. Cable." *Century Magazine* 29 (April 1885): 909–17.

Greeson, Jennifer Rae. "The Pre-History of Possessive Individualism." *PMLA* 127, no. 4 (October 2012): 918–24.

Gustafson, Sandra M. "Reimagining the Republic: Tourgée on Citizenship." In *Reimagining the Republic: Race, Citizenship, and Nation in the Literary Works of Albion W. Tourgée,* edited by Sandra M. Gustafson and Robert S. Levine, 97–109. New York: Fordham University Press, 2022.

Hahn, Steven. "Class and State in Postemancipation Societies: Southern Planters in Comparative Perspective." *American Historical Review* 95, no. 1 (February 1990): 75–98.

Hall, Stuart. "Race and Moral Panics in Postwar Britain." In *Selected Writings on Race and Difference,* edited by Paul Gilroy and Ruth Wilson Gilmore, 56–70. Durham, NC: Duke University Press, 2021.

———. "Race, Articulation, and Societies Structured in Dominance." In Gilroy and Gilmore, *Selected Writings on Race and Difference,* 195–245.

Harris, Cheryl I. "Whiteness as Property." *Harvard Law Review* 106, no. 8 (1993): 1707–91.

Hine, Darlene Clark. "Rape and the Inner Lives of Black Women: Thoughts on the Culture of Dissemblance." *Hine Sight: Black Women and the Re-Construction of American History,* 37–48. Bloomington: Indiana University Press, 1994.

Howells, William Dean. "A Psychological Counter-Current in Recent Fiction." *North American Review* 173, no. 541 (1901): 872–88.

Hutner, Gordon. "Reenvisioning Reconstruction: An Introduction." *American Literary History* 30, no. 3 (2018): 403–6.

Ignatiev, Noel. "'The American Blindspot': Reconstruction According to Eric Foner and W. E. B. Du Bois." *Labor / Le Travail* 31 (Spring 1993): 243–51.

Immerwahr, Daniel. "Caste or Colony: Indianizing Race in the United States." *Modern Intellectual History* 4, no. 2 (2007): 275–301.

Johnson, Walter. "Agency: A Ghost Story." In *Slavery's Ghost: The Problem of Freedom in the Age of Emancipation,* edited by Jarod Roll, 8–30. Baltimore: Johns Hopkins University Press, 2011.

Karcher, Carolyn. "Introduction." In *Bricks without Straw,* by Albion Tourgée, edited by Carolyn Karcher, 1–64. Durham, NC: Duke University Press, 2009.

———. "Rape, Murder, and Revenge in 'Slavery's Pleasant Homes': Lydia Maria Child's Antislavery Fiction and the Limits of Genre." In *The Culture of Sentiment: Race, Gender, and Sentimentality in Nineteenth-Century America,* edited by Shirley Samuels, 58–72. Oxford: Oxford University Press, 1993.

Kelly, Adam. "Dialectic of Sincerity: Lionel Trilling and David Foster Wallace." *Post45* 17, no. 14 (October 2014): 1–15.

Kelly, Brian. "W. E. B. Du Bois, Black Agency and the Slaves' Civil War." *International Socialist Review* 100 (Spring 2016): 48–68.

Kendall, Mrs. John S. "Cable, George Washington (1844–)." In *The Library of Southern Literature,* edited by Edwin Anderson Alderman and Joel Chandler Harris 2:619–54. 17 vols. Atlanta: Martin and Hoyte, 1909–13.

Knadler, Stephen. "The Bright Side: African American Women and the Affective Archive of Southern Racial Uplift." In *The Oxford Handbook of the Literature of the U.S. South,* edited by Fred Hobson and Barbara Ladd, 231–50. Oxford: Oxford University Press, 2016.

———. "Narrating Slow Violence: Post-Reconstruction's Necropolitics and Speculating beyond Liberal Anti-Race Fiction." *J19: The Journal of Nineteenth-Century Americanists* 5, no. 1 (2017): 21–50.

———. "Traumatized Racial Performativity: Passing in Nineteenth-Century African-American Testimonies." *Cultural Critique* 55 (Fall 2003): 63–100.

Kreyling, Michael. "Introduction." In *The Grandissimes: A Story of Creole Life,* by George Washington Cable. London: Penguin, 1988.

Marler, Scott. "Fables of the Reconstruction, Reconstruction of the Fables." *Journal of the Historical Society* 4, no. 1 (Winter 2004): 113–37.

Marrs, Cody. "Three Theses on Reconstruction." *American Literary History,* 30, no. 3 (Fall 2018): 407–28.

Marrs, Cody, and Christopher Hager. "Against 1865: Reperiodizing the Nineteenth Century." *J19: The Journal of Nineteenth-Century Americanists* 1, no. 2 (Fall 2013): 259–84.

Marx, Karl. "Address of the International Workingmen's Association to Abraham Lincoln." In *An Unfinished Revolution: Karl Marx and Abraham Lincoln,* by Robin Blackburn, 211–12. London: Verso, 2011.

McInnis, Jarvis C. "'Behold the Land': W. E. B. Du Bois, Cotton Futures, and the Afterlife of the Plantation in the U.S. South." *Global South* 10, no. 2 (2016): 70–98.

Monteith, Sharon, and Suzanne W. Jones. "Introduction: South to New Places." In *South to a New Place: Region, Literature, Culture,* edited by Sharon Monteith and Suzanne W. Jones, 1–19. Baton Rouge: Louisiana State University Press, 2002.

O'Brien, Michael. "C. Vann Woodward and the Burden of Southern Liberalism." *American Historical Review* 78, no. 3 (1973): 589–604.

Peterson, Carla L. "Commemorative Ceremonies and Invented Traditions: History, Memory, and Modernity in the 'New Negro' Novel of the Nadir." In McCaskill and Gebhard, *Post-Bellum, Pre-Harlem,* 34–56.

———. "Frances Harper, Charlotte Forten, and African American Literary Reconstruction." In *Challenging Boundaries: Gender and Periodization,* edited by Joyce W. Warren and Margaret Dickie, 39–61. Athens: University of Georgia Press, 2000.

Phillips, Lily Wiatrowski. "*The Black Flame* Revisited: Recursion and Return in the Reading of W. E. B. Du Bois's Trilogy." *CR: The New Centennial Review* 15, no. 2 (2015): 157–69.

Phillips, Ulrich B. "The Central Theme of Southern History." *American Historical Review* 34, no. 1 (1928): 30–43.

Piep, Karsten H. "Liberal Visions of Reconstruction: Lydia Maria Child's *Romance of the Republic* and George Washington Cable's *The Grandissimes.*" *Studies in American Fiction* 31, no. 2 (Fall 2003): 165–90.

Poulantzas, Nicos. "The Problem of the Capitalist State." In *Ideology in Social Science: Readings in Critical Social Theory,* edited by Robin Blackburn, 238–53. London: Fontana Press, 1972.

Rabinowitz, Harold. "More than the Woodward Thesis: Assessing *The Strange Career of Jim Crow.*" *Journal of American History* 75, no. 3 (December 1988): 842–56.

———. "Reconstruction and Disfranchisement." *Atlantic Monthly* 88 (1901): 433–37.

Renker, Elizabeth. "Reconstruction Literature." In *American Literature in Transition, 1851–1877,* edited by Cody Marrs, 322–36. Cambridge: Cambridge University Press, 2022.

———. "What Is 'Reconstruction Poetry'?" *American Literary History* 30, no. 3 (2018): 508–30.

Rogin, Michael. "The Sword Became a Flashing Vision: D. W. Griffith's *The Birth of a Nation.*" *Representations* 9 (1985): 150–95.

Romine, Scott. "Fables of the Bloody Shirt: Reconstruction and the Problem of National Violence." In *A History of the Literature of the U.S. South,* edited by Harilous Stecopoulos, 185–202. Cambridge: Cambridge University Press, 2021.

———. "Southern Affects: Field and Feeling in a Skeptical Age." In Hobson and Ladd, *Oxford Handbook of the Literature of the U.S. South,* 161–79.

———. "Things Falling Apart: The Postcolonial Condition of *Red Rock* and *The Leopard's Spots.*" In *Look Away: The South in New World Studies,* edited by Jon Smith and Deborah Cohn, 175–200. Durham, NC: Duke University Press, 2004.

Rosenthal, Debra J. "The White Blackbird: Miscegenation, Genre, and the Tragic Mulatta in Howells, Harper, and the Babes of Romance." *Nineteenth-Century Literature* 56, no. 4 (2002): 495–517.

Saks, Eva. "Representing Miscegenation Law." In *Interracialism: Black-White Intermarriage in American History, Literature, and Law,* edited by Werner Sollors, 61–81. Oxford: Oxford University Press, 2000.

Saman, Michael J. "Du Bois and Marx, Du Bois and Marxism." *Du Bois Review* 17, no. 1 (2020): 33–54.

Samuels, Shirley. "The Identity of Slavery." In Samuels, *Culture of Sentiment,* 157–71.

———. "Introduction." In Samuels, *Culture of Sentiment,* 3–8.

Sanborn, Geoffrey. "Mother's Milk: Frances Harper and the Circulation of Blood." *ELH* 72, no. 3 (2005): 691–715.

Schurtz, Carl. *Report on the Condition of the South.* 1865; Salt Lake City: Project Gutenberg, 2005. https://www.gutenberg.org/cache/epub/8872/pg8872.html.

Scott, Rebecca. "Public Rights, Social Equality, and the Conceptual Roots of the *Plessy* Challenge." *Michigan Law Review* 106, no. 5 (2008): 777–804.

Sexton, Jared. "The Social Life of Social Death." *InTensions* 5 (2011): 1–47.

Short, Gretchen. "The Dilemmas of Reconstructing the Nation in Albion W. Tourgée's *A Fool's Errand* and Charles W. Chesnutt's *The Marrow of Tradition.*" *REAL* 14 (1998): 241–67.

Singh, Nikhil Pal. "On Race, Violence, and So-Called Primitive Accumulation." *Social Text* 128, vol. 34, no. 3 (September 2016): 27–50.

Smith, Stacy L. "Emancipating Peons, Excluding Coolies: Reconstructing Coercion in the American West." In Downs and Masur, *World the Civil War Made,* 46–74.

Sollors, Werner. "Charles W. Chesnutt's Historical Imagination." In *Passing in the Works of Charles W. Chesnutt,* edited by Susan Prothro Wright and Ernestine Pickens Glass, 3–8. Jackson: University Press of Mississippi, 2010.

Spillers, Hortense J. "Mama's Baby, Papa's Maybe: An American Grammar Book." *Diacritics* 17, no. 2 (Summer 1987): 64–81.

Stein, Jordan Alexander. "American Literary History and Queer Temporalities." *American Literary History* 25, no. 4 (2013): 855–69.

Stein, Judith. "'Of Mr. Booker T. Washington and Others': The Political Economy of Racism in the United States." In *Renewing Black Intellectual History: The Ideological and Material Foundations of African American Thought,* edited by Adolph Reed Jr. and Kenneth W. Warren, 19–50. Boulder: Paradigm Publishers, 2010.

Stevens, Erica. "Absolutely Novel: The Event and Charles Chesnutt's *Paul Marchand, F.M.C.*" *Studies in the Novel* 50, no. 4 (Winter 2018): 523–42.

Stevens, Thaddeus. "Reconstruction: Hon. Thaddeus Stevens on the Great Topic of the Hour. An Address Delivered to the Citizens of Lancaster, Sept. 6, 1865." *New York Times,* September 10, 1865.

Stewart, James B. "Psychic Duality of Afro-Americans in the Novels of W. E. B. Du Bois." *Phylon* 44, no. 2 (1983): 93–107.

Sumner, Charles. "Are We a Nation?" *The Works of Charles Sumner,* 12:187–249. 20 vols. Boston: Lee and Sheppard, 1870–83.

———. "The Question of Caste." *Works of Charles Sumner,* 13:131–83.

Swann, Charles. "*The Grandissimes:* A Story-Shaped World." *Literature and History* 13, no. 2 (1987): 257–77.

Taylor, Christopher. "The Plantation Road to Socialism." *Amerikastudien / American Studies* 62, no. 4 (2017): 551–65.

———. "Sharing Time: C. L. R. James and Southern Agrarian Movements." *Social Text* 111, vol. 30, no. 2 (2012): 75–98.

Tennyson, Alfred. "The flower in the crannied wall." *Major Works,* 379. Oxford World's Classics. Oxford: Oxford University Press, 2000.

Thomas, Brook. "The Literature of Reconstruction and the Worlds the Civil War Might Have Made." In Diffley and Hutchison, *Cambridge Companion to the Literature of the Civil War and Reconstruction,* 169–82.

Tourgée, Albion. "Brief of the Plaintiff in Error." In *Undaunted Radical: The Selected Writings and Speeches of Albion W. Tourgée,* edited by Mark Elliott and John David Smith, 296–327. Baton Rouge: Louisiana State University Press, 2010.

———. "The Claim of 'Realism.'" *North American Review* 188, no. 388 (March 1889): 386–88.

———. "The South as a Field for Fiction." *Forum* 6 (1888): 404–13.

———. "Topics of the Time: Battles and Leaders of the Civil War." *Century Magazine* 28 (October 1884): 943–46.

Tuhkanen, Mikko. "'Out of Joint': Passing, Haunting, and the Time of Slavery in Hagar's Daughter." *American Literature* 79, no. 2 (June 2007): 335–61.

Van Wienen, Mark, and Julie Kraft. "How the Socialism of W. E. B. Du Bois Still Matters: Black Socialism in *The Quest of the Silver Fleece.*" *African American Review* 31, no. 1 (2007): 67–85.

Wagner, Bryan. "Disarmed and Dangerous: The Strange Career of Bras-Coupé." *Representations* 92, no. 1 (Fall 2005): 117–51.

Warren, Kathryn Hamilton. "Empathetic Persuasion in Albion Tourgée's *A Fool's Errand.*" *American Literary Realism* 44, no. 1 (Fall 2011): 46–67.

Warren, Kenneth W. "Tourgée, Democracy, Romance, and the Art of Fiction." In Gustafson and Levine, *Reimagining the Republic,* 110–23.

Weinbaum, Alys Eve. "Gendering the General Strike: W. E. B. Du Bois's *Black Reconstruction* and Black Feminism's 'Propaganda of History.'" *South Atlantic Quarterly* 112, no. 3 (Summer 2013): 437–63.

Wilderson, Frank, III. "Gramsci's Black Marx: Whither the Slave in Civil Society?" *Social Identities* 9, no. 2 (2003): 225–40.

Wilson, Woodrow. "The Reconstruction of the Southern States." *Atlantic Monthly* 87 (1901): 1–15.

Womack, Autumn. "W. E. B. Du Bois's Apocalyptic Ambivalence." In *Apocalypse in American Literature and Culture,* edited by John Hay, 239–51. Cambridge: Cambridge University Press, 2020.

Yeats, W. B. "Easter, 1916." In *The Poems,* edited by Daniel Albright, 228–30. London: Everyman's Library, 1992.

Zimmerman, Andrew. "From the Second American Revolution to the Third International and Back Again: Marxism, the Popular Front, and the American Civil War." In Downs and Masur, *World the Civil War Made,* 304–36.

———. "Introduction." In *The Civil War in the United States,* by Karl Marx and Friedrich Engels, edited by Andrew Zimmerman, xi–xxx. New York: International Publishers, 2017.

Films and Websites

Downs, Gregory P., and Scott Nesbit. *Mapping Occupation: Force, Freedom, and the Army in Reconstruction.* March 2015. https://www.mappingoccupation.org.

Griffith, D. W. *The Birth of a Nation.* 1915; Chatsworth, CA: Image Entertainment, 1992. DVD.

INDEX

abjection, 77, 106–7, 108, 137

abolition, 3, 14–15, 31–32, 55–56, 58–59, 88, 99, 100, 104, 110–12, 113, 116–20

"abolition-democracy," Du Bois, 58–59, 70–72

Absalom, Absalom! (Faulkner), 165–66, 178n49

activist state, 58, 63, 64, 77, 85

"African Roots of War, The" (Du Bois), 146

agency, 70, 121, 135–36, 192n1

allegorical structure in Cable, 29–31, 35–38, 42–49, 52–53

allegory, impasse of sincerity as, 64, 67

allegory, sentimental poetics as, 112

allusions, 52, 97, 108–9, 111

Althusser, Louis, 13

ambiguity, 22, 55–56

ambivalence, 140–41

"American grammar," Spillers, 78

American Left, 121–22, 193n3

American realists, 19, 181n35, 191n58

American Revolution/revolutionary tradition(s), 8, 10, 59, 60–61, 76–77

Ammons, Elizabeth, 188n23

anachronisms: "abolition-democracy," Tourgée, 72; anachronistic historicism, Cable, 28–34, 53; anachronistic temporality, Du Bois, 124, 128, 139–41, 145, 147, 152–54; counterfactual narrative mode, Du Bois, 125–26; historical novels, reconstructing, 18–24; necessary anachronism,

18, 90, 105; racial custom, Chesnutt, 108–9; segregation, 104–6; sentimental poetics, Harper, 120; sentiment's anachronistic character, Chesnutt, 113

anagnorisis, 137, 142

Apartheid South Africa, 37

apocalyptic treatment of time, 131, 141–42

apolitical developmentalism, 65

aporias, 13, 124, 126, 158–59

Appeal to Caesar, An (Tourgée), 75–77

Arendt, Hannah, 7, 59–60, 68

"Are We a Nation?" (Sumner), 61

aristocracy, 32–33

Armstrong, Tim, 114

art and politics, 126–27, 131

Atlantic Monthly, 15, 20

Atlantic slave trade, 44, 174n63

authenticity, 68–69

baby-swap narratives, 144–45. *See also* kinship

Badiou, Alain, 12

Bakhtin, Mikhail, 94

balance of forces, 71–72

Bancroft, George, 8

barbarism, 33, 65

Barthes, Roland, 111–12

"Battles and Leaders of the Civil War" (Cable), 33

Baucom, Ian, 174n63

Beard, Charles, 155, 199n9

Beard, Mary, 155, 199n9

thinking in Cable, 51–53; plantation idea, 31–33; public and private, 33–34, 39–40, 48; regional critique of in Cable, 38, 41–42, 43–49

Castronovo, Russ, 188n29

Century Magazine, 33–34, 40

Chakkalakal, Tess, 4, 183n58

Chandler, James, 19

Chase, Richard, 178n49

chattel slavery, 3, 6–7, 60, 79, 81, 87–88, 106, 107–9, 112–20, 135, 148, 190n46, 190n49. *See also* slavery

Chesnutt, Charles, 24; as American realist, 19; background, 14; canonization, 102; color line, 95, 97, 101, 105–6, 107; conjure stories, 102; debt images, 107–13, 191n55; and Du Bois, 130; elliptical treatment of Reconstruction, 94, 105–6; historical sense, 166; history of slavery for the Jim Crow era, 102–3; inheritance plot, 161–62; passing genre, 87–90, 94–101, 107–13; and print, 161; racial custom, 97, 107–13; segregation, 105, 108; sentimental fiction/poetics, 106–7, 112–13, 160; somnolent reading, 100

Chesnutt, Charles, works of: *The House behind the Cedars,* 15, 18, 22, 87, 94–97, 101–2, 105, 112–13, 161–62, 187n19, 189n31, 191n55; *The Marrow of Tradition,* 102, 130, 160–63, 186n8; "Marse Jeems' Nightmare," 109; "The Sheriff's Children," 191n55, 199n5 (*see also* slavery); "What Is a White Man," 190n44; *The Wife of His Youth and Other Stories of the Color Line,* 102, 199n5

Child, Lydia Maria, 88

Christian Recorder, 15, 119

"chronotope," 94, 120

Ciccariello-Maher, George, 136

citizenship, 15–16, 32, 58, 74–75, 77–80, 81–86, 160, 183n57

civic virtue, 59–60

civil rights: "abolition-democracy," Du Bois, 58–59, 70–72; Civil Rights Act of 1875, 33, 38; *Civil Rights Cases,* 33–34, 38, 74, 82–83, 88; civil rights legislation, 32–34, 38–39, 82, 88; civil rights movement, 1, 30, 103–4; historical narrative of post-Reconstruction politics, 3, 6; literary approach to Reconstruction, 16; possessive individualism, 74–75, 79; radicalism/radical tradition, 169n3

civil society, 37, 71

Civil War, 6–9, 16–17, 33, 55, 60–61, 64, 83, 88–90, 123, 128–29, 133, 140, 155, 170n13, 199n9

Clansman, The (Dixon), 21–22

class identity, 125, 137, 148

class perspectives, 40, 71, 128–29, 141–42, 150–51, 153–54

class subject, 7, 128–31, 135–36, 144–45, 155, 158. *See also* "new world peasantry," Du Bois

Clegg, John J., 190n49

Clotel (Brown), 108

Clukey, Amy, 167

"Code Noir," 44

colonial economy, 177n30

color line, 87–90, 95, 97–98, 100–101, 102–6, 107, 112–13

"color question," 127–28

Comité des Citoyens, 84, 185n81

commencement address, University of Mississippi, 28–29

commodification, 107–9

commodity cultures, 153

communal property, 85

Communist Party, 125, 164

Compromise of 1877, 65

concubinage, 116

Confederacy, 62, 70, 73, 109

Congress, 38, 40, 61–62

Congressional Reconstruction, 57, 64, 76

consensus, 41

Constitutional Convention, South Carolina, 163–64

constitutionalism, 59, 61

imperial futurity, 20–21
imperialism in slaveholding, 146
imperial management, 32
Imperium in Imperio (Griggs), 4–6, 12, 22, 159
incest, 108
Incidents in the Life of a Slave Girl (Jacobs), 117
industrial working class, 136
inheritance plots, 77–79, 84–85, 88, 92,
  161–62, 179n60, 183n59
instrumental identity, 84
instrumental power, 60–63
insurrection, 5, 9–10, 21, 45, 123, 140–41, 166
integration, 104
international slave trade, 128–29, 152
International Workingmen's Association, 55
interracial, 84–85, 93, 95, 103–4, 128–29, 139
interregnum, 37–38
Invisible Empire, The (Tourgée), 65–66
Iola Leroy (Harper), 15, 18, 22, 87, 94, 101–2,
  113–20, 188n23, 192n69
irony/ironies, 57–58, 63, 68–70, 72–73, 83,
  85, 97

Jacobs, Harriet, 117
Jamaica, 59
James, Henry, 33, 69
Jameson, Fredric, 12–13, 48, 137, 174n68
"Jean-Ah Poquelin" (Cable), 36
jeremiad, 8–11
Jim Crow South, 31, 102–3, 163–64, 185n80
John March, Southerner (Cable), 41–42, 67, 130
Johnson, Andrew, 11, 94
Jones, Suzanne W., 34
justice, 113, 114–15, 184n69

Kelly, Brian, 192n1
Kendall, Mrs. John S., 49–50
Kennedy-Nolle, Sharon, 13, 172n48, 183n61
Key to Uncle Tom's Cabin, A (Stowe), 14, 65
King, Edward, 49, 65
kinship, 88, 99–100, 115, 142, 183n57, 188n24
Knights of the Golden Circle, 128–29, 146, 151
Kosselleck, Reinhart, 7

Kreyling, Michael, 178n49
Ku Klux Klan, 14, 56, 65–66, 72–74

labor, 111, 148–55
Ladd, Barbara, 30, 45, 176n10, 178n49,
  179n60
language, absence of, 142
language for reading the past, 90
leadership, 147
legal personhood, 77–81
legal segregation, 103–4
legitimacy, 51
Leopard's Spots, The (Dixon), 20–22, 138
Lewis, David Levering, 126–27
liberal historicism, 30
liberalism, 18, 29–30, 31–35, 38, 42, 104, 176n9
liberal public sphere, 32, 41, 158
Library of Southern Literature, The, 49–50
Lincoln, Abraham, 1, 9, 55
liquidity, 109–10, 190n49
literary convention, 107–8, 130
literary form and historical emplotment,
  Ricoeur, 126
literary realism, 14, 19, 69, 112
lived experience, 17, 19, 173–74n62
local color fiction, 28, 175n1
locality, 28
Logan, Rayford, 89–90
Louisiana, 43, 46–47, 93
Louisiana Separate Car Act, 81–84
Lowndes County, AL, 123
Lukács, Georg, 18, 19, 23–24, 174n69, 174n71

MacPherson, C. B., 80
Madame Delphine (Cable), 36–37
Marable, Manning, 126–27
Margolis, Stacey, 102, 108
marriage contract, 78, 114
marriage plot, 46–47, 93, 107–8, 129, 162–63,
  183nn57–58
Marrow of Tradition, The (Chesnutt), 102,
  130, 160–63, 186n8
Marrs, Cody, 16

www.ingramcontent.com/pod-product-compliance
Lightning Source LLC
Chambersburg PA
CBHW030302100426
42812CB00002B/545